What people are
Enjoying India

"Being an Indian myself, I can tell you that this book is an authentic account about India. It is obvious that the author is someone who has lived and traveled in India over a long period of time. India is such a vast country that it is difficult for even Indians to gain such a depth of knowledge about the country as this author has achieved.

"From the insights that the book oozes, it is evident that the author has travelled the breadth and height of India. I have read a few other accounts about India by westerners and was always disappointed by the superficial nature of those books and observations.

"However, this book was a surprise. With a very humorous point of view, it was thoroughly enjoyable and I read it in almost one sitting. It is a must for anyone to carry and read if they are visiting India even for a brief time. This book prepares you for the surprises that await here.

"The author's observations are presented without bias and prejudice. It was an open minded thesis that delved deep into the psyche of the Indian phenomenon. This is obviously an effort that should have spanned several years of unrelenting research and observation.

"Whatever it is, this certainly is not anything that falls under the genre of books that typically stereotype India. It looks beyond the usual shocking point of view of India as a country of elephants and tigers. This book is about the real contemporary India and about real Indians.

"I thoroughly enjoyed this book and would highly recommend it to anyone with an interest in India. I also commend and thank the author for an unbiased view of my country that I so love."

— Satyanarayana Pamarty (Chennai, India)

• • •

With one billion people, there is a whole lot of culture to embrace in India. "Enjoying India: The Essential Handbook" is a guide filled with simple and recommended wisdom as J. D. Viharini walks readers through the best ways to enjoy the cities and culture of the this massive country well. From overcoming language barriers, cultural taboos, safety concerns, and many more, "Enjoying India" is a strongly recommended read for trying to avoid the pitfalls of culture shock.

— Midwest Book Review

• • •

"*Enjoying India* by J. D. Viharini is at once an insightful and practical handbook, covering a wide range of topics without either oversimplifying or getting bogged down in too many exceptions, the rock on which so many India books inevitably founder. Viharini strikes an excellent balance between the big picture—cultural differences, spirituality, doing business—and the details, such as safety and security, food and health, money, bargaining, and shopping. She is a lively writer and a keen observer. I was most impressed at how she was able to be simultaneously fair and respectful towards India without pulling any punches concerning the less savory features of life on the subcontinent. She is not afraid to be frank, which foreign observers often are, and this made me trust her immediately."

— Craig Storti, author of *Speaking of India:*
Bridging the Communication Gap When Working with Indians

• • •

"This is my favorite travel book on India. Every page is worth reading, as the author obviously has years of experience traveling in India. If you are planning to go to India, this is the top book on the market. Take it with you — you'll find that the advice given is like having your own personal guide, telling you things that you may never have thought about. I fully recommend this book!"

— Thomas Egenes (Fairfield, Iowa)

• • •

If there is one book you are going to read to prepare for going to India, this is the one. It is not only of value in preparing for a trip, those who have since returned from India will enjoy it and learn a great deal from reading it as well.

Having lived in India off and on for over 7 years I can say from experience that the detailed insights that you will find here will most definitely save you from a myriad of little problems, and quite possibly from some really big ones. However, Ms. Viharini goes far beyond helpful hints on how to handle the various challenges that may baffle the visitor (such as how to figure out a railway booking with all the confusion of 8 or more classes of carriage, booking windows, platform tickets, journey tickets, porters, etc.) She presents you with a colorful portrait that is quite comprehensive and subtle in its appreciation of the culture. For example, she carefully explains traditions and customs of India that the traveler really needs to know. I am not referring here to understanding ancient festival traditions that a tourist may witness so much as the description of "the way India works." She depicts most accurately the way people relate to each other, customs of everyday dress, what is considered proper behavior in many different contexts, and the key differences between the Indian and the Western visitor in these and so many other areas. Years of lessons learned are gracefully folded into its pages.

The title could not be more apt. This "handbook" should be kept "at hand" as it will inevitably prove itself essential again and again when it comes to enjoying India on a deeper level. It will serve as a real boon for those who wish to delve more deeply into the unfathomable mystery that is India.

— L. Geeslin

• • •

Enjoying
India
The Essential Handbook

J.D. Viharini

Tara Satara Press
Fairfield, Iowa

© 2010–2012 JD Viharini

Tara Satara Press
www.tarasatarapress.com

ISBN: 978-0-9819503-0-3

Cover photo by Teri Tucker

With unbounded gratitude to
His Holiness Maharishi Mahesh Yogi,
who has given me far more blessings
than I could ever have imagined

• • •

Table of Contents

Introduction

THE PURPOSE OF THIS BOOK is to help you feel comfortable in India and to enhance your enjoyment of the time spent here by understanding the culture, how to communicate effectively and how things work, and also by helping you determine what you need to do to keep yourself healthy, safe and in tune with what is going on around you.

Everyone's needs are a little different, so you have to figure out what works for you. If it happens that you or someone in your group has a delicate immune system or merely a delicate stomach, it might be necessary to be extra careful about food, while someone who is stronger could be a bit more relaxed. Moreover, context is extremely important, so what is essential in one context may not be necessary in another. Rural communities, for instance, are generally far more conservative than cities, while hygienic standards are almost always much lower. This means that you may often find yourself needing to adjust on many levels as you move around.

In any case, don't be too rigid about following every suggestion in this book. That could make you feel a bit paranoid about getting sick etc., which would definitely spoil your enjoyment of India. There are certain recommendations with respect to health and safety that are essential for virtually everyone, but many others are not necessary in all circumstances. Talking to other travelers can help you decide what you need, but be wary of consulting those with a devil-may-care attitude towards everything—such an attitude is all too likely to land you in circumstances you will soon regret.

Knowing how to do things in harmony with the Indian way will help you avoid a lot of frustration and difficulties. The Indian way of doing things has its own logic, which is often very different from the way things are done in other countries. Trying to force things to happen as they do back home only creates difficulties for everyone concerned (especially yourself), so it is necessary to relax and go with the flow. You'll not only enjoy India more, but Indians will also enjoy you more. Understanding how things function in India can also help you avoid costly and embarrassing mistakes. Learning how to communicate effectively will make your time in India much happier and more productive.

It's really not all that hard to learn how to get along well in India. Although there's always something new and we can never know it all, the basic information presented in this book will help you figure out how to deal with just about anything that comes your way here. Also, you'll find that whatever effort you put into understanding and respecting the culture will be well rewarded.

In spite of all the years I've spent in India, I do make mistakes sometimes. Everyone does. We just have to do our best and try not to get caught up in feeling bad about it. Given the enormous cultural diversity, it's impossible to know what's appropriate in all situations. But even though I may know the right thing to do intellectually, if I'm not really thinking about it, some inappropriate but deeply ingrained American habit can just take over. Fortunately, most Indians don't expect visitors to know everything and they are pretty forgiving when we goof up, especially if they see that we are trying to get it right.

The idea for this book came after I gave a lecture to some university students preparing for a trip to India. Looking around to see if there was any book that could answer most of the questions they asked, I was unable to find anything that I felt was even close to adequate.

Although all the guidebooks address various practical and cultural issues, they do it in a rather sketchy way. There are many important aspects of life in India that they skip over altogether because it's not part of their purpose to address them. Seeing this, I decided to step in and fill the gap. It has taken several years, but I feel that it was well worth the time and effort.

I love India, and this book is my way of giving something back to my adopted country.

• • •

Nine Keys to Enjoying India

ENJOYING INDIA IS EASY once you learn to relax, to be respectful and patient, to pay attention, to be flexible, to keep your perspective, to keep your sense of humor, and to open your heart and mind. Having the right attitude and using your common sense are essential, but to really feel at home in India you have to respect the culture, you have to open your heart, and you have to understand the importance of culturing relationships in every aspect of life.

The ancient culture that underlies contemporary life in India is an exceptionally rich one, and gaining familiarity with it can be extremely rewarding. However, a disrespectful attitude will leave the most delightful doors firmly closed. In fact, you usually won't even know they are there, which means that you will be missing the best that India has to offer.

Life in India is first and foremost about relationships. Although family relationships take center stage in the drama of Indian life, even interactions that are relatively brief or that seem insignificant in the general scheme of things are meaningful in their own way. That you may never pass this way again is of no consequence. The more attention you give to establishing good relationships with the people you meet, the more India will open itself to you and the more rewarding your time here will be.

When you give the time to understanding people, to seeing how their lives are, to sitting and chatting with them over endless cups of tea, or on buses and trains, in offices and shops, you will find that they are almost always happy to help you. Indians are among the most hospitable people in the world and they love to do things for others—this is a central part of the Indian character.

India is not an individualistic society. If you rush around on your own agenda, focused solely on your own interests, doing everything as quickly as possible, you may not only offend many people, but you will find that it is difficult to get things done. Nothing will go as smoothly as it could, and help may not always be as generously forthcoming as it otherwise would. You'll also miss much of the best that India has to offer.

On the other hand, if you present yourself as a person who is sincerely interested in other people and concerned about their welfare, and who is appropriately respectful of them and their culture, and if you give the time and attention needed to understand how to get along well in India, your experience is likely to be a wonderful one.

Take It Easy

The pace of life in India is more relaxed than in most countries, and ways of doing things are different. Relax. Take it easy. Get into the local rhythm. Do your best to stay rested. When you are tired or tense, you are more likely to hastily reject things that are unfamiliar. Sitting back easily and soaking in the culture is the best way to appreciate it. Try to keep your itinerary or schedule relaxed and flexible. Give time to chatting with people you meet over cups of *chai,* not minding the time. Don't be in a hurry all the time.

Be Respectful

If you respect the people, the culture, the Indian way of doing things, and the religions—even if you privately believe them to be misguided—India will start to open itself to you, and it is likely that you will really enjoy your time here. Respect has many aspects. For instance, dressing appropriately communicates to the people you meet that you are someone who respects their culture, and, as a result, they are likely to be much more open with you and to help you. Never allow yourself to descend into contempt for those around you or you are certain to get it back. And do remember that, whether you want to be or not, you are an ambassador of your own country, so your behavior and attitudes will greatly influence how the people you meet perceive your country and its people, as well as how they treat you as an individual.

Be Patient

Nearly everything in India happens at a slower pace than in the West. Don't try to rush the world around you. Indians are a people who are eager to please—so eager that they often say *yes* to things they know aren't possible, or today when they know it will be tomorrow, or tomorrow when they know it may be next week—or never. They don't like to disappoint anyone, especially a guest. Just be patient and accept the fact that things happen more slowly here—and are often much more complicated because you don't know the language or understand the system.

Pay Attention

Traveling anywhere in the world today requires vigilance, and India is no exception. While there are certain precautions one must take, and there are a few troubled areas to be avoided, India is on the whole a safe place. Just be alert whenever you are moving around and make a point of noticing what is happening around you. And although there are diseases endemic to India that you may not encounter at home, with a reasonable amount of precaution and common sense you are unlikely to get anything worse than a little Delhi Belly. For the sake of your own wellbeing, you need to pay attention to your environment and your own body and mind, as well as to those who are with you. Giving your attention to what's going on around you is also necessary in order to enjoy India fully.

Be Flexible

You will constantly encounter the unexpected because ways of doing things here are often completely different than what you are used to and things change without notice. There are inevitably plenty of challenges, but that's part of the adventure. Try to have an easygoing attitude. Don't hold on to the idea that things have to be as you expect them to be. Don't mistake inflexibility for strength. Be willing to change your plans according to changing circumstances. Take it as it comes. You can hardly spend a day in India without encountering something you have never seen or imagined in your life, which can be a great delight—though it can also challenge your flexibility to the extreme. And you will find that no matter how carefully you arrange everything, India loves to get creative with your plans. Try to regard the unexpected as an adventure or a challenge rather than as an obstacle.

Keep Your Sense of Humor

You need a sense of humor to get along well anywhere, and this is also true in India. Your sense of humor will be challenged often, to be sure. Try to laugh at yourself whenever you make a mistake, but try to avoid laughing at other people—it's much better to laugh with them instead, and you will make many more friends that way. Just remember that almost everything is funny once enough time has passed . . . all your trials and tribulations will make for great travel stories when you return home. As G.K. Chesterton said, "An inconvenience is only an adventure wrongly considered; an adventure is an inconvenience rightly considered."[1]

Keep Your Perspective

Since you are from another country and were able to buy a ticket to get here—which cost more than many Indians make in a year—you will inevitably be seen as a wealthy person, especially by people on the lower rungs of the economic scale. In comparison with the majority of Indians, who struggle to live on less than $2 a day, even the poorest foreigner is affluent. It is impossible to avoid being overcharged at times, especially since the government actively promotes the idea that foreigners should pay more for everything. But, if you can avoid taking this personally, you will have an easier time here. Non-Indians in general, but especially Westerners, are perceived as being wealthy. No matter how poor you feel or how tight your budget is, you are still relatively affluent compared to most Indians.

Open Your Mind

When you come with an open mind, you will be greatly rewarded. Don't be judgmental. Try to be aware of your own cultural biases and realize that they don't apply here. Leave your prejudices back home. Don't try to change the culture. Don't try to convert everyone to your way of thinking and doing things. Do your best to be tolerant of other people's beliefs, no matter how much you disagree with them. If you come with the idea that your culture is the only great culture in the world and your way of doing things is the only right way, you might as well stay home. A cocky attitude is of absolutely no use in getting to know another culture.

Cultural differences inevitably create many aggravations and conflicts, so try your best to avoid getting angry when things don't work the way you expect. If you make an effort to understand the motivations of the people you are dealing with and the challenges they have to face in doing whatever it is you need, you may find yourself getting less annoyed.

Open Your Heart

Indians are among the most warm-hearted, hospitable, friendly people on Earth, and it's usually very easy to make friends with them. If you open your heart to those you meet, you'll find friends to treasure for your whole life, and perhaps a "second family" that you will want to visit again and again over the years. Since interpersonal relationships are primary in Indian culture, without an open heart, you can't even begin to get beyond the surface values of India. The best of India is only available to those with open hearts, open minds and a respectful attitude.

• • •

Preparation & Arrival

THERE ARE TWO ASPECTS TO PREPARING for India: internal and external. The internal aspect is concerned with minimizing culture shock. India's culture is incredibly diverse, and will no doubt differ radically from what you are used to. This is something you should start working on as soon as you have decided to go to India.

The second level of preparation is on the practical level: documentation (passport, visa, etc.), what to take along, planning for special needs, arrangements for arrival, etc.

Prepare Yourself First

You can minimize culture shock by getting a good idea of what to expect before you come to India. People who come without any idea of what is about to confront them generally have a harder time. But the more you have prepared yourself—by reading, talking to other people who have spent time in India, etc.—the easier it will be. By already having an idea how to deal with situations that may be much different than anything you have ever experienced, you will be much better able to really enjoy India.

When you first arrive you'll inevitably be a bit overwhelmed by the noise, colors, smells and sheer number of people. But don't let yourself be overshadowed by the beggars and the heartbreaking poverty. There is so much beauty in India—and many other wonderful things as well. Make an effort to look for the positive aspects as much as possible. Be happy for or compassionate towards those you meet, according to their circumstances, but don't allow yourself to become caught up in other people's misery.

There's always a danger in generalizing the characteristics of any group of people, but it is impossible to understand a new culture without doing so. Whatever your expectations, you should try not to be thrown off balance when you meet up with exceptions, as you certainly will. Just keep an open mind and don't let yourself fall into the habit of stereotyping people. When you stereotype someone, you are virtually robbing them of their individuality. A stereotype is simply a rigid and oversimplified preconception. If you consider a person only in terms of what you believe about the group they belong to, you are ignoring that person's individual characteristics and, consequently, doing them a grave injustice.

Judging people on the basis of the prejudices of our parents or our community—especially if we have never personally known any members of the ethnic or religious groups against which we are prejudiced—is the most damaging kind of stereotyping. Inherited prejudices are truly blind because we rarely question them, but they prevent us from seeing people and things as they really are. If you are able to set these prejudices aside, you will soon notice that while some or many individuals in any group may possess the despised characteristics, they are usually not the majority, and virtually never every member of the group. To assume otherwise is a big mistake. Every individual deserves a chance to be appreciated for his or her best qualities. Anyone may blow that chance instantly, of course, but that's another matter.

Ask yourself how you feel when other people are judgmental towards you without making any effort to get to know you as an individual and to understand you, especially if it is because of some totally irrational prejudice. Of course you don't like it, and you're not alone because everyone else feels the same way, too.

Many people make the mistake of lumping different cultures together. Maybe you know someone with an attitude something like this: "Well, all Asians are pretty much the same. Anyway, I can't tell the difference between a Chinaman and an Indian, so what works in China will surely work just fine in India, too." This kind of bigoted thinking invariably causes problems because it has no basis in reality. In business, such an ignorant attitude spells certain disaster. Cultural differences can't be disregarded.

It's not just that India is different from other Asian nations. Indian culture is not a single homogenous culture. Rather, it is made up of a huge number of extremely diverse subcultures. For this reason, you'll find yourself constantly needing to readjust your thinking as you move around India. The differences between metropolitan and rural India are enormous, and sometimes villages just a few miles apart can have radically different cultures. You'll also notice that, in general, southern India tends to be much more relaxed and easygoing than the north.

By consciously avoiding stereotyping, and by making a point of seeing people as individuals, you'll be culturing a greater ability to see things as they are rather than as you would like them to be. It is up to you to adapt to India's unique environment since it's certainly not going to adapt to you! And whenever you meet up with problems resulting from different ways of thinking and acting, try to resolve the differences in a way that is acceptable and beneficial all around.

Try to understand why the people you meet think and act as they do. Do your best to appreciate what life must be like for the people you meet, what their challenges and needs are, and how they experience the world. Don't rely too much on your imagination, though. Ask people about their lives, and then adjust your ideas accordingly. In fact, you should keep on adjusting your ideas, and with each adjustment, ideally you will come just a little closer to seeing things as they really are. Nevertheless, even if you think you understand why someone is behaving in a particular way, there's always a good chance that you are wrong, so you shouldn't get too attached to your ideas.

In any case, try to refrain from being judgmental and don't try to change the way people think. Don't go around telling people that the way they are doing things is wrong, especially when you don't thoroughly understand the cultural context, which you undoubtedly don't. India's cultures are highly complex, and people here have a different way of doing things. In many cases, the differences are extreme.

Our cultural conditioning gives us a particular view of the world, but this is only one manifestation of reality, and other perspectives are also valid. Do your best to appreciate all that is best in Indian culture and the people you meet.

Get Your Documents in Order

In order to enter India, you must have a valid passport with a valid visa. With certain specific exceptions, visas are not issued on arrival. The Indian government has recently been revising visa regulations, so you should check for updates.

India is now outsourcing their Indian visa application processing to private agencies in many countries. Check with your embassy to find out what the procedure is for your country. In the US, visa processing is handled by Travisa Outsourcing Inc. You can submit an online application at their website (https://indiavisa.travisaoutsourcing.com). VFS Global (http://www.vfsglobal.com) handles visa processing for many other countries.

Don't wait until the last minute to apply for your visa. On the other hand, avoid applying too far in advance if you plan to stay in India for a while as Indian visas are valid from the date of issue, not the date of entry.

Previously, it was possible to get routine visas in one day, but that's no longer the case. Now it tends to take a week or two. Processing may take much longer (up to three months) in the case of film-makers, researchers, journalists, missionaries and others requiring prior approval from authorities in India, or for non-US citizens. It's a good idea to call well in advance to find out about estimated processing times and recent updates.

Tourist Visa. Most people come to India on a multiple-entry Tourist Visa valid for three or six months, though Americans can also get one valid for five or ten years that allows stays in India for up to 180 days at a time. If you are planning more than a couple of trips to India, this option is much cheaper and more convenient than getting a new visa every time you go.

Anyone holding a Tourist Visa is no longer allowed to re-enter India within two months of their last departure from India if their last visit was longer than ninety days or if they have stayed longer than 180 days during the past year. However, it is possible to go to neighboring countries such as Nepal and Sri Lanka for a visit and then return without waiting for two months. You may want to check what the situation is before you go, as regulations keep changing. In fact, as this is going to press, the word is that the two-month gap rule is about to be eliminated.

A Tourist Visa is not available to anyone with a residence or occupation in India. You can spend your whole visit in one place or you can travel every day. The Tourist Visa is intended only for activities such as sightseeing and recreation, as well as visiting friends and family.

When you apply for a Tourist Visa—even if you are applying for a ten-year visa—keep it simple. Just put "tourist" or "visiting friends," etc. in the space on the application that asks why you want the visa. Detailed explanations of your intentions are unnecessary and can delay your visa. The approval personnel don't want to know about all your wonderful plans. Nonessential explanations just create more work for them, and can also cause processing delays.

Student Visa. A Student Visa (S–Visa) is required for anyone enrolling in regular programs in an Indian university or other recognized academic institution. If you want to study in India but are not sure exactly where, you can get a *Provisional Student Visa* for the purpose of checking out various programs. If your admission is confirmed while you are still in India, you can apply for a regular Student Visa without going home.

Research Visa. A Research Visa (R–Visa) is required for scholars and is valid for the period of research. You have to provide a certificate and letter from the institution or Ministry that is sponsoring the research, as well as approval from the Ministry of Human Resources Development.

Business Visa. If you are involved in signing contracts or setting up joint ventures with an Indian business, you need a Business Visa. However, there is a bit of a gray area here because at present there is no legal definition of the term "business trip." However, if you are in India on a Business Visa, you aren't supposed to get paid in India.

Employment Visa. You need an Employment Visa (E–Visa) in order to work in India. E–Visas are mainly granted to consultants and skilled, qualified professionals or those who will be working in the tourist industry. Indian companies can hire foreigners without any government approval, but you have to get your visa from the Indian consulate in your own country before coming to India to take the job. On the other hand, if you are doing work for which you are being paid in your home country rather than in India, you might not need an Employment Visa, but you should ask. You have to earn a salary of at least $25,000USD in order to qualify for an E–Visa.

Conference Visa. You should get a Conference Visa if you are coming to India just to attend a conference, but you might be able to attend on a Tourist Visa if the conference is not a high-profile event. A Conference Visa requires an invitation from the organizers and takes several weeks to process. Visas for international conferences and for conferences on certain sensitive subjects are issued only after clearance for the conference is received from the Government of India.

Medical Visa. You can get a Medical Visa (M–Visa) if you are coming solely for medical/dental treatment. You'll need a medical certificate or letter from a recognized or specialized hospital in India. Your assistant can get a *Medical Assistant Visa* (MX–Visa).

Journalist Visa. If you're a professional journalist or photographer coming to India on assignment, you have to get a Journalist Visa (J–Visa). If you are a freelance writer or if you are just writing a casual weekly travel column for your local newspaper while you travel around as a tourist, you may be OK with a Tourist Visa. But if you are a feature writer, photographer or reporter on assignment for a major news agency, magazine, etc., you are required to get a J–Visa. This visa is valid for all media purposes except filmmaking. You need prior approval in order to shoot films and documentaries in India, and it's a lengthy process. Contact the consulate for information about getting the necessary approval.

Missionary Visa. Missionaries are required to get a Missionary Visa, which is a single-entry visa of specified validity. According to the U.S. State Department: "Immigration authorities have determined that certain activities, including speaking at religious meetings to which the general public is invited, may violate immigration law if the traveler does not hold a missionary visa. Foreigners with tourist visas who engage in missionary activity are subject to deportation and possible criminal prosecution. [Certain states] have active legislation regulating conversion from one religious faith to another. . . . [Anyone] intending to engage in missionary activity may wish to seek legal advice to determine whether the activities they intend to pursue are permitted under Indian law. Foreigners suspected of or actually proselytizing Hindus have been attacked in several conservative, rural areas in India."[2]

Entry Visa. The Entry or X–Visa is available primarily to family members of people on certain types of long-term visas, as well as to people doing volunteer work for charitable organizations.

Special Visas. Special visas are available for teams undertaking major expeditions, including mountaineering expeditions, botanical expeditions, canoe/rafting expeditions, as well as trekking, and for teams or individuals participating in international sporting events that are being held in India.

Visa Application Tips. Review your application carefully to be sure that it is complete and accurate, so that it doesn't get rejected for some trivial reason. Indian visas are not automatically granted to everyone who applies for one. If yours does get rejected, you may not be told why.

If your visa application requires an explanation of your plans, keep your statements as concise and clear as possible. Use short sentences and common words. The longer and more complicated your explanation, the greater the risk of rejection or delay either because the clerk might not understand your meaning or because you may have used some word or phrase that automatically gets a red flag. Any nonstandard visa applications may be sent to India for approval, which means they can take a few months to process.

Before submitting your application, make copies of your passport and all documents you are submitting. You should also make photocopies of your visa once you get it. Keep the copies separate from your passport. This will help in replacing it in case of loss.

Take good copies of all the documents with you to India. If possible, you should also scan all the documents and e-mail them to yourself or copy them to a secure online storage site, so you'll always have copies no matter what happens. If you email them to yourself, be sure that your account is extremely secure. If you're staying in India for more than six months or if you are on a long-term visa, you'll have to register after you arrive (*see below, pp. 37–38*), and for this you will need to provide copies of everything. Never part with your only copy of any document.

If you are a professional journalist, photographer, film-maker, writer, researcher, etc. and you are applying for a Tourist Visa, you should allow much more time to process your visa even though you're not coming to India for professional purposes that require a special visa. This is one case in which a slightly more detailed description of your plans might help convince the visa processors that you are coming as a bona fide tourist.

If you are applying for a visa from a country other than your own, it could take an extra couple of weeks for processing.

Visa Extensions and Conversions. If you won't be able to leave India before your visa expires, or if you won't have finished your studies, etc., you can apply for an extension. You can easily get a 15-day extension on any visa from the Foreigners' Regional Registration Office (FRRO) in emergency cases or for non-availability of flights, as long as you have a confirmed ticket for your departure within that time. Longer extensions must be approved by the Ministry of Home Affairs (MHA). The process of applying for one can give you a bit of a grace period while they consider it. It's important to note that if you stay in the country illegally beyond the period of your visa, you may face fines, deportation and/or up to five years in prison.

Visa conversions and extensions are handled by the MHA only between 10 A.M. and noon, Monday to Friday. The address for the main office is Foreigners' Division, MHA, Lok Nayak Bhawan, Khan Market, New Delhi. If you want to change your visa status from one category to another, you should go in person to the office. In case of serious illness, you can send a representative. If you aren't in Delhi, go to the nearest Foreigners' Registration Office (FRO), which will forward your case to the MHA for approval. Applications for extensions or conversions should be made a few months before your current visa expires, if possible.

In general, you can't change the category of your visa while you are in India; e.g., if you are in India on a Tourist Visa, you can't just decide to take up a job. In such a case, you have to go back to your own country to apply for a new visa. The MHA does have the authority to give you a different visa if there are extraordinary circumstances, but they rarely do it.

PIO Cards and OCI Status. If your parents, grandparents or great-grandparents were Indian nationals, or if you are the spouse of an Indian citizen or PIO, or if you once held an India passport, you can get a PIO (Person of Indian Origin) Card that is valid for 15 years. This card allows visa-free entry to PIOs living abroad, but you do have to register if you stay more than 180 days.

There is also a status called Overseas Citizenship of India (OCI) that is available to PIOs or others who either are or were eligible for Indian citizenship at a certain time. This is not dual citizenship. Rather, it's essentially a permanent visa that allows you to come and go as you wish and to stay as long as you like without registering. It gives you most of the privileges enjoyed by Indian citizens, except that you can't vote, buy agricultural land, or hold certain public offices.

Exit Visa. If your passport is lost or stolen, you have go to the FRRO so you can get your visa transferred to the new passport. Or you can get an Exit Visa, which will allow you a certain number of days in which to leave the country legally. Without one or the other, you won't be able to leave India. To get an Exit Visa, you need to present your new passport, a letter from your embassy giving details of the lost or stolen passport, and the original police report, as well as proof of date of entry into India (i.e., your boarding pass, a letter from the airline on which you arrived verifying the date and place of your arrival in India, or a photocopy of your visa and entry stamp).

Special Permits. In order to visit certain restricted or protected areas, including the Andaman Islands, Lakshadweep, parts of Ladakh, and some of the Northeastern States, you will need a special permit. Some permits (excluding Inner Line permits for border areas of Ladakh, which take only a day) may take a week or two to get, so you should apply well in advance. You can get permits for

Sikkim from embassies and consulates abroad before you come, or from the Foreigners' Registration Offices in India, and in Darjeeling and Siliguri, as well as at certain major airports.

What to Bring

Have your reservation confirmations, tickets, passport and any other important documents organized well before you are ready to leave so you aren't scrambling around at the last minute. Bring an ATM card and a credit card, if possible. Leave extra credit cards, social security card and other items you won't need at home. Photocopy your cards and documents, and keep the copies separate from the originals. Remember to bring all the phone numbers of anyone you might need to contact and any other information you might possibly need.

Bring as little luggage as possible. Although there are porters *almost* everywhere, it is better to travel as light as possible. In addition to all the usual travel gear, a water purifier is a necessity for most travelers. You'll also need a mosquito net most places in India, but the ones you get locally are bulky, so it's better to bring one. A few pairs of good earplugs are highly recommended, even if you are not normally sensitive to noise. You don't need to weigh yourself down with shampoo, laundry soap, toothpaste, etc. Except for very special imported brands, everything is available.

Be sure to bring any medicines that you must take regularly, as well as the prescriptions. Keep essential medications in your carry -on, with a separate supply in your checked bag, as well.

It's best not to bring expensive or irreplaceable jewelry. If you do, you should get insurance that covers loss or damage.

You are usually better off buying clothes in India, as they are more suitable to the culture and the climate. Lightweight, loose clothes made of cotton or linen are by far the most comfortable fabrics for hot weather, as synthetics feel sticky in no time.

Clothing Tips for Women

You'll probably want to bring only two or three sets of clothes from home, and then go shopping for more suitable clothes when you arrive. Many of the clothes that we wear at home are not appropriate for India, either in terms of the climate or in terms of the culture. As far as the culture is concerned, India is simply not a country where one can safely go around dressed as most of us do in the West, so it's important to be familiar with the Indian dress code and the reasons behind it.

Whether you believe it should or not, how you dress profoundly affects how people respond to you, and this is perhaps even more the case in India than in most other countries. Women who dress and act modestly are much more highly regarded than those who flout the cultural norms, and they are safer from sexual harassment. (See *Safety Tips for Women*, p. 148, for a better understanding of why this is so.) Wearing clothing that is indecent by Indian standards is insulting to the culture, and it also gives men the idea that you are available for sexual favors to anyone who wants you—even if your behavior emphatically indicates the opposite.

Since standards vary from place to place, you can look around at how most of the local women dress (not the tourists), and try to cover up to a similar extent. Nevertheless, there is a kind of basic Indian dress code, and it's important to understand it. What kind of clothes you choose to wear is not as important as how you wear them. If you don't want to always be thinking about what to wear, you can just follow the general guidelines below to feel comfortable virtually anywhere in India.

While it's fine to wear Western clothes, it's essential to wear them in a manner that is respectful to the very modest Indian culture. Nearly every Indian, including both men and women (not to mention several foreigners), to whom I mentioned this book told me, "I hope you are going to tell the women how to dress!" Most Indians are much too polite to tell you to your face if you are inappropriately dressed, but they certainly notice. If you don't believe me, just walk behind a woman in shorts or other attire that is similarly deficient by local standards for a few minutes and observe the expressions of the locals as she passes. The ones who avert their eyes are also making a statement.

It's true that many girls and women—especially in Mumbai and Delhi and other places that see a lot of tourists, as well as on college campuses—tend to dress in ways that are considered really immodest by traditional standards. However, as a visitor, you are already at a disadvantage due to common preconceptions, so it is much safer to dress a bit more conservatively. And don't look to Bollywood or fashion magazines for cues on how to dress. They have nothing to do with real life.

Basic standards of modesty in most of India require that you cover your knees, upper arms, shoulders, cleavage and midriff. It's acceptable for your midriff to be exposed when wearing a *sari*, but not otherwise. Shorts and short skirts are generally not acceptable. Underwear should always be worn discretely under your clothes where it belongs, and it should not show at all. A bra is essential unless you are as flat-chested as an eight-year old. Tops should not show your cleavage or be too tight or revealing. Leave your sheer blouses, shorts, spaghetti-strap dresses, bikinis, tank tops, etc., at home. While sleeveless tops are becoming more common in some of India's big cities during the hot season, in general they are not acceptable. Short sleeves are usually OK, except in the more conservative areas.

When wearing pants, go for loose, tunic-style tops that cover your crotch and buttocks. At home, many of us like to wear our blouses neatly tucked into jeans or slacks, but here, it's better to let them hang out.

If you bring a swimsuit, it should be a conservative one, no matter where you plan to wear it. A one-piece is preferable. Although there are certain beaches where it seems that 'everyone' wears biki-nis, I'd advise against it. On the way to or from the beach or pool, or whenever you are interacting with locals, put something modest on over your swimsuit.

In certain conservative locations and in many places of wor-ship, you will also need to cover your head. Observe what the local women do, and do likewise.

Traditional Indian clothes are often more comfortable than West-ern clothes, especially in the heat. Even in extremely hot weather, having your arms and legs covered with very light cotton actually keeps you cooler than shorts and halter tops can.

Most Indians love it when you wear Indian dress because it shows your appreciation of their culture. Wearing traditional clothing also serves as a great icebreaker. Many people will comment on it, and you will find that the comments are generally very appreciative.

If you'd like to try Indian clothes, you'll probably want to start with one of the two basic varieties of ladies' pantsuits: the *salwar-kamiz* (a.k.a. *Punjabi suit*), which consists of a long tunic top (*kamiz*) over baggy pants (*salwar*) which are banded at the bottom, or the *churidhar-kamiz*, which has the *kamiz* over skinny straight pants (*chu-ridhar*) that are worn bunched around the calf and ankle. Inciden-tally, *churidhars* are mainly worn by young women and teens, and not so much by older women in most places. A scarf draped across the front completes the outfit. The scarf (*chunni* or *dupatta*) is an essential part of the ensemble, without which you may be regarded as an immoral woman, especially in small towns and villages. You can buy suits readymade or else you can buy a "suit piece," which consists of three coordinated pieces of fabric (for the top, pants and scarf), and have it made up by a tailor. For a more international look, get the pants made with a straight leg.

In many parts of South India, as well as a few other places, ankle-length skirts (*lehngas*) worn with an overblouse and a large scarf are common. However, do pay attention to which styles of dress are worn by women of your own age to avoid unwittingly parading around in something considered childish or inappropriate. Long dresses are not traditional. The ankle-length dresses you see for sale everywhere are really nightgowns. While it's OK wear one, say, to the corner market for some milk, or while having morning *chai* with friends on the veranda, it's not acceptable to wear one all day.

The *sari*, which is arguably the most beautiful style of dress in the world, is the most common form of women's clothing. It's worn almost everywhere in India, although it's wrapped in different ways according to local custom. *Saris* are comfortable and easy to wear once you get used to them. It's fun to learn to wrap one, and any Indian woman will be happy to show you how to do it.

Although it's not essential, you can pin the *sari* to make sure it stays on. Use a big safety-pin at the waist that goes through all the pleats from the inside of your petticoat so that it doesn't show, and a smaller pin or brooch at the shoulder to keep the end (*pallu*) from sliding down.

Saris can be both modest and sexy, depending on the blouse and style of wearing the *sari*, but don't go to the extreme of wearing very skimpy blouses. Wearing your *sari* too low on your hips, whether for a sexier look or because you are tall, is also not acceptable. *Saris* should be worn long so that the bottom is no more than about an inch or so off the ground with your shoes on; your ankles are not sup-posed to show. If you are tall, you may need to have an extra piece of matching fabric added to the part you tuck in. It won't show, and you will look much better than if you wear the *sari* inappropriately.

Although *saris* seem to be a one-size item, they really aren't. Most are 44" wide, but some *saris* that are made in certain parts of the country are up to a few inches narrower or wider. If you are exceptionally tall or short, look for one that is the appropriate width. Many *sari* merchants who get their merchandise from only one or two sources are unaware of the regional differences. Saris also come in different lengths, 5.5 meters being the most common.

Incidentally, *sari* petticoats may look like long skirts, but they are undergarments that are worn under *saris*. If you wear one as a skirt, people will stare at you mercilessly.

The blouse (*choli*) that you wear under a *sari* is typically a fitted, midriff-revealing style with short sleeves that is fastened in front with hooks. However, you can always have it made with long sleeves for cooler weather, or long enough to tuck in if you are uncomfortable with your midriff exposed, or a bit looser if wearing such a tight blouse makes you feel like a stuffed sausage. Blouses are normally made with wide margins (seams) so they can easily be let out if one's figure grows more 'prosperous'.

Most *saris* come with a blouse piece, which consists of about a meter of fabric. It's usually attached to one end of the *sari*. You can take it to a tailor to have made into a blouse. If you don't have a blouse piece, go to a matching store, which is a shop that typically has a huge array of colors in cotton rubia and similar fabrics out of which you can make your blouse and matching petticoat. If you want some different fabric, you can easily get it dyed to match.

A conservative Western-style dress or business suit (i.e., below knee length and not too tight or low-cut) is appropriate for doing business in India. If you prefer a pantsuit, it should cover your buttocks and crotch.

For social meetings with business associates, you can wear conservative dresses, or nice pantsuits, either Indian or Western style. Long pants and modest tops are the norm for sports activities. Shorts are generally not acceptable except in some exclusive health clubs (but you would normally change there rather than wearing the shorts en route). See what the Indian women you are working with wear for casual attire and follow their example—as long as it's not too immodest, of course. Evening attire can be extremely fancy, depending on the occasion. *Saris* can be worn for many celebrations.

Even if you are a budget traveler, you'll probably want to have at least one nice outfit to dress up in if the occasion calls for it. Whenever you go somewhere that requires getting dressed up, ask your friends what is appropriate. If you are invited to a wedding or other fancy event, ask an Indian friend or acquaintance to take you shopping for clothes. You might also be able to borrow something for the occasion. Incidentally, Indians are generally much too polite to tell guests that they are dressed inappropriately even when asked directly, so you have to figure out in advance what is the right thing to wear.

If you are invited to a temple for an important celebration, do dress nicely. At the least, you should wear something clean, modest and pressed. If you choose to wear a *sari*, it doesn't have to be an expensive one. Happily, you can get a beautiful *sari* for much less than you would pay for a new pair of jeans at home.

If you have long (below shoulder-length) hair, it's good to wear it tied back or up in some way. Leaving it loose can be seen as immodest.

Clothing Tips for Men

In the cities, most Indian men wear Western clothes—but only long pants, not shorts, with certain exceptions. Just see what the locals wear, if you want to fit in. Going shirtless or wearing sleeveless undershirts in public is not acceptable unless you're at the beach— with the singular exception that certain temples in South India require you to take off your shirt to enter.

It's essential to maintain a dignified appearance when doing business. If you are in India on business, wear a suit and tie. In hot weather you can often dispense with the jacket, though you may want to bring it along in case the air-conditioning is too cold. In many places, long-sleeved shirts are the norm, even in summer. See what the people you are dealing with are wearing and dress at least as well, if not slightly better.

For casual activities involving business associates, short-sleeved shirts and long pants or jogging suits are preferred. Shorts are generally not acceptable except in the gym, the beach or perhaps out jogging in more Westernized neighborhoods. Even casual attire should be relatively nice. Bring a pair of swim trunks. Modest ones are best.

Traditional Indian clothes are naturally well suited to the climate. A nice cotton *kurta-pajama* (long shirt over pajama-style pants) is exceptionally comfortable, and a well-pressed, classic white or cream one in fine cotton or silk can be very dignified. A *khadi* (hand-spun cotton) *kurta-pajama*, on the other hand, is good for casual wear. What you wear depends on what sort of image you want to project and where you want to fit in. Some Western men like to wear *dhotis*, but it takes practice to wear one with dignity (a *dhoti* is a single piece of unstitched fabric wrapped around the waist that is worn with either an unstitched upper cloth or *kurta*). *Lunghis* are similar to *dhotis* but are more casual. They are acceptable for beach wear and lounging around.

Evening attire for men is about what it would be anywhere, depending on the venue. A sport coat and slacks will do for just about any occasion, though a nice shirt and slacks will often be OK if you don't have a jacket with you.

And for Your Feet

Sandals are appropriate most of the year for both men and women. In hot weather, they are much more comfortable than closed shoes. They definitely look better with Indian clothes.

Avoid wearing sandals with a business suit, even if it's really hot. Observe what your Indian business associates are wearing and do likewise.

Rubber thongs (*chappals*) are indispensable for many purposes—sharing a bathroom, going to temples, going to the pool or the beach, etc.—but you can get them everywhere in India. Keep a pair handy even if you don't expect to need it.

Good walking shoes are also essential. Many major international brands are now available in India, but if you can't find any shoes you like in the shops, you can get some made to order. In Delhi, Mumbai, Bangalore, etc., you'll find expert shoemakers who can make beautiful custom shoes for you at a fraction of the price you would pay for the same quality in London. If you will be in rural areas where there are snakes, you'll need a pair of sturdy boots to protect your feet.

Children's Needs

Indians love children and are quite tolerant and welcoming of them in almost any situation. However, you do have to be extra-vigilant about health and safety. And you'll need to plan ahead for their comfort and security.

As soon as you know you will be coming to India, start preparing your children for the adventure. Let them know that this is really something exciting and wonderful. Find some appropriate books and documentaries about India, and go through them together, explaining as well as you can.

Naturally, your children will want to bring some of their favorite things from home, including items such as a favorite stuffed toy or security blanket for younger children, some favorite photos of friends and family they may particularly miss seeing while they are overseas, and anything else that will create a more familiar environment for them.

Make sure they have complete identification with them at all times—something they can't easily lose—as well as your complete up-to-date contact information. Bring copies of their medical records with you and record their fingerprints as well. If you give them cell phones, be sure that they are programmed with your number as well as other emergency numbers.

Like women, young girls (even if they are quite small) should be also dressed decently by Indian standards. Yes, shorts, short skirts, halter tops, tights worn with short tops, etc. are cute and comfortable, but in India they really aren't suitable. There's more latitude for young girls under age 10 or so, of course, but older girls need to observe the general dress code as much as women, which can be tough given the social pressure to look trendy.

Children should wear hats when they go out in the daytime when the weather is hot, or at high altitude. Let them choose their own so they will be more likely to keep them on when they are out of your sight. The sun can be extremely intense, even when it is overcast, and too much exposure can bring about flu-like symptoms, heat stroke, heat exhaustion, irritability, headache, sunburn, etc. Bring a really good, long-lasting sunscreen and make sure they use it when they go out in the middle of the day. Also make sure that they drink plenty of water. Children get dehydrated more easily than adults.

Don't allow your kids to run around outside without shoes as they can pick up worms or parasites from the soil, especially in places where there are dogs. Also, the ground is usually covered with many rocks, broken bottles, pieces of metal, etc., that could cut bare feet and require tetanus shots. Keep their feet healthy with a good foot cream, preferably one that has tea tree oil or neem in it.

If you have young children, you may want to hire an *ayah* (nanny) to help you look after them. Be sure to get one from a reputable agency, and verify that all documents are in order. No matter how busy you are, do not neglect to get the *ayah* verified by the police *before* you hire her. This is essential—as it is for any other servants you may hire.

It's really not safe to let young children run around outside by themselves, so if you can't be with them all the time, do get an *ayah* to help you.

For infants, try to use cloth diapers as much as possible rather than depending entirely on disposables, especially if you are living in one place. You'll save a lot of money this way. Getting cloth diapers washed is so cheap and easy that it makes little sense to use disposables all the time. Cotton diapers are much more comfortable and healthy for your baby, anyway.

Breastfeed your baby, if possible. Doing so will help him or her in acquiring immunities, and it is safer unless you are sick.

When traveling, make up games to get the children interested in the culture and help them learn about their new surroundings. Make a point of engaging them in their surroundings and pointing out and explaining new things as they come up.

If your children are old enough to understand, remind them frequently that they shouldn't accept food or drink from anyone except in your presence or with your express permission, including from their classmates if they are in school. Also that they should never, ever swallow the tap water or water they are bathing or swimming in. If they are too young to understand, you'll simply have to be extremely vigilant. It's also best to give them pure water for brushing their teeth.

Teach them not to put their hands in their mouths or to rub their eyes or to pick up things off the street. It's essential that they wash their hands after using the toilet and also before eating. Keep some moist towelettes or hand sanitizer gel available in case there is no place to wash hands (excellent gels are readily available all over India from Himalaya Herbals and other companies).

Don't let your children hang their head or hands or anything else out of any vehicle they are riding in. Indian drivers tend to cut extremely close to each other and serious injury can result even from resting an elbow on the car's window ledge.

Never allow your children to feed or tease or attempt to play with monkeys. Monkeys may be cute, but they are also dangerous, and even the youngest ones are likely to bite. They will also steal your glasses, camera or anything else they can grab—usually with the intent to ransom these items for some food. Don't get too close to them and don't even think of trying to hand-feed them. It's just not worth the risk, no matter how much you love animals. The same goes for other animals, including dogs and cats. Be particularly careful of the street dogs, which are often mean and aggressive. Moreover, they invariably have fleas and often other afflictions as well. Rabies is not uncommon in India, so any animal scratch or bite requires immediate medical attention. With house pets, always ask the owner if it's OK to pet them.

Even cows, which are generally pretty benign animals, can be dangerous—they are, after all, large animals with sharp horns, and even a casual toss of the head can inflict considerable damage—so teach your children to be careful of them.

Planning for Special Dietary Needs

If you will be eating out a lot, write out your requirements in English, and, if possible, get someone to write everything out for you in the local language. Make a complete list of the things you don't eat as well as anything you must have, at the same time keeping the list as clear and simple as possible. It's helpful to keep a few copies with you, since your list may not always make it back from the kitchen. You can often get by with English, especially along well-worn tourist routes, but in many places you may have trouble finding someone who speaks enough English to help you. Other foreign languages are much less common outside of the popular tourist areas and major business centers.

If eating out isn't going to work for you, you may need hire a cook who understands your needs or else cook for yourself. It's pretty cheap to hire a cook, so that's not as extravagant as it sounds.

And cooking for yourself is not really so difficult. If you equip yourself with a small camping stove and cook set, a few utensils, spices and other essential ingredients, you can carry your own kitchen with you even when you are traveling. It's possible to make a fairly well equipped portable kitchen that weighs less than 2kg and takes up about as much space as a shoe box. You can buy fresh fruits and vegetables locally, as well as very small quantities of grains, etc. It's not a problem, as very small purchases are not unusual in most places.

Wheelchair Access & Other Special Needs

In spite of the enormous number of physically challenged people in India, few places are wheelchair accessible by design. Most of the major tourist attractions are inaccessible, to say nothing of many other places you may want to visit. Hotels, temples, private homes, restaurants, shops and other buildings usually have steps up, especially in places with heavy monsoon rains.

If you require wheelchair access, you'll need to find out in advance about every single place you plan to visit or stay. For many people, a specialized travel agency could be the best option for making such arrangements. Otherwise, you will need to spend enormous amounts of time and energy planning every step in advance. Whether you use an agency or do it yourself, it's essential to articulate your requirements as fully and clearly as possible.

Although the situation is slowly improving, few hotels are truly accessible. When making hotel reservations, be sure that your reservation is for a particular room, one that meets your exact requirements, and get the room number. In India, the first floor is not at street level. It's the second floor by American reckoning. For a street level room, ask to be on the ground floor.

Speak with the manager rather than a desk clerk, and be sure to write down the person's name. Remember that Indians never like to say *no* to a guest, and you will inevitably find some cases where you have been assured of a particular situation that simply doesn't exist when you get there.

Asking detailed questions will produce the best results, though getting specific answers can be challenging. Indians are frequently hesitant to answer questions if they don't understand why you want to know—or if they aren't sure which answer you are hoping for! General questions will almost invariably get *yes* answers, whether they are appropriate or not, because they want to make you happy—and they may also be afraid that you won't come if they can't satisfy your needs. If the hotel has a website, look at the photos carefully, though of course they can be quite misleading.

Make your questions as specific as possible, for example:
- How many stairs between the street and the entrance?
- How many stairs between the entrance and the room?
- Are there elevators? Does the backup power run the elevators?
- How big is the room? Does it have an attached bath?
- How big is the bathroom? Is the toilet Western-style?
- How wide are the doors (including the bathroom door)?
- How much space is there next to the bed?
- Can I make and receive outside calls from the room?

When speaking with the reservation agent, trust your intuition. If she seems vague or evasive or uncertain, take it as a sign that she is just trying to please you without actually knowing whether she can accommodate your needs. Verify that you are speaking with the manager (and not an assistant). If she *is* the manager, then you'll probably be much better off staying elsewhere.

Reserve as far in advance as you can, then call ahead a day or two before you arrive to confirm that the particular room you have reserved will be available and that you haven't been switched to another one that may not meet your requirements. Again, speak only with the manager.

When you arrive, take time to make friends with the manager, owner and other key people. It will make a big difference in how successful you are in getting what you need. If they have taken good care of you, when you leave, write a letter saying so. It will be deeply appreciated. Tipping as you go rather than waiting until the end can also help to assure good service.

Travel by private car is by far the best option if you can afford it. Again, you need to be extremely specific in asking your questions. If, for instance, you will need the driver to lift you in and out of the car, that has to be clearly spelled out in advance.

If you will be traveling by plane within India, check with the airlines before making reservations. The airlines have requirements that will definitely spoil your trip if you don't check ahead; e.g., you'll need a medical form and doctor's certificate to fly, and also to bring the wheelchair. And most Indian airports have stairs leading up to the planes.

Regular train carriages are difficult, as the aisles may not be wide enough for a wheelchair, and the toilets are not accessible, so there could be a lot of carrying involved. However, First Class is spacious enough that it could be OK for many people. Many mail/ express trains now have special accessible carriages with accessible toilets, though you'll need to ask before you book your tickets. All the trains are quite high off the platform. Often the only ramps are freight ramps, and many stations have long flights of stairs to get to the tracks. Passengers are not supposed to use the freight crossings, though an authorized *kuli* (porter) can push a wheelchair across.

Buses are worse than trains, since the aisles are narrower, but everything is possible if you have someone to help you. Delhi has recently begun replacing city buses with ones that that are wheel-chair accessible (and other cities will eventually follow suit), but other buses are not at all accessible.

If you are fully dependent on your wheelchair, you will defi-nitely need someone to assist you, whether you bring a companion with you or you arrange for someone in India. Solo travel is not advised in such a case because it would require constant requests for assistance to whoever is at hand, and there would inevitably be times when help wouldn't be available.

Many people recommend bringing the smallest and lightest wheelchair possible, or else an all-terrain one. Streets and sidewalks (when there are any) are generally rough and uneven, with lots of cracks and holes for the wheels to get stuck in, and curbs tend to be high with no access ramps, so larger wheels are certainly an advantage. Although trying to get around with an electric wheelchair is difficult in many ways (e.g., they can't be taken on a domestic airplane), some people prefer them because of the large wheels.

Toilets and bathrooms are extremely challenging, especially because most Indian toilets are of the squat variety, and the Indian-style toilet rooms are typically tiny. Although Western-style toilets are fairly common, especially in more upscale places, the rooms are usually too small for a wheelchair. A portable urinal is a necessity. It will save you from a lot of distressing situations. Be sure to carry a large shawl so you can use it discretely.

Bathtubs are quite rare in India. And except in more upscale hotels, which often have showers, you'll usually have to take a bucket bath. You may need to bring a folding commode, although you can get an adapter for Indian squat toilets in medical supply shops in the big cities.

Touching Down

The international airports have two customs clearance channels. If you have nothing to declare, you go through the green channel. But f you have dutiable items, including commercial merchandise, you go through the red channel.

Cash or travelers' checks equivalent to US $10,000 or more must also be declared. Foreign nationals aren't allowed to bring Rupees into India. There ATMs and 24-hour banks at the major airports, so you can change money when you arrive. The exchange rate at the airports is really poor, though, so you may want to just change enough for a day or two.

There are also restrictions on meat, dairy products, seeds and plants. You can bring all the usual personal effects, including small electronic items and one laptop computer for your personal use, but other electronic equipment should be declared at Customs on arrival. Weapons must be licensed and declared.

It is strongly recommended that you book your first night in advance even if you plan to be completely spontaneous the rest of the time—especially if you arrive at night. Hotels in all major cities can be booked on the Internet, so it's easy to have something lined up for your first night. Another option is to stay in one of the Retiring Rooms at the airport and wait until morning. Retiring Rooms are hotel rooms or dorms, but they are almost always full, so you can't depend on one being available.

If you arrive in the middle of the night, you should arrange for someone to pick you up at the airport, especially if you are a woman traveling alone. It's comforting to have someone standing at the airport exit with your name on a placard when you arrive. Ask for the name and mobile number of the driver so you can call him if necessary.

If a prearranged ride is not possible, get a prepaid taxi. There are usually two or three options, ranging from basic to luxurious. The cheaper ones are OK in the daytime, but at night the risk of breakdowns is more serious as these taxis are almost all pretty decrepit, and you are more likely to have problems with the drivers themselves. Be sure that the registration number on your slip of paper matches the vehicle, and insist on keeping the slip until you reach your destination.

Relying on the advice of a taxi driver or auto-rickshaw driver for a hotel is foolish, and usually ends up being much more expensive than a prearranged room would have been, since the hotel will pay him a substantial commission on top of the normal room rate.

Even if you know where you want to go, prepaid-taxi drivers will sometimes claim that your hotel is closed for repairs even if you have a confirmed reservation, or else that the hotel is no good and they know somewhere better. Don't believe it. Firmly insist on going where you want to go. Threaten to inform the Traffic Police if they won't cooperate.

If possible, allow yourself at least a day or two to relax and get used to the time difference before you start racing around. Being rested can make all the difference in whether or not you are overwhelmed by being in a new culture and environment.

Foreigners' Registration

The Indian government requires foreigners traveling on certain visas to register shortly after their arrival. This does not apply to holders of Tourist Visas or other short-term visas. If you are in India on a long-term Student Visa, Research Visa, Employment Visa, Medical Visa, Medical Attendant Visa, or Missionary Visa, you have to register in person within 14 days of your first arrival at the nearest Foreigner's Registration Office (FRO) or Foreigner's Regional Registration Office (FRRO), no matter how long you plan to stay. In small towns, the office of the Superintendent of Police or the LIU (Local Intelligence Unit) is the FRO. For other types of long-term visas, including Business and Entry Visas, you don't need to register if your stay is not more than 180 days on a single visit. If your plans change, be sure to register well before the end of the 180 days.

You only have to register once during the validity of the visa, even if you take trips out of India. You will only have to register again if you enter India on a new visa or if you move to a new district. However, you must inform the FRO whenever you move or if you leave the district for more than a few weeks (be sure to ask for the current requirements when you register). They may check periodically to see if you are residing at your registered address.

For registration, you need your passport, a photocopy of your passport and visa, four recent passport-size photos, proof of address, photocopies of your appointment letter and all the documents you had to provide to get your visa, including passport and visa. Take four or five copies of everything in case they ask for them, which they often do. If you are staying more than a year and are between the ages of 15 and 60, you will also need an AIDS test certificate (be sure to keep a copy).

If you are staying in a hotel because you haven't found your own place yet, you can bring a notarized letter on their letterhead as your proof of address. If you're staying with friends, you'll need a notarized letter along with a photocopy of their identity card and proof of address, and maybe a photo as well.

Call ahead to make sure the office is open. They close for lunch and all possible holidays. Getting registered is an intensely bureaucratic exercise that often requires more than one trip to the office, so don't wait until the last day. Go early, and bring something to do while you wait, as you can expect to be there for a few hours, especially if you are in a big city.

There is no fee for foreigner's registration, but there is a penalty for late registration. Failing to register altogether when required brings much harsher penalties. Children under the age of 16 years don't have to register.

After you have registered, add a good color photocopy of your registration certificate to your document portfolio. It's good to carry a copy with you, too.

Getting Your Bearings

No matter how well you have prepared yourself, some degree of culture shock is unavoidable. There will inevitably be many things you haven't anticipated, and at times it may be a real stretch to accept them.

If you are feeling overwhelmed by the foreignness and immensity of India, try approaching the culture in small steps. Especially if you are staying for a while, start by making friends with one or two of the local people. Indians are typically warm and approachable people who easily respond to overtures of friendship, and they are usually happy to help you make sense of your new environment.

By making friends with local people, you will also find your world expanding and getting richer. If you start including your new Indian friends in social gatherings or outings and accepting their invitations, life can quickly become much more interesting. By getting to know and really enjoy the country and its people, you can have fabulous memories to treasure for a lifetime.

If you are living on your own in India and you feel a desperate need to be with people from your own country, go to your embassy or consulate and ask about social programs or clubs. You can also try to strike up some friendships with the people who work there. Most of the big cities have expat clubs that you can join. However, while it is natural to seek the company of other people from one's own culture, and most people need to do so fairly often, try not to spend all of your free time with them.

If you are stressed out from your work or anything else, instead of getting drunk, smoking a joint, or doing whatever you can to blot the situation from your awareness, consider taking up meditation or yoga to calm your mind, and then do it regularly. Don't think you don't have time to meditate. If you are more relaxed, you will find that you can work much more efficiently. Anyone can meditate. It doesn't have to be hard.[3]

What you focus your attention on grows stronger in your life. If you focus on your misery, you will inevitably become more and more miserable. Don't sit around feeling sorry for yourself, thinking all the time about how lonely and isolated you feel or you will inevitably continue to feel like that. Focus on what you lack and lack is what you will have. Instead, look around for all the positive things you can find in your circumstances and surroundings, and do your best to appreciate them. You'll definitely feel better.

If you are living in India with your family, try to spend plenty of time together doing fun and interesting things. Expand your interests: take up yoga; learn the local language; volunteer to help at an orphanage; join a local sports team; the possibilities are endless. Rather than always seeking out expat activities, go for local fairs, sporting events, nearby parks, etc.

To get to know a place, spend some time walking around slowly and aimlessly, just exploring, stopping to talk to people, making friends, asking a lot of questions if language is not a barrier, using sign language if it is. Keep your eyes and ears open, take the back roads and alleys, avoiding the tourist places, and you'll be richly rewarded for your efforts. This is one of the best ways to get in tune with India.

Sticking to a rigid agenda or always being in a hurry results in a lot of frustration. If you aren't relaxed and flexible, it always happens that just when you have met someone or spotted something really interesting, it's time to leave. India doesn't open itself up to people dashing around the country on an "if today is Monday, this must be Ajanta" kind of itinerary. The hidden treasures of India only reveal themselves to those who move slowly.

Photography

Always be respectful of people you want to photograph. Ask permission beforehand, especially from women, as taking photos of people can be an extremely sensitive issue. You don't need to know the local language. It's enough to smile and hold your camera or camcorder up in a questioning sort of way.

Remember that colorfully dressed tribal people and others are simply living their lives. Refrain from encroaching on their privacy without their permission. India is not a giant theme park that is here for your pleasure. Even if you come to India on an expensive photo tour, your fee does not entitle you to take photos of anyone and everyone without their consent.

Some people will ask for a little payment, or *bakshish*, for having their photo taken. A rupee or two is usually sufficient, but certainly no more than five or ten rupees, unless you are a professional photographer shooting for commercial purposes and you need a model release, in which case it is appropriate to give more. If anyone refuses to let you take his or her photo unless you pay, then don't take the photo unless you are willing to give something. This is their prerogative, and you shouldn't resent it. After all, you are intruding on their lives, so it is reasonable for them to expect some little compensation. In the case of children who hang around tourists hoping to get their photos taken as a form of begging, however, don't encourage them by giving them money, chocolates or anything else.

Most people will be delighted if you take the time to show them the photos you have taken of them. It's a great way to make new friends, and this simple courtesy can open the doors to places you would never have seen and experiences you would never have had otherwise.

Photography is commonly forbidden in temples and other places of worship, at least in the inner sanctum. There are many exceptions, but if there is no sign you should always ask. Instances of angry priests seizing cameras and destroying them are not unheard of. Some temples that do allow photography will charge a camera fee as well as a much higher video fee, and if there are parts of the temple that are off limits to photography there will normally be a sign to that effect.

Temples that don't allow photography will usually make you leave your equipment outside. Be cautious about checking expensive cameras at the shoe stall. It's helpful to carry a lightweight, lockable day-bag that is big enough for all of your equipment so you can lock it up and hand the whole thing over. Pilferage is the main risk in these places. In any case, avoid packing up expensive equipment in public view. When checking items at a shoe stall, you'll usually be given a token of some sort. A lockable day-bag is also useful for keeping extra gear safe when you have to leave it in a taxi.

Always be respectful of places of worship and other holy places, and of people performing religious ceremonies in any setting. Don't photograph cremations, in Varanasi or anywhere else, except maybe from a long ways off.

Many visitors wander around India with a camera or camcorder in hand at all times. India and her people are fabulously photogenic, so irresistible photo opportunities present themselves constantly. Unfortunately, camcorders and cameras inevitably create a barrier between you and your subjects. Try putting your camcorder down fairly often and involving yourself with what's going on around you in a more direct way. Incidentally, while professionals naturally take a lot of photos or videos, even they don't go around indiscriminately shooting everything in sight. The best photographers carefully observe what is around them, and not only through the lens.

Have you ever gotten home and looked at your photos or videos only to realize that you have no idea of where many of them were taken? If so, it's a sign that you weren't fully there, or else that you were moving too fast. Take the time to enjoy wherever you are in a leisurely manner. If you walk around with a camcorder running constantly, not only will you offend countless people without realizing it, but you'll hardly see anything with your own eyes—you may as well stay home and look at someone else's photos and videos for all you will have experienced of India.

Whenever you feel inspired, take a photo or video, by all means, but try to be discriminating, and try to refrain from gratuitously shooting everything you see. When you try to capture an image of every moment for the future, you are missing those real moments in the present. And what's the point of reliving through photos something you never truly lived in the first place? Would you rather take a photo of a ripe, juicy, delicious mango, or would you rather eat it? You can do both. Just don't forget to eat the mango.

If you discard most of your shots eventually, or if they're almost all of poor quality, you are probably taking way too many. Take enough photos to remind you of your time in India, but make each one count. Just making a little effort to compose and focus each shot well makes a huge difference.

Many Internet cafes and photo shops have facilities for downloading digital photos and burning them to disk. Memory cards are easily available. You can also get film most everywhere, but it's not easy to find high-speed or other specialty films. Be sure to check the date and whether the package is faded or not-quite-right looking. Take care to protect your camera from dust as it may not be easy to get it reliably repaired on short notice.

• • •

Cultural Differences

INDIA DOES NOT HAVE A SINGLE homogeneous culture that pervades the whole country. There are actually a huge number of distinct cultures. This is because India has been formed from many different states that have been joined together over time, many of which have little in common. And it's not always an easy alliance. It is often said, "no matter what you say about India, the opposite is also true." For this reason, it is impossible to make any definitive statements about Indians in general. Nevertheless, there are some qualities and tendencies that most Indians seem to possess to a greater or lesser degree, and the following descriptions attempt to address them.

Indians are typically friendly and hospitable people. Although there are certainly many Indians who are highly intellectual, it is the heart that rules interpersonal relationships in India. Consequently, Indian logic is significantly different from the Western variety. For Indians, the feeling level is primary, and it is essential not to hurt people's feelings, make them lose face, or embarrass them in any way.

Indians have developed a subtle and complex style of communicating that gives priority to preserving each other's emotional wellbeing, and even though that style seems vague, it's just as clear to them as our more overt Western style is to us. In India, this approach works most effectively, so you need to learn to operate in the same way. However, because India is a hierarchical society, this principle applies to guests, elders, equals and superiors, but not necessarily to those of a lower status.

The Importance of Honor

The concept of *izzat* is fundamental to social interactions in India. It's one's honor as well as one's self-respect, one's self-esteem. There is also a collective *izzat* that belongs to families, clans, castes, the various Indian cultures, tribes, religious groups, political parties, and, of course, the nation as a whole. How much respect is given to a person is determined by strict but unwritten hierarchical rules, which every Indian learns from infancy. These rules govern all aspects of behavior in India, and how individuals and groups relate to each other.

As outsiders, we have to tread with care so that we don't insult either the collective honor or anyone's personal honor. At the same time, in order to function well in Indian society, it's important that we maintain our own honor. When visitors go around flagrantly disrespecting cultural norms, either out of ignorance, prejudice, or because they simply don't care, they are insulting the collective honor. In the process, they are undermining their own honor and showing themselves to be undeserving of respect, which is not a good position to be in. This kind of behavior also tarnishes the collective honor of the country to which they belong.

Be especially careful about religious honor. It is essential to respect all the religions of India, no matter what your private opinions may be. Never insult any religion—doing so can be dangerous. Fortunately, most Indians are pretty tolerant and somehow manage to keep silent in the face of ignorant mistakes or even bad behavior on the part of visitors, especially if it is to their advantage to do so. On the other hand, if one fails to give the respect that a person feels is due to his religion, his family, himself, etc., it " . . . can provoke an irrational response totally disproportionate to the level of the slight."[4]

Most Indians don't expect visitors to be perfectly tuned in to the nuances of the local culture, so if you are seen to be doing your best to be respectful, people will notice, and you will be treated with greater respect as well.

An essential aspect of *izzat,* honor, is face. The enormous importance Indians place on saving face can be difficult for Westerners to grasp, especially because many face-saving situations seem so extreme to Western eyes. It can be as if an elephant has been "hidden" behind a palm leaf, and everyone is pretending that the elephant is not there. If you point out the elephant—which everyone can plainly see—then the people involved lose face. But if you pretend there is no elephant, then there is no loss of face.

Face, as an aspect of *izzat,* is collective as well as personal. Pointing out any deficiency or error, no matter how grave or obvious, causes loss of face. This is why, when visitors are critical and outspoken about India's problems, such as poor sanitation, dowry deaths, caste problems, corruption, etc., it upsets people, but doesn't tend to bring about change. The dynamics of change in Indian society are different from those in the West. In any case, change has to come from within a society, not from outside it.

Family and Relationships

Because India is a collective rather than an individualistic society, learning to live together harmoniously is a high priority. For this reason, consensus and cooperation are highly valued, and relationships are of prime importance to Indians. The extended family is the basic unit of society rather than the nuclear family, so Indians have to learn how to get along with many people from earliest childhood. Indians are typically close to their families and separation tends to affect them deeply.

Resourcefulness

It is commonly said that necessity is the mother of invention, and nowhere will you find greater inventiveness than in India. Resources for most people are limited, so you'll often encounter highly unusual solutions to problems. While some are astoundingly brilliant, many are barely adequate, and others are downright hilarious even in their efficiency.

For those of us who have grown up in relatively affluent environments with adequate tools and resources for accomplishing most anything, it can be a revelation to see how people manage with almost nothing. But in India, it's completely normal to make do without what we would consider the proper tools, though it's not always due to poverty. Take an appliance in to have the plug changed and the electrician might simply bite the old one off with his teeth because there isn't a wire cutter handy. You will often see grass being cut with shears rather than a lawnmower, or you may even see people simply sitting on the lawn and using their hands to carefully trim the grass, putting it in little piles, then sweeping up the piles with their hands. In some places, grain is harvested with the bare hands. On the other hand, many good hotels with wall-to-wall carpeting have a boy come each morning with a whiskbroom and carefully brush the carpet.

Indians know how to make do, and they tend to do whatever needs to be done without a fuss. For instance, poor people do not have the luxury of being finicky about where and how they sleep. Many people simply spread a cloth or newspaper on the floor and wrap themselves up in a blanket, or even lie right on the ground without anything. This is the norm for poor people everywhere in India, as well as *sannyasis*, religious mendicants.

On the other hand, circumstances are not always what they seem when viewed from the perspective of our own culture. "A visitor may pity men and women sleeping rough at a railway station, only for it to be revealed that they are actually people from all walks of life simply waiting for a train. Preconceived signs of poverty we may recognize are sometimes just plain old cultural differences. In some places, people favour [sic] sleeping on mats on the floor [rather] than in beds, prefer walking barefoot and are accustomed to eating with their fingers."[5]

Jugarh is a word that means improvisation, finding alternative ways of doing things, making do with resources at hand, or taking adverse situations and finding a way to turn them around. This creative ability is an essential part of the national spirit and you find it everywhere: in the educated and uneducated, the rich and the poor alike. However, many of the greatest masters of *jugarh* are extremely poor people who have little or no education. They have to be in order to survive. They have almost no resources, yet sometimes they come up with solutions to problems that any engineer or executive would envy, even though they are often temporary fixes or work-arounds rather than long-term solutions.

Get into the spirit of creative problem solving. Let yourself be entertained by this inventiveness, which you will encounter everywhere, but never ridicule it. You will often be challenged to come up with creative solutions to problems yourself—there's always something that requires a bit of innovation and resourcefulness.

Indians are, on the whole, a naturally creative and resourceful people, especially when they haven't had these tendencies educated out of them. Unfortunately, the majority of Indian schools—especially those for the poor—are so useless and irrelevant that many children drop out before they reach their teens. Most schools are primarily focused on rote memorization for the purpose of scoring well in exams rather than preparing students for life in any meaningful way. The education provided by this system is so stultifying that it's astounding how many people manage to rise above it. The art of creative thinking is rarely taught or encouraged in Indian schools, but if it were, India could easily become the most creative country in the world.

Communicating Effectively

Whenever you have any difficulty communicating, remember that the problem is that you don't speak the local language, not that the local people don't speak yours. Even English may be hard to understand due to widely varying pronunciation and usage from place to place in India, but the biggest difficulty is in the style of communication rather than the language itself.

Since India was a British colony until 1949, many visitors assume that everyone speaks English. However, the British did not institute universal English education, nor has the Indian government done so. Very few of the English-medium schools actually teach spoken English. Probably most Indians who speak English really well have been educated abroad or in one of India's more elite schools.

When you are speaking with someone who doesn't understand English well, keep it simple. Use uncomplicated sentences and the simplest expressions possible. Use short, common words as much as possible. If you are not getting through, patiently repeat what you are saying a few times slowly, or try changing the words or the syntax; but don't raise your voice. Speaking louder not only doesn't help unless the person happens to be hard of hearing, but it can also be highly offensive to the person you are speaking to.

Speaking clearly and a little slowly, without the use of slang or other idiomatic expressions, will help others to understand you better. Avoid punctuating your speech with words that add no meaning to what you are saying (inserting the word "like" in every sentence, for example). Enunciate your words and don't run them together. Avoid usages like "d'ya wanna" for "do you want to," etc. Many people have difficulty understanding contractions like "don't," "we'll" or "they're," so it's helpful to use the long forms, i.e., "do not," "we will" or "they are."

Learning even a few words of the local language can be extremely rewarding since Indians do not expect foreign visitors to know their native languages. You'll find that people suddenly become much friendlier when they see that you are not merely a careless tourist. Any effort to speak the local language, however poorly, will be appreciated. Perhaps you don't feel that way about visitors to your country, but Indians do. Knowing even a few words of the local language can make a big difference in how successfully you are able to interact with people who don't know English. It's especially useful for essential communication such as bargaining and ordering food in restaurants.

Since Indians have mostly learned English from the British, they commonly have difficulty understanding North American accents and manners of speaking. No matter where you are from, use the best English you know and enunciate your words clearly. On the other hand, there are circumstances where it helps to learn some Indian English if you have to interact much with people who aren't fluent in English and you are having trouble making yourself understood. There are actually many varieties of Indian English. *Hinglish* is the version spoken by Hindi-speakers, which typically adds many Hindi words to the mixture, but there are also many other varieties of Indian English. For instance, in Tamil Nadu, where Tamil is the main language, it's *Tanglish*. Indians who speak British or American English well (or who think they do) tend to look down on Indian English, especially if they were educated abroad.

If your listeners simply can't understand your normal speech, which is often the case with those who are not well educated, try to imitate their accent and manner of speaking as best you can, but *not* in a comical or patronizing way. Learning Indian English is like learning a foreign language, and sometimes it is necessary. Don't make a habit of using it all the time, though. Do it only when nothing else works or you will sound condescending, and people may also wonder about your own intelligence or ability to speak English. Moreover, educated people would be offended if you addressed them in pidgin Indian English. Resort to speaking like this *only* when your own natural manner of speaking isn't being understood. Nevertheless, you may find that if you stay in India long enough and are surrounded mostly by people who speak Indian English, certain words or expressions may creep into your normal speech and it can be pretty hard to get them out again, at least while you are still in India.

It's all too easy to slip into making fun of Indian English because many of the expressions tend to sound humorous, especially to North Americans. However, it's better to keep your amusement to yourself to avoid offending people.

One feature of Indian English that visitors often find quite entertaining is the wonderfully flexible spelling of English words, especially on menus and signs. Words in most Indian languages are spelled phonetically, i.e., as they sound, so it is natural for Indians to spell English and other foreign languages the same way. Some Indians may appreciate having their spelling mistakes rectified, but most will feel that they are of no importance at all. For Indians who don't have a solid English education, English spelling is something that is not fixed. Since most people spell words as they sound, the spellings can sometimes vary beyond recognition as pronunciations vary enormously from place to place.

Curiously, if you ask a native Hindi speaker to repeat something, she is likely to say it faster rather than slower, so you may have to keep asking her to slow down. If you are learning to speak Hindi and people don't understand what you are saying, try speaking faster and they are more likely to get it. Speaking slower in Hindi seldom helps. In fact, it usually makes matters worse. Moreover, it often happens that if you speak Hindi or another Indian language to an uneducated person, he may not understand you (even if your accent is good) simply because he doesn't expect or believe that a foreigner would be speaking the language.

Most frustrating for non-Indians is the problem of understanding the subtleties that Indians use in communicating *yes* and *no*. Because the conventions are so different from those of most other cultures, non-Indians typically have trouble understanding the tendency of

Indians to say *yes* when they really mean *no*. To Westerners who don't understand the cultural context, this may seem really insincere, but it's really just a different style of communicating. Someone may be saying the word *yes*, but simultaneously signaling *no*—and other Indians generally know perfectly well what is meant.

Because the culture gives great importance to honor—for which reason it's considered rude to cause someone to be uncomfortable, embarrassed or upset—Indians typically will do almost anything to avoid overtly saying *no*. The word *no* is considered harsh and even downright rude in many circumstances. This is why you need to learn to read the subtle cues that tell you what Indians are really saying; these cues are easy to miss if you don't know how to listen and watch for them.

When an Indian wobbles his head from side to side it means *yes* or *OK*, rather than *no*, as many Westerners might expect. This wobble is a movement of the head from side to side in sort of a figure eight, which makes the head appear to be loosely connected to the neck. If you watch closely, however, you will notice that this movement is actually quite different from the side-to-side shaking motion that we Westerners use when we mean *no* (which, in fact, many Indians also do). If you are bargaining, this head wobble means that your offer is accepted. In other contexts, however, this same gesture may just mean, "OK, I hear what you are saying"; it doesn't always mean *yes*. Although this head-wobble is common in many parts of India, there are also many places where it is not used at all, so you have to observe what the local custom is.

OK or the Hindi equivalent, *thik hai* (pronounced something like "teak hey"), is used interchangeably with *yes*. However, it doesn't necessarily mean *yes*. If you ask someone a question that requires a *yes* or *no* answer, you are likely to get nothing more than an *OK*. For example, if you ask a driver if he knows how to get to a certain place and he answers *OK*, it just means he will do his best to get you there, even if doing so means asking a dozen people along the way. His *OK* doesn't imply that he knows where it is.

When Indians say *yes*, they will give you other cues that can be either verbal or nonverbal, and these have to be interpreted to understand what their *yes* really means. *Yes* by itself may mean that: they simply understand what you are saying, although they aren't necessarily agreeing or disagreeing; they understand what you are asking, and what you want seems to be impossible, but they are hoping that you will be satisfied with something else, or maybe they can even get someone else to take care of you; even though they disagree or know that something is impossible, it would be rude to disappoint you; or maybe they have no idea what you are asking but they want you to be happy. In other words, it really doesn't mean anything. *No problem, sure, OK,* and other similar expressions have the same essential function. Without any other positive indications, they are just polite words of acknowledgment, and nothing more.

A genuine *yes* answer will normally be followed by a definite statement that clarifies the matter, and may also be accompanied by the head-wobble described above or the local equivalent. In any case, watch the body language as you listen to what the person says as well as what she doesn't say, which is equally important. Indications of discomfort usually mean that the answer is *no*, or at least that it's not entirely positive.

Negative answers are necessarily subtle, and this is where you get into trouble. When a person is not saying a clear and definite *yes*, she is most probably saying *no*, especially if there is any feeling of evasiveness about the reply. If she says, "I will try," she might mean exactly that, but she more often means *no*. You have to listen carefully to what else she says or doesn't say, as the case may be.

A long silence or hesitation in response to a question can be taken to mean *no*, unless the eventual response indicates that the person was just taking time to think carefully about the answer.

Naturally, someone may repeat your question to clarify what you mean simply because he hasn't quite understood your language or your accent—but if he has understood, then the repetition tends to mean something like: "Are you sure you want that? It's really not OK, so let's come up with a better plan." For instance, if you ask, "Do you want to meet before lunch?" and he or she replies, "Do *you* want to meet before lunch?"—the answer is *no*. Such an answer is your cue to ask what the other person would like to do instead. If you keep pressing for what you want, you will probably be disappointed. You really have to pay attention.

Changing the subject instead of answering the question is a clear indication of a negative answer. In this case, you could rephrase your question, maybe so that it requires a little less doing on their part, depending on what you are asking. If you get the same type of response, you are probably at a dead end unless you can somehow figure out what she would like, although if she feels the need to be so evasive, she may not be willing to tell you directly. Indirect questions are often more successful.

Responses that contain words like *maybe* usually mean *no*, but you should look for other indicators. *Maybe later* usually means *no* unless a definite time is then fixed up. Indians will generally do their best to honor their commitments, so they are reluctant to make them unless they know they can follow through.

A common nonverbal way of saying *no* is to hold the hand up and rotate it from side to side, as if in greeting (so don't wave like this to mean hello). It can also mean "go away" or "I really don't care." Accompanied with a smile, however, it can also mean *maybe*.

Learn to respond as the Indians do and get out of the habit of saying *no*. Reserve it for those occasions where it is really necessary and anything softer simply will not do.

Since disagreeing openly would be rude, especially in a group where it could cause the other person to lose face, Indians will often defer the matter to someone else or a later time when it can be discussed privately. For this reason, if you are giving a presentation or are engaged in a group discussion, keep an eye on those around you. If you notice that your listeners are fidgety or too quiet, stop and ask for their input. If it's not forthcoming, try changing the subject and then coming back to it from a different angle in some way that will allow the others to say what they are feeling without any risk of loss of face for you or anyone else. If that doesn't work, pull someone aside afterwards and ask for advice. If you want to get honest feedback, don't project any feelings of attachment to what you were saying no matter how you feel inside. Of course, if you have been going on and on enthusiastically about something without noticing the group's reaction, everyone may be afraid to say what the problem is, even later in a private conversation.

Now, to an Indian, all these signals are pretty obvious, so he is usually quite surprised when a foreigner misses the point—especially when the foreigner keeps asking over and over a question that he feels he has clearly answered. This approach is fruitless and frustrating for everyone involved, since, out of politeness, he'll keep saying *no* in his usual subtle manner while avoiding saying it overtly.

On the other hand, Westerners often inadvertently insert verbal cues for *no* into their speech when they don't intend to say *no* at all, which is confusing to Indians. Conditional answers or answers that mix positive and negative elements are commonly misinterpreted by Indians as meaning *no*.

To communicate successfully, you need to learn both to frame your responses in the Indian way and to listen in the Indian way. When you need to say *no* to an invitation, for instance, instead of refusing directly, simply give a vague and noncommittal answer. Say you will get back to them later or else that you'll try to come.

It's virtually always counterproductive to ask questions in either a *yes*-or-*no* or *either-or* format, so it's better to take a more specific angle. Questions that involve the word *or* are particularly problematic with native Hindi speakers. The Hindi word *aur* (which is pronounced about like the English *or*) means *and* in English, so this may create confusion even in a native Hindi-speaker who knows English pretty well.

Frame your questions in ways that do not require a *yes*-or-*no* answer. For instance, instead of asking a driver whether he knows how to get to such-and-such an address, ask him where it is. If he says he will ask someone or if he simply can't answer coherently, it means he doesn't know.

Try to ask your question in a way that doesn't give any clue to the answer you are hoping for. Otherwise, the answer you want is exactly the one you'll get, no matter what the real answer should be. You don't want to lead the witness, so to speak.

For example, if you are trying to buy a pure cotton shirt, ask what the shirt is made of rather than asking if it is pure cotton. The merchant may keep trying to find out what you want before she answers, but just patiently repeat the question instead of letting her know what you want or she will simply tell you what you want to hear. You could take the approach of first asking her to show you the no-iron shirts (which you aren't interested in), and then asking if the others on the shelf are pure cotton. Asking the difference between various items is often the best way to get what you want or at least to find out that it is not available. In this example, it may be that the merchant doesn't have any pure cotton shirts, and this approach will usually enable you to figure it out.

Another example: if you are trying to determine whether a supplier will have your order completed by a certain date, don't ask directly. Instead of asking *if* it will be ready, ask *when* it will be ready. However, you may need to take a more roundabout means of finding out how it's going, and listen carefully to what isn't said as well as to remarks that seem extraneous to the topic. For instance, if the supplier keeps slipping in comments about an upcoming exhibition or his daughter's wedding or a shortage of staff, you can expect delays. In this case, asking about the preparations for the exhibition or the wedding, or the reasons for the shortage of staff and how they might affect your order would probably give you a better idea of what to expect. If the situation seems unsatisfactory, ask what could be done to get the order ready for delivery on time.

If you really must have something delivered or accomplished by a certain time, make sure they understand why you need it so quickly, e.g., you are leaving town Alternatively, you could offer to pay an extra "rush order" charge if the person can get it ready on time (but pay only if he actually does). Whenever possible, allow extra time in case of problems and delays. Be aware that demands by family, friends, long-time customers, police officers and politicians will always be given priority over those of a one-time customer. If you are living in India, developing good relationships with merchants and suppliers will make a big difference in how you are treated.

Often a shopkeeper will ask you to wait while he sends a boy out to another shop or *godown* (warehouse or storeroom) to get the item you have asked for, though the boy may come back with something completely different. In the meantime, the shopkeeper may show you everything in the shop that even faintly resembles what you have asked for (at least in his mind, there's some resemblance). Or he may tell you to come back tomorrow. Of course, he still might not have your item when you return, but he may have something more to show you that he believes to be similar. He's just trying not to disappoint you, but he really doesn't have what you want or know where to get it and is hoping you will be satisfied with something else. However, if you listen carefully during your first visit, you may realize that he simply can't help you.

Sometimes Indians, especially those who aren't so well educated, are curiously reluctant to answer your questions if they don't understand why you want to know. Also, uneducated people are more prone to saying *no* openly, if only because they don't have more subtle words at their command. On the other hand, some Indians—even if they don't belong to a high caste themselves—tend to regard foreigners as belonging to a low caste, in which case they may simply not see a need for any particular politeness. You may notice that Indians are not necessarily polite to people of lower status than themselves. Who they will comfortably say *no* to is very much a matter of status.

You will find the Indians often don't volunteer extra information when to a Westerner it would be obvious and courteous to do so. For example, if you ask how to get to the museum, but you forget to ask if it is open, they may not mention if it's not.

If you ask how to do something, Indians will almost always insist on coming and doing it for you rather than just telling you, especially if you ask over the phone. A simple question such as "Where's the light switch?" often seems to baffle the descriptive powers even of many people who speak English fairly well. They always want to come and show you, although it may also be because doing so is also considered more courteous.

Many Indian languages, including Hindi, have polite, ultra-polite and familiar forms, so words meaning *please* and *thank you* are often superfluous and therefore seldom used, and in many languages they are nonexistent. Although many Indians who are used to being around foreigners may use these words, not everyone does. This should not be chalked up to bad manners—especially since it's not customary for Indians to give appreciation for ordinary courtesies or any services rendered as part of one's duty, which include serving guests. Instead of saying *thank you*, Hindi-speakers might say *meherbani hai* ("it is a kindness"). If you are praising someone for doing their job well, you can say *shukriya* or *shabash* (both of which mean *well done*, though the latter is a bit more emphatic).

Directions & Street Addresses

When you are asking for directions, give the name of the family or business as well as the address. Write the address on a piece of paper that you don't need to get back. If your destination is not well known, have someone write it in the local script. It's best to give a piece of paper with nothing else written on it. Any extraneous information tends to cause confusion, even if it is clearly separated from the address or on the other side of the paper.

Be a little selective about who you ask. Drivers are usually a good choice if they are local. Sometimes people will give directions that have no relation to where you want to go. They just don't want to disappoint you by saying they don't know. This is part of the culture, so you may as well get used to it.

Indian addresses can be extremely confusing. Street addresses (when they exist at all) are often not arranged in any way that is obvious. The numbering system can vary radically even within the same city or within the same colony (community). To make matters worse, if a street has been renamed, there will always be people who will continue to use the old name for many years.

An address may include a block number and a house number, e.g., A/16 (pronounced "A by 16" or else "A oblique 16"), or a district name and a number, or just a house name. A-Block may not be next to B-Block. C-Block might be split so numbers 1–45 are on one side of town and 46–90 on another, with G-Block and H-Block in between. Numbers might run up and down a street for a ways, and then mysteriously go out of sequence.

Some addresses are extraordinarily complicated. You can have many different elements in an address, e.g., "B19/84a, 3rd Floor, Behind 58, M.G. Rd., 8th Crossing, 29th Main, BLM Layout, 2nd Stage, 1st Phase, Anna Nagar." Where there is no street number, the address may contain some point of reference, such as "behind Regal Cinema" or "near the Electric House" or "behind the petrol pump."

Or the address might just be the name of a street, or even just the village and nothing more.

Words like *near* and *opposite* are much more loosely defined in India than in other places. *Opposite*, for instance, could be as much as a few blocks away down the street on the opposite side, or even back a couple of blocks, while *near* could be half a kilometer away.

Sometimes you may ask twenty people for directions before you can find the address. On rare occasions, you may never find it. On the other hand, if the person you are visiting is well known, you may not even need a specific address because everyone in town knows her, and someone will probably take you to her. This is more often the case in villages and very small towns, of course.

Mind Your Body Language

Many physical gestures have different meanings in India than in the West. You can beckon someone to come to you by holding your palm down and bringing your hand towards yourself in a sweeping motion. This gesture is also the proper way to hail a taxi, rickshaw, etc. The American custom of holding the palm up and motioning with the forefinger is likely to be taken as an insult.

Pointing at people with the index finger is considered rude and accusatory in India. Indians gesture with the whole hand instead. Indians sometimes point with their chins, though this is not acceptable if pointing to someone older or of higher status.

Avoid standing with your arms akimbo (hands on hips with elbows out), or Indians may think you're angry and aggressive. This is the classic stance of a Bollywood villain plotting revenge.

A jerky forward thrust of the chin is an unrefined way of asking people what they want. It can also mean something like, "What's this all about?" But in some places, tossing the head back, if accompanied with a smile, can also mean *yes*.

Most Indians gesture with their hands when they are talking, so standing with your hands in your pockets or keeping your arms folded in front of you while speaking can seem a bit arrogant.

When the hand is held up with the fingers splayed outward and twisted in the direction of the little finger in a single motion, it is a rather impolite gesture that can mean something like "What a stupid idea!" or "What is this nonsense?!" or "What the *bleep* do you think you're doing?!"

Winking is considered rude because it has sexual connotations.

Many Ways to Say "Hello"

There are many different traditional greetings in India, but the most common is *namaste*, which is said with hands pressed together at chest height with fingers pointing up. *Namaste* is understood almost everywhere, even if other greetings are locally preferred, and is used for both formal and informal greetings—it's all in how you do it. When greeting an older person, or someone of higher status, you can also say *namaskar*, which seems slightly more formal, though some people always prefer to use *namaskar*. If the person you are greeting is held in great reverence, you can indicate deep respect by holding your hands in front of your forehead instead of your chest. You can also bow your head slightly, but you should generally look at the person you are greeting while you do it. It is enough to perform the gesture without speaking, and the meaning will be understood. Many people just touch their right hand to their heart in silent greeting.

Although *namaste* and *namaskar* are the most common ways to greet and take leave of others, in various communities other greetings may be preferred. Muslims say *salam aleikum*. Near the source of the Narmada River, it's *Narmadey Har*, while in Ladakh, *jullay* is the usual greeting. English greetings like *hi, hello, good afternoon*, etc., are also common, especially among young people and in the metropolitan areas. When someone greets you, it's usual to respond with the same greeting.

Because India's culture is hierarchical, you should always greet the eldest and most senior people of a group first, and then continue down the social scale to the youngest, most junior person. You should also take leave of each person individually. This is especially important in business contexts, where it is expected.

Forms of Address & Names

When asking someone's name, many Indians say, "What is your good name?", so it's polite to do likewise. Always address people formally until invited to do otherwise—especially people whose status is equal to or higher than yours and those who introduce themselves with a title. Elders should be addressed as *Sir* or *Madam* or *-Ji* (see below) unless they specifically ask you to call them by their first names, but it's OK to be more informal with youngsters. Traditionally, people are addressed by their personal names only by family, superiors, close friends and elders. Of course, in tourist areas, many people are used to being on a first-name basis with new acquaintances, and they may introduce themselves accordingly.

When addressing a person who has a professional title, such as *Doctor, Professor* or *Pandit*, always use it, at least until you know the person better. Use *Mr., Mrs.* or *Miss* for those without professional titles, followed by the name with which they were introduced to you. For women, this is more likely to be their given name, e.g., *Miss Gita* or *Mrs.* (or *Madam*) *Gita*. Indians attach great importance to their titles and expect them to be used, especially by new acquaintances. Always use professional titles when doing business or dealing with bureaucrats.

If you are introduced to a Mr. Ram Prasad Sharma, you can address him either as *Mr. Sharma* or *Sharma-Ji*. Once you know him well, you might be invited to just call him by his given name or nickname, if he has one, or perhaps his initials, *R.P.* If you meet a man named Dr. Satish Shukla, then you would normally address him as *Dr. Shukla* or *Dr. Satish*, depending on the introduction, but the form of address can be a little more complicated for women. A Doctor Shankari Gaur may be introduced as *Dr. Mrs. Gaur* or *Dr. Mrs. Shankari*, though you could address her as Dr. Shankari or Dr. Gaur.

Titles can be further complicated for both men and women because military and other professional titles may accumulate, and all of them are normally retained for one's whole life. A woman might be known as *Dr. Professor Mrs. Bharati Aggarwal*, while a man could be *Dr. Air Marshall Professor V. P. L. Rawat*. Anything is possible. For verbal address in formal situations, use the first title in the string if you're not sure, but in writing, use the full name with all of the titles, e.g., *Pandit Dr. Prof. R. K. Chaturvedi.*

Don't call a person by his or her given name or nickname until the person has invited to you to do. If you want a small step down in formality, use a man's last name with *-Ji* (pronounced *jee*) rather than the first name. If you are on a first-name basis, you can append *Ji* to the first name unless the person really doesn't like to be called *Ji*, as some people don't. *Ji* can be either a term of great respect or great intimacy. As a respectful honorific, it has a similar force to *Sir*, but it can also be applied to women. You can also use it with children or anyone with whom you are on familiar terms. It can be attached to a first name, last name, title, or nickname, or else it can be used alone. It's extremely useful when you can't pronounce someone's name or can't remember it, or even when you never knew it in the first place. *Ji* (which is Hindi) is so widely used and understood that it's safe to use it almost anywhere, although other forms may be preferred in various parts of India.

Use *Ji* when addressing *sadhus*, yogis, pandits, teachers, police officers, bureaucrats, officials of any kind, etc. However, even when you are speaking to a lowly government clerk, you may want to add *Ji*. If you need that person to get something done for you, a show of respect is important. You can also use *Ji* with a title, e.g., *Doctor-Ji*.

Never address beggars or menial laborers as *Ji*. You would also not address most servants as *Ji*.

Many people have a guru of one sort or another. A guru is traditionally a spiritual preceptor, but can also be a music teacher, dance teacher, etc. A spiritual guru may be addressed or referred to as *Guru-Ji*, or *Guru Dev*. Orange-robed *sadhus* and *sannyasis* may be addressed as *Swami-Ji* or *Maharaj*. Respected pandits (learned Brahmins) are usually addressed as *Pandit-Ji*.

Among certain traditional segments of society, a wife won't address her husband by name, or even say his name aloud. When referring to him, she may use *Ji* with his last name (e.g., *Sharma-Ji*) or refer to him as the father of their child (e.g., *Anil's father*) or even just as *he* or *him*.

Nicknames are extremely common. Often they are merely a shortening of a longer name: Vikas, a boy's name, might be transformed into *Vicky*, for instance, and Tejaswini, a girl's name, may become *Teju*. English nicknames are common among Westernized Indians. Women may have names like *Lucky, Smarty, Beauty, or Pinky*, and men might be called *Bunny, Bittoo, Munna* or *Dumpy*. Many men prefer to be known by their initials. It is also common for people to shorten a long name. For instance, Mr. Kumaraswamy might shorten his name to *Mr. Kumar*.

After titles, most people will use their given names first, followed by a family, caste, or clan name. There are plenty of exceptions, though, and you will only know for sure by asking.

The wife and children may take the husband's or father's given name as their second name; e.g., Anjali, the wife of Narayanaswamy, might become *Anjali Narayanaswamy*. There are also cases where the given name may be preceded by the mother's family name. After marriage, women may take the husband's name, which is typically the family name in the North and the first name in the South. It is, however, no longer uncommon for professional women to keep their maiden name after marriage.

Traditions differ in various parts of the country. In the North, Hindus usually have a first and last name, but many names that seem to be surnames are actually caste names, e.g., Sharma, Varma, Gupta, Gujjar, etc., and sometimes surnames will be occupational names, such as Pilot. To avoid being identified by caste, people may take their father's name or village name as a surname. In the South, men normally use the name of their ancestral village and/or the names of their father, but these names are typically used in front of the given name as initials.

Within a family, relationship names are used more commonly than given names. In Hindi, for instance, the paternal grandfather and grandmother are *Dada* and *Dadi*, respectively, while the maternal grandparents are *Nana* and *Nani*. The father's elder brother is *Chacha*, while mother's elder brother is called *Mama*. Each relationship is named in a particular way. There is a whole special set of names for one's in-laws, so instead of all of one's spouse's brothers being called *brother-in-law*, for example, each has a specific term. A woman's husband's younger brother is *Devar*, and his wife is called *Devarani*, while the elder brother is *Tayi*, etc. The elder brother's wife is called *BhabhU*. The wife's brothers and their wives have a whole different set of names, and so on. The eldest sister is called *Didi*, but younger sisters are called by their given names or nicknames.

Cousins are often referred to as *cousin brother* or *cousin sister*; however, people may also use these terms to refer to more distant relatives, or sometimes to close friends who are not related at all. In this case, these terms are a way of saying that "he is like a brother to me" or "she is like my sister."

A man's name may be followed in writing by *s/o*, i.e., "son of," and the father's name (especially for official documents or announcements). A woman's name may be followed by *d/o*, or "daughter of," with the father's name, or *w/o*, "wife of," with the husband's name, if she is married.

Sikh men usually have *Singh* as a middle name or surname, and most Sikh women have the name *Kaur*. However, not all Singhs and Kaurs are necessarily Sikhs, and some Sikhs have changed their names for various reasons. Address a Sikh by his or her given name preceded by *Mr.* or *Mrs.* rather than saying *Mr. Singh* or *Mrs. Kaur*. Sikh men are also referred to as *sardars*.

Muslim names are typically of Arabic derivation. The given name of a Muslim man is generally followed by *bin* (son of) and his father's name, e.g., Abdul bin Mohammed. A Muslim woman's name usually includes *binti* (daughter of) plus her father's name. Westernized Muslims often drop the *bin* or *binti* from their names. The title *Hajji* (for men) or *Hajjah* (for women) indicates that the person has made the pilgrimage to Mecca (the *Hajj*), which all devout Muslims hope to do once in their life.

Indians generally address all adult women over the age of about 25 as *Mrs.* or *Madam* whether they are married or not. It's quite usual to find *Ms.* as an option on forms; and in written communication, there's no problem at all. However, if you are a woman who prefers to be called *Ms.*, you may often find that insisting on this form of verbal address is an exercise in frustration. Of course, people will try to honor your request because they want to please you, but their cultural habits are so deeply ingrained that they will inevitably forget.

Peons in many organizations have been trained to address everyone, including women, as *Sir*. Trying to correct them is often a complete waste of time. For them, it's the same as saying *Ji*, which is used for men and women alike, so you should accept it as it's meant.

Depending on your age and your relationship with them, your Indian friends may address you as if you were a relative: *Auntie, Uncle, Mother, Father, Mataji* (respected mother), *Didi* (elder sister), and so on. Children are commonly taught to call adults *Auntie* or *Uncle*, whether they know them or not.

Conversing with Indians

As Indians will typically start off by asking personal questions about you and your family, it's good to reciprocate with similar questions about theirs. Indians—especially those who are used to seeing foreigners—are prone to asking questions that may seem too intimate, often within minutes of being introduced. This is because they are trying to zero in on your social and economic coordinates to know who you are in terms of social standing, wealth, power, family, education, connections, religion, respectability, etc., all of which comprises a person's *auqat,* or place in the social hierarchy. The rules of social interactions, which have everything to do with *auqat,* are deeply ingrained in every Indian from infancy. For most Indians, caste is still a major part of this equation. *Auqat* determines how much respect you will be given and how you will be treated in any particular situation, so it is intimately connected with your *izzat* or honor (see pp. 45–46).

Indians tend to be extremely curious about how our thinking and lives are different from theirs. After the first question, which is almost invariably which country you are from, you may be subjected to a barrage of personal questions about your family, your marriage (or why you aren't married, if you are single), your job, your education, your home, your income, where you are staying, why you are in India, how you like India, your religion, etc. Don't take offense. This is not considered impolite, as it might be in other cultures. You don't necessarily have to answer, though. If you are asked an uncomfortable question, you can always reply with a question of your own to try to change the direction of the conversation. Or you can smile and be politely vague. To bluntly tell someone that it's none of his business would be extremely rude.

On the other hand, Indians will expect you to ask such questions of them as well, and if you don't, many people may feel you are impolite or have no real interest in who they are. They know all these sorts of things about the people around them, but the only way they can find out about you as is to ask.

Questions about art, culture, religion, history, food, and the local region are good conversation topics because people are naturally inclined to appreciate any effort to understand their country better. Since cricket is an obsession with many Indians, learning a little about the game and the top players will nearly always give you something to talk about. Indian cinema, if you are fond of it, is also a good topic of conversation. It is always good to mention the things that you love about India.

When talking about life in your own country, make an effort to present a balanced picture. Don't just glorify the culture and lifestyle; also mention the realities of inflationary prices, stress, pollution and other problems. Many Indians idolize the West in an unrealistic way, thinking that if they could only get to America, for instance, they could make lots of money and their problems would be over. This is certainly not true for the vast majority of Indians, so it's more helpful to disillusion them a little. Indians who emigrate are often so unhappy being away from their own culture that all they want to do is to come home.

Since Indian society is exceptionally hierarchical, if you are in a group where there is any significant inequality in terms of age or social standing, you may notice a certain amount of avoidance of one sort or another, while in a group of peers, you usually won't see this. For instance, as a sign of respect, Indians typically don't make eye contact when talking to someone who is older or of a higher status. On the other hand, Indians often stare quite openly when they are not talking to you, especially if they are not used to foreigners. You really can't do anything but smile and ignore it.

Indians tend to show much more appreciation for each other than Westerners do, so make a point of expressing your appreciation for your Indian friends—not thanking them exactly, but telling them how wonderful or kind they are, how much you enjoy being with them, or how much you like anything about them.

Most Indians are extremely reluctant to express disagreement overtly—except with close, trusted friends or people who are lower in the hierarchy—because doing so would be regarded as rude or even aggressive. Disagreements are usually expressed indirectly, so it's best if you try to do likewise.

For the most part, at least in casual conversation, it's best to avoid topics like poverty, dowry, widows, foreign aid and anything that shows India in a bad light. If an Indian starts the conversation, you can join in, but on the whole it's better to mostly listen and keep your opinions to yourself.

When visitors start a discussion on sensitive topics, their comments are likely to be seen as criticism. It's also best to avoid discussing anything to do with the military, even if you happen to be really interested in it, or you could find yourself suspected of spying. Indian politics can also be a touchy subject, especially if you are with people who have diverse views and allegiances, though many people will be interested in your views of foreign politics. Pakistan and Kashmir are particularly sensitive subjects. Avoid getting into discussions about sex. And try not to mention the weather. Those of us who have grown up in milder climates tend to complain far too much about India's weather.

You will also find that Indians are prone to giving advice on just about everything, which you should acknowledge politely, whether it seems useful to you or not.

Sexual Issues

When it comes to sex, most Indians are extremely conservative. Sexual matters are considered private and are rarely discussed. Also, men and women don't mix as freely as in Western countries. Physical contact with a person of the opposite sex is a cultural taboo that should be respected when you are in public. Since Indian society is generally conservative, avoid greeting members of the opposite sex with hugs and kisses. Even holding hands is not acceptable in most places. In some places you can even be arrested for kissing in public![6]

But what about the erotic carvings at Khajuraho? No one really knows their purpose, but they have little to do with modern Indian life. And the *Kama Sutra?* Most Indians would be too embarrassed to walk into a bookstore and ask for a copy.

In the West, if a man wants to protect a woman from sexual harassment, he may put his arm around her or hold her hand as a means of sending a clear message to other men to leave her alone. In India the opposite is true. Here such behavior sends the message that she is a loose woman and fair game for any man. So in order to protect your woman, refrain from touching her in public. By treating her in a way that Indians see as being respectful, you are signaling that others should do likewise. Refrain from even looking at each other in an intimate way in public. Even though many Westernized Indians may behave more intimately in public, it is not a good idea to do likewise.

In traditional Indian society, there is considerable separation between men and women. Men are expected to keep a respectful distance from women they are not married to, and they are also expected to refrain from any physical contact with their wives in public, however slight. For a man to touch a woman in public, regardless of the intention behind it, is offensive almost everywhere in Indian society. In extremely conservative communities, it is forbidden for any man but the husband to even look at the face of his wife. In a typical gathering, men and ladies won't mix much, and they may be seated on opposite sides of the room.

Men should refrain from addressing a woman who is walking or sitting alone. It's inappropriate and may be taken as a sexual proposition no matter how innocent the intentions.

Once in a while, someone may ask you about your sex life, e.g., whether you and your friend sleep together, etc. No matter what the reality is, looked shocked and refuse to answer, or else say something negative. Saying *yes* is an invitation to trouble of one sort or another. Most Indians are not so rude. You'll get questions like this only from young men whose hormones are raging out of control and who are desperately looking for an outlet. A *yes* answer may lead them to believe they have found one.

If you are used to casually touching people when you talk to them, get out of the habit in India, at least when you are speaking to someone of the opposite sex. Even shaking hands with someone of the opposite sex should be avoided except in international corporate settings. If you are a woman and an Indian man wants to shake your hand, you can just *namaskar* instead. Sometimes the man may pretend to be offended, but this is just an act. Most men wouldn't treat an Indian woman that way. If you are a man, don't initiate a handshake with an Indian woman. It's much better to stick with the traditional greetings unless the woman holds out her hand to you.

On the other hand, Indians often hold hands with people of the same sex as a matter of friendship. This is not usually an indicator of homosexuality. If someone of the same sex takes your hand or puts his or her arm around you and it makes you uncomfortable, try to refrain from squirming. If you pull away, the person will be deeply offended. Just accept their action as the gesture of friendship it is meant to be. If someone touches you in an inappropriate way, however, immediately push him away and let him know that his advances are unwelcome.

Although it has recently become legal, homosexuality is not well accepted in Indian society, so if you are so inclined, you may find it easier to keep your preferences private most of the time, especially in conservative areas.

It is considered inappropriate for a man to compliment an Indian woman who is not his wife or a close relative. And refrain from complimenting young children. Many people are afraid that compliments will attract envy or misfortune, so you should try to resist the temptation to tell a mother how beautiful or how cute her children are, especially if she is from a traditional family.

Public nudity is unacceptable everywhere (except for *naga babas* and small children), and a swimsuit or other clothes must be worn even when bathing in a remote location. No place is so remote that someone might not come along. Men should wear swim trunks, especially at the beach or pool, although it's common for Indian men to go for a dip in holy rivers in their underwear.

For ladies the situation is much more complicated. In some hotels and beaches, bathing suits are the norm, but these should be modest—leave your bikinis at home. In other places, especially holy rivers, watch what most of the Indian women are doing and follow suit. Some places have separate pavilions where women can bathe out of the sight of men, but mostly this is not the case. You usually go into the water wearing your clothes, which you then change as soon as you emerge. Avoid wearing clothes that will become transparent when wet. On the other hand, don't wear anything heavy or it will weigh you down.

Indian ladies are extremely clever at changing clothes modestly in public. They may wrap a large cloth around themselves and change under it, or use a *sari* petticoat tied loosely around the neck as a private cabana. This isn't as hard as it might seem, although wet fabric is extremely clingy. See what the local custom is and try your best to do likewise.

Few people in India know how to swim well, so if you want to take a real swim anywhere other than in a swimming pool, you will have many people watching you with great interest and possibly alarm, especially if you are a woman.

Indian Hospitality

Indians are extraordinarily hospitable people. For most people, it's a point of honor and a sacred duty to feed one's guests and take care of their needs. Likewise, being a guest is equally important, as it gives others the opportunity to serve you.

It is traditional to greet guests with a garland, although you may not get this treatment very often. The garland is usually accompanied by a *tilak* (application of sandalwood paste or a red powder on the forehead). Whenever you are given a garland, the proper response is to take it immediately off to show humility.

When you are visiting someone's home, however casually, you will usually be offered tea, and maybe biscuits or fruit or other snacks as well. The polite response is to refuse at first and to accept the second or third offer. Your hosts may be insulted if you don't take something. Serving guests is often considered a religious act, so it is important to accept some little thing. It doesn't have to be much. Even a few sips of tea can be enough.

When someone invites you home for dinner, you should always say that you would love to come, whether you really want to come or not. If you intend to accept the invitation, you should arrange a specific date and time. Otherwise, the plan will likely be forgotten. Refusing an invitation outright is impolite, no matter how gently you have phrased your refusal according to Western standards, and doing so may even be regarded as a sign of arrogance. It is considered far more polite to evade a request or invitation. You should avoid making a definite commitment if you know you may not be able to keep it.

Be sure to let your hosts know in advance if you are vegetarian, if you can't eat spicy food or if you have a special diet. They would be extremely uncomfortable if they prepared a meal that you couldn't eat—to say nothing of how you would feel! You can also ask to have your water boiled. Most middle class homes have water purifiers these days, but if they aren't cleaned or serviced regularly, they don't really do the job, so boiled water or tea is safer.

When you are invited to eat in someone's house, you should generally arrive about 15–30 minutes late. Arriving right on time for a social event is generally considered impolite. You will rarely sit right down to dinner as soon as you arrive. Dinner can easily be served an hour or two later. Indians don't usually eat dinner before 8PM, so you may be offered tea and a light pre-dinner snack when you first arrive. Most socializing is done before dinner. Indian guests typically leave immediately after dinner, so you should do likewise unless your hosts ask you to stay longer.

If you are invited to dinner with a family, don't come empty-handed. Flowers (except white flowers, which are associated with funerals), European chocolates or other sweets are always appropriate. For children, toys or books will be appreciated.

Often a prayer is recited at the beginning of a meal, so you should wait until everyone starts eating or until your host or hostess urges you to start. Also, refrain from serving yourself unless you are asked to do so.

In a traditional Indian home, the whole family rarely sits down together. When there are guests, they are served first, then the men of the family, then the women and children. The cook, whether it's the wife or someone else, generally eats last. In any case, a traditional wife usually doesn't eat until she has finished serving everyone else. If you have come at an odd time, you may even be the only one eating, while your host sits and keeps you company.

Take small quantities at first. In this way you can decide what you want more of—and you won't risk taking too much of something you can't manage to eat, which will not be appreciated. In many parts of India, leaving a little on your plate is a signal that you are full; otherwise, your hosts will keep piling it on. In other places, however, it is considered disrespectful not to finish everything that is on your plate.

When you pass the salt, put it on the table close to the person rather than handing it to them, which is felt to be unlucky.

Don't enter the kitchen unless invited to do so. Also, it's customary to take your shoes off before entering the kitchen even if you are told you can keep them on in the rest of the house. If you feel like offering to help, note whether your hosts have servants. If they do, your offer would be inappropriate.

It's impolite to thank your hosts for a meal, so try to avoid doing so. Instead, tell your hosts how delicious the food is. Even if in your opinion the meal isn't particularly good, you should always find something to praise. It's part of your duty as a guest.

You can also invite them for a meal in return, which will show them that you value the relationship you have with them. It should, however, be a similar sort of meal, not one that is much more lavish. If you have had a simple meal at their home, for instance, you shouldn't invite them to a five-star hotel for dinner, even if you'd like to give them a treat. It would make them feel extremely uncomfortable.

Although casual visitors are usually welcome at almost any time, never enter anyone's house without being invited to do so, especially on your first visit. Some people may prefer to entertain you outside for one reason or another.

It is normally much safer to eat in homes than in restaurants, as long as you avoid the usual hazards such as uncooked food, etc., and it is typically a delightful experience.

Gracefully Evading Hospitality

While you are sure to enjoy Indian hospitality in general, there may be times when you don't feel up to eating anything for one reason or another. In that case, you can often get away with just having tea. You can just pretend to sip it if you really don't even want to take tea.

If you really don't want to eat, getting out of a meal can be tricky when your hosts are determined to feed you. If you say you are sick, they will almost always have something they are sure will be good for what ails you (which may be the case). If you tell them that your doctor has given you a special diet, they will send someone out to try to get what you need. If they can't get it, they will either come back with something as close as possible or else they will feel bad about their failure, so this approach isn't useful if you don't want to eat at all.

By far the surest and most polite way to get out of eating is to tell your host or hostess that you are fasting, regardless of the real reason you don't want to take anything. Fasting is understood and appreciated by virtually everyone, and no offense will be taken. "I am fasting just now" is the best way to put it. Since "just now" doesn't refer to any specific period of time, your statement will be true no matter how short your fast may be. It's usually not necessary to give any reason for your fast, though you might have some vague answer ready in case they do. Fasts are often for religious reasons, though it's also common to fast for health reasons as well. Sometimes the fasts are complete, but more often they involve abstaining from certain foods or drinks for a specified period of time, so you can easily adapt your fast to fit the circumstances.

In any case, take care not to insult your hosts. If you have accepted a dinner invitation but realize when you arrive that there may be a problem (e.g., the food has been sitting out and is covered with flies), it is extremely difficult to extricate yourself without hurting your hosts' feelings. Take only the items that are obviously freshly cooked and hot, but avoid the dairy products, especially if the weather is hot. If nothing feels safe, you could say you have a sudden tummy ache and ask for tea or Coke™.

If you don't accept their hospitality on one occasion, your hosts may insist that you come back when you are not fasting. Just smile and say you would love to come, whether you mean it or not (remember, this is not regarded as insincere as long as you don't make a definite commitment you don't plan to keep). You could suggest meeting at a restaurant where you feel comfortable, but this is a bit delicate because you must be careful not to let your hosts feel that there is any deficiency in their home or hospitality. Also, if you invite them, you'll be picking up the tab, so be sure you can afford it.

Staying With an Indian Family

If you remain in India for a while, you'll probably be invited to stay with a family at some point. Since Indians are such wonderfully hospitable people, living with an Indian family is generally a delightful and rewarding experience. You should be aware, however, that you may not have complete freedom to come and go, and you may have to surrender your own agenda in the face of all the hospitality that will be showered on you.

When you go to stay with a family, be sure to bring a gift of some sort. Something from your own country would be much appreciated, as would a nice arrangement of flowers or sweets.

Most Indians feel that by honoring a guest, one is honoring God and this idea that hospitality is a sacred duty is deeply embedded in the culture. Hospitality is a quality you will find in most Indians irrespective of religion, class, or economic level. Indians love to have guests, and even the poorest people will generously share whatever little they have. Most Indians would feel ashamed to allow a guest to walk out the door without having partaken of their hospitality. Traditionally, no guest should go away dissatisfied or hungry. Invitations are often offered with the words "please come home," in the sense that "our home is also your home." Such expansive hospitality is delightfully irresistible.

When you stay in an Indian home, you will usually find that all the members of the extended family who are living in the same house or compound will come to greet you, and sometimes half the neighborhood as well. Many people consider it a special honor to have a visitor from overseas in their home and they will often go to incredible lengths to care for your every need.

Some Indians are so eager for visitors that they could be described as aggressively hospitable. You may meet complete strangers in airports or on trains who insist that you must come and stay with them literally within the first minute of your conversation! When this happens, you should be on guard. In such a culture, their motives could easily be pure, but they could also have a hidden agenda that you wouldn't want to be involved in, or even something sinister, so be careful. It's not recommended to accept hospitality from strangers, especially if you have met them on the train or bus. For the sake of courtesy, however, you should say the usual vague but noncommittal *yes*, whether you plan to show up or not, but don't let yourself be bullied into going with anyone against your will. You aren't obligated to give in to their agenda. If someone keeps pressing you for a commitment and won't accept your excuses, you may have to say a firm *no*.

On the other hand, if you receive such insistent offers from a person who has been introduced to you by friends, the situation is entirely different. Being a friend of a friend means a lot in India, and by offering hospitality to such a person, one is honoring one's friend as well. In this case, you should feel free to accept as long as you feel comfortable with the situation. But if you don't feel comfortable, then you can simply evade the invitation in the usual manner, or else you might agree to come for tea instead.

Entertaining

If you are giving a dinner party, a buffet is easiest. Be sure to have more food than you think you will need. If the event is important, get the invitations printed and send them out early, but don't expect everyone to RSVP. Replying to invitations is not a particularly common Indian habit. A few days before the party, try to contact everyone personally, though don't be surprised if you still have trouble getting commitments from many of your guests.

Indians generally don't show up at the specified time for social events, since punctuality is considered poor form in most circles. Most guests will be at least 15 minutes late, and some may not show up at all, perhaps due to some family or business crisis that has suddenly arisen. On the other hand, some of your guests will probably bring friends—another quite normal practice in India under most circumstances. If this happens, receive the friends as warmly as if you had been expecting them and simply adjust. If you have arranged for extra food, you shouldn't have a problem hosting additional guests. Just be sure to keep some aside for late arrivals.

If you are serving a buffet, always arrange the vegetarian and non-vegetarian items separately and mark them clearly. Finding out your guests' preferences (or at least their religions) in advance will help avoid awkward situations. This is essential, as religion must be taken into account when planning your menu.

While traditional Hindus and Jains are vegetarians, many Westernized Hindus eat some non-vegetarian food, but not beef. Jains are usually pure vegetarians, and strict Jains don't eat dairy products, eggs, onions, garlic, potatoes or other root vegetables, and sometimes chillies. Most Buddhists (with the exception of some Tibetan Buddhists) and many Sikhs are vegetarians. Muslims are usually non-vegetarians, but they don't eat pork, and many don't eat crab and duck. Since most cheese contains rennet that comes from slaughtered cows, you'll be safest serving cheese that is specifically vegetarian. To further complicate matters, many Indians observe specific dietary restrictions during certain religious festivals, abstaining from certain foods and/or from alcohol, or only eating specific foods at that time. If you don't know everyone's preferences, include some vegetarian dishes that even traditional Jains and other pure vegetarians can eat. That way you won't risk having any guests who can't find something to eat.

Most religions forbid the consumption of alcoholic beverages. Although many Indians do drink alcohol, from the point of view of religion, it is generally unacceptable except among Christians. If you are unsure whether or not your guests drink, you're safer not serving alcohol. It would be awkward if the hosts were the only ones drinking. In any case, always keep some non-alcoholic beverages on hand for your guests who don't drink. Since many people would be offended if you offered them alcohol, simply ask what they would like to drink instead of offering them a beer or a glass of wine. Most Indian women don't drink even if their husbands do.

If you invite anyone out to a meal, it is assumed that you will pay. In India, the host always pays. A person would feel offended if you invited him out and then expected him to pay his own way.

Indians rarely eat anything without offering some to whoever else is present, and you would do well do follow their example. It would be considered extremely rude, for instance, if you were out with friends and stopped to buy yourself an ice cream without offering to buy one for everyone.

Here Comes the Groom

Hindu weddings traditionally last a few days. Many different ceremonies are involved, most of which you will not be likely to witness. The one you will see most often is when the groom rides a white horse or horse-drawn chariot through the streets to the marriage hall. The groom is typically preceded by a uniformed band playing cacophonous tunes at ear-splitting levels; several people carrying tall arrays of flashing lights on their heads; a big, noisy generator to provide power for the lights and amplifiers; and a group of male friends dancing wildly as the procession moves slowly through the streets, along with an entourage of relatives, friends, and curious bystanders.

The actual marriage rites, which are almost always religious in nature, are typically followed by a reception with music blaring from poor quality loudspeakers at top volume for several hours. Alas, musical ability does not seem to be a prerequisite for most bands! If you are invited to a wedding, unless you are hard of hearing and love music that is deafeningly loud, bring along some earplugs and comb your hair so it covers them, if possible. They won't even begin to block out everything, but at least they should prevent any damage. Most Indians seem to be a little hard of hearing, and weddings are surely one of the chief causes!

After the marriage, the bride typically goes to the groom's house, which may be shared with a large joint family including parents and grandparents together with several brothers and their families along with, perhaps, a few others under the same roof or in the same compound. In a traditional family, the mother-in-law instructs the new bride in her duties, and the bride serves her in-laws as well as her husband. In a large extended family, the oldest married (not widowed) woman in the house rules over all the others, so there is a certain pecking order. Although most interactions between them will be behind the scenes, this point may help you understand the household politics in an extended family, as well as the hierarchy.

If you are invited to an Indian wedding, expect to get dressed up, especially if the people involved are affluent. If the wedding is particularly fancy, you may need to borrow or buy something appropriate. A fancy *sari* or suit is always appropriate for ladies. Since your friends probably will not expect you to go out and buy something expensive for the occasion, they are likely to tell you to "just wear anything," but don't take them seriously. If you show up in casual clothes, you will feel out of place. Ask your friends what they will be wearing. If possible, ask to see what they are planning to wear since they may understate the description considerably in order to make you feel comfortable about whatever you have. You may not need to wear something quite as fancy, but you will get a good idea of what is appropriate.

Although the men may not always dress up to the extent that the women do, blue jeans and a T-shirt would definitely be out of place. Slacks with a nice shirt would be much more appropriate, and you might add a blazer for fancier weddings.

Upscale big city weddings are astoundingly flashy: the ladies typically wear designer silk *saris* or suits covered with gold embroidery, beads, sequins, crystals, etc., and accessorized with an incredible amount of flashy jewelry as well. Even for modest weddings, people put on their best clothes and jewelry. It's amazing what can come out of the cupboards for such occasions.

Most marriages are still arranged by the relatives of the bride and groom, although this trend has been changing, especially in the metropolitan areas. Foreigners from cultures where individuality and personal freedom of choice are valued most highly tend to be extremely critical of arranged marriages. However, this issue is not as simple and clear-cut as it may seem. In India, family and tradition are far more important than the individual; and marriages arranged by families who care deeply about their children's happiness and wellbeing are often very successful.

For weddings in India, the families nearly always put on the best celebration they can. Unfortunately, they sometimes go to extremes they can't afford, and may even spend the next ten or twenty years working to pay off the debt. A family typically spends maybe 10% of their wealth on a wedding; but for a family that can barely make ends meet, it can prove to be an immense burden. It's usually the bride's family that has to bear the burden of the wedding, which is frequently made much heavier by payment of dowry. Dowry has been illegal for many years, but it's still a widespread practice. You may notice that few of the matrimonial ads in the newspapers say "no dowry." But even if there is no dowry, weddings are still an enormous expense, as there is immense social pressure to make them as lavish as possible.

Dowry is a touchy issue in India, so you should avoid the subject or at least keep your questions about dowry general and refrain from getting personal. And try to refrain from mentioning it at all during wedding celebrations. As noted above, although most people agree, at least in public, that dowry is a bad thing, the practice continues anyway. Even though there are significantly more boys than girls in India, the parents of girls are often afraid that without giving dowry they won't find husbands for them.

It's traditional for women to have *mehendi* (henna) designs drawn on their hands and sometimes also on their feet when they are attending weddings or other celebrations. They are essentially temporary tattoos that usually take several days to wear off. If you choose to get *mehendi*, be aware that black henna often contains a dye that can cause serious skin reactions.

Married women who are Hindu typically wear a *bindi* or decoration on their forehead between the eyebrows. These are distinct from *tilaks*, dabs of red or orange paste on the forehead that are a form of *prasad* given at a temple to both sexes of any ages. In addition to the *bindi*, many women wear red powder *(sindur)* along the part in their hair that also symbolizes their status as a married woman.

Giving and Receiving Gifts

Never give or take anything with your left hand. Always use the right hand or both hands together. You should always give and receive gifts with both hands. The left hand can be together with the right hand or else just supporting the right wrist. It is customary to wash your hands before giving or receiving *prasad*—which is any food or other item that has been offered in a religious ceremony or at a temple—or any sacred item.

In Indian culture, the act of giving is much more important than the gift itself or even whether the recipient actually likes the gift. But gift giving should never be careless. When given with sincerity, a humble gift is greater than the most expensive and beautiful gift given reluctantly or from a mere desire to impress, etc. Whatever is given should come from the heart. If you have put some special thought or effort into a gift, and especially if you've brought it from home, it will be appreciated.

In general, you should avoid giving expensive gifts, especially if the person might have any difficulty reciprocating comfortably. Expensive gifts are normally only given on occasions such as weddings, and only between family members and close friends.

It's necessary to take religion into account when you are selecting a gift for someone. If you aren't sure, then keep your gifts as neutral as possible—and keep them simple. Don't give leather or alcohol, either of which would offend many Indians.

Muslims dislike dogs, which are considered unclean, so even a box of chocolates with a picture of a cute puppy would be objectionable. Anything made of pigskin would be highly offensive as pigs are also considered impure. For Muslims, it's also best to avoid giving cards and gifts that have images of people on them.

High-tech gifts are well valued, and are especially appropriate in a business context, but they shouldn't be too expensive. Pens are almost always good gifts, especially the preferred brands, which are Parker and Cross.

For traditional women, a *sari* or suit piece is generally appropriate. If you give a *sari* as a gift, always include a blouse piece. The quality should correspond to what she usually wears. A man shouldn't give a gift to an Indian woman unless it is also from his wife or sister or another relative. Traditionally, expensive jewelry is given only between family members. For men who wear them (more common in the South and especially among Brahmins), a *dhoti* is an appropriate gift. It should also include the upper cloth. Shawls are good gifts for either men or women.

Keep gifts for children simple and inexpensive. Sweets are generally appreciated. A paper kite or a cricket bat is a good gift for any boy. For girls, jewelry or clothing is appropriate, or colored pencils. Books are excellent gifts, as long as you give something that is neither too easy nor too advanced.

As with weddings anywhere, what you give depends on how well you know the couple. Economic status is also a factor, but almost any gift brought from your home country will be cherished. Even at weddings of wealthy people, gifts don't have to be so expensive. Anything that looks impressive (even if it is inexpensive) or has a well-known brand name is good.

A framed photo of yourself together with people you have lived or worked with will usually be much appreciated, especially if you have become close to them, because it shows them that you really value the relationship.

Red, yellow and green are the most auspicious colors for wrapping gifts; black and white are considered inauspicious.

Whenever you give money as a gift, as you might on the occasion of a birth or marriage, or as a bonus or donation, it's traditional to give an odd number. The numbers 11, 21, 51, 101, 501 and 1001 are considered especially auspicious, and giving these or similar denominations will make your gift more special. Every stationery shop has little decorated envelopes that are specially designed for giving money.

It is customary to bring a box of sweets as a gift when you visit people during *Diwali (Dipavali)* and other festivals.

When someone gives you a gift that is wrapped, you should accept it graciously and set it aside. Don't open it in the presence of the giver unless she insists. Also, don't expect gifts you give to be opened in front of you, as this is not the usual Indian custom.

In Indian culture it is not necessarily considered rude to ask friends for gifts, so if people ask you to bring them some item from home or to give them, say, your new iPod, you needn't feel offended. However, you don't have to do it, even if they keep asking. Their requests can be seen as an indication of intimacy—they are comfortable enough with you to ask, and you are comfortable enough to refuse (by evasion, of course).

Of course, if people you barely know ask for something, they may simply be out to exploit you. Many people whose jobs bring them into contact with foreigners are in the habit of asking for favors and gifts. Sometimes they have a sob story and ask for money, but it is best not to give in to these people; their stories may be made up or heavily embellished, and you have no way of knowing. They may request an expensive gift like a camera, or they may want you to help them come to your country. Your best course here is to smile and say something noncommittal such as, "OK, I'll see what I can do," and then forget about it unless they become good friends over time and you really want to do something for them.

Privacy is a Foreign Concept

Privacy is a foreign concept in India. It is not considered essential or even desirable except in certain situations. India is a relatively small landmass with a population of more than 1.3 billion people, so with such a population density, the habit of privacy is not the norm. For the vast majority of people in India, sleeping alone in a room is almost unimaginable, and it's not something they would do by choice. In fact, most Indians would feel lonely, or even a little frightened, if they had to sleep alone.

Of course, everyone would like privacy in the bathroom, but many people don't even have access to bathrooms. You'll often see people bathing in rivers or ponds or at outdoor pumps, though only children bathe in the nude in public. Men typically bathe in their underwear or with a cloth wrapped around their waist. For women, the situation is more delicate, but it is astonishing how much modesty Indian women can maintain while bathing and changing clothes in public, which they do more-or-less fully clothed. But by far the worst thing is the shortage of decent toilet facilities, and it's extremely common to see rows of people relieving themselves out in a field in the early morning.

In any case, the absence of privacy creates a much deeper intimacy between people than exists in the West, an intimacy in which the essence of Indian life is structured. Such intimacy is unnerving to those who are used to hiding their feelings and themselves behind a veil of materialism, and it takes getting used to.

If you don't keep your door locked all the time—even in your own house—people are likely to come wandering in at just about any time. Friends and servants may walk into your room day or night without knocking. If you are staying with a family, you may have trouble convincing them that you are uncomfortable having people walking in on you unannounced at any hour of the day or night. And, if another guest shows up, no matter what the hour, you could suddenly be asked to make room for the person. If this happens to you, do your best to adjust, if possible. Even if the situation is miserable, try to wait until the next day to decamp for more comfortable quarters or everyone will certainly be upset.

If you insist on your privacy, people may wonder what you have to hide, and they may take offense sometimes, especially if they are not used to foreigners, because their expectation is that friends have nothing to hide from each other. However, you can try explaining that customs in your country are different and you need a little more privacy to feel comfortable.

Patience, Anger & Tact

Life in India tends to move a bit slowly, especially outside the big cities, so India is a good place to learn patience. If someone says something will take one minute, it will usually be five or ten. If they say ten minutes, it will probably be at least thirty. If they say an hour, it may be tomorrow. If they say tomorrow, it may be next week or even never.

Yelling at someone to try to get something done sooner is worse than useless. In fact, getting angry will frequently bring progress to a standstill. Soft, sweet words of encouragement and praise will nearly always be much more effective. Keep smiling, and keep your voice even. You may often need to be firm and insistent, but try not to get angry.

Although Indians tend to be extraordinarily patient in most situations, they can become surprisingly impatient in others. When sitting around, most Indians can easily wait for hours, days, weeks or even months without growing impatient, but when standing in a line or driving, they often become impatient and sometimes extremely aggressive, especially the men. If you are in a line at the bank or post office, for instance, you may have to be quite assertive if you don't want to be elbowed out of the way. You may get to the head of a line only to have some man (or several) reach over you with his papers, or simply wedge himself in front of you as if you weren't there. (Indian women might behave like this with other women, but not with men.) In this situation, you can just politely mention that you were in line ahead of him. Thus reprimanded, most people will apologize and stand back because you are a guest in their country. Often there is no line as such, just a crowd of people reaching for the counter.

If in spite of your best efforts to be patient, you lose your temper and yell or are rude to someone, you should always apologize as soon as you have calmed down—even, if possible, when you truly feel that the other person was in the wrong. Of course, in that case you need only apologize for losing your temper. Always apologize if you have inadvertently offended someone in some way, especially if religion was involved. Never criticize or make fun of any religion or any religious idol, no matter what your private feelings may be. You could find yourself in deep trouble if you do.

A sincere apology will almost always be graciously accepted, and it will definitely influence the way you are perceived in the eyes of those around you. Why should you care? Well, if, for instance, there is even a slight chance that you may ever need that person to do something for you in the future, your apology will make a big difference in their performance. More importantly, anyone who may have witnessed your outburst will have formed a negative opinion of you, and word is sure to spread quickly that you aren't a good person to deal with. If you are living here, a bad reputation can lead to major problems. Even if you are just passing through, remember that such behavior on your part will reflect on other foreigners who will come after you (especially those from your own country), making things just that much more difficult for everyone.

Indians will generally go far out of their way to avoid hurting other people's feelings, so you should try to learn to do likewise. If you hurt their feelings by speaking harshly, you will find that they can really shut you out. For this reason, even when you are angry or upset, speaking kindly and respectfully will always be far more effective than swearing or speaking harsh words.

Any difficult situations should be handled with tact. If you have to send something back in a restaurant, for example, try to soften your complaint with a compliment about something else. If you just can't come up with something to compliment about the restaurant or the food, try to think of something nice to say about the person you are addressing. Almost anything that will take the edge off your complaint will do.

Mind Your Hands & Feet

In India, everyone who is physically able to do so uses the left hand for toilet functions, so it is considered unclean. Avoid eating and giving or taking anything with the left hand.

Never point your feet at any person or at any religious shine or image of a deity, especially the soles of the feet, because doing so is a great insult. The feet are considered to be unclean—and shoes are even worse than bare feet. Avoid sitting American-style with one foot resting on the other knee, because your foot will almost always be pointed at someone, and that person may be offended.

Always apologize if your shoes or feet accidentally touch another person. This apology doesn't have to be verbal, though. Indians often make this kind of apology with a little gesture, first extending the palm of the right hand towards the person and then bringing it back towards the heart.

If you put your feet up on a chair or train seat, take your shoes off. Shoes should always be kept on the floor. Try not to step over people who are lying on the floor (such as in a train station.) If doing so is unavoidable, step over their feet only.

You may sometimes notice young people touching the feet of elders. This is a way of showing respect or seeking blessings. By tradition, people also receive the blessings of saints by touching their feet. In many other circumstances as well, people will touch the feet of someone, but the person whose feet are being touched is always superior in position and/or age.

If a child touches your feet, accept this gesture gracefully and touch her lightly on the head or shoulder as a blessing. Just as soon as they learn to walk, children from traditional families are taught to touch the feet of elders to receive their blessings. If an adult touches your feet, it's customary to tell him that it's not necessary and take his arms to raise him up, though you can also give your blessing in the same way. In India, the head is regarded as the seat of the soul; so apart from giving your blessing when someone touches your feet, never touch anyone's head.

If a beggar tries to touch your feet, you can just back away and say *no*. Putting your hand up with palm directed towards the beggar to indicate that she should not come closer also serves the purpose of giving a blessing because the gesture is essentially the same, though it's not what she is after.

Shoes are often left at the door of Indian homes and always outside of temples and shrines. Anytime you see shoes at the door, you should always assume that you should take yours off, too. Keep a pair of socks with you if you don't like going barefoot.

Smoking

As is appropriate everywhere, you should always ask whether anyone objects before you light up indoors.

Although India is way behind the West in regulating tobacco, and there is still little general awareness of its dangers, India is making progress in this direction. Smoking is now prohibited on buses, trains, airplanes, restaurants, places of worship, government offices, and nearly all other public places. Most people will comply if you politely ask them not to smoke. Few Indian women smoke. It's simply not acceptable in the eyes of most Indians.

Other Points of Etiquette

Always let people do their duty, especially when you are a guest in someone's house or even at a hotel. This is especially important in business contexts, where you should take care not to lower yourself in any way. Indians get upset if they see you doing any work that they consider part of their job, especially when it's something menial—even something as simple as carrying your own suitcase to the door, or taking a cup to the kitchen.

Whistling is considered rude because it has sexual connotations, so if you are a habitual whistler try to remember not to whistle in public.

Strong profanity is regarded as disrespectful, so if you are in the habit of swearing a lot, try to tone down your language.

It is inappropriate to smell flowers that are for sale in a shop or that are to be offered for a religious ceremony or at a temple, or to be given to someone as a gift. The reasoning here is that smelling a flower is like taking a bite out of an apple, only it's much subtler. It doesn't matter that you can't perceive the missing fragrance. From an Indian's point of view, to partake in any way of something you are intending to offer either to another person or in a religious ceremony is disrespectful. Even if you don't understand the logic here, you should go along with it anyway in order not to give offense.

About the Caste System

Caste is still an essential part of the average Indian's identity. You have only to look at the matrimonial ads in the newspaper to see the extent to which this is true. So even though many people would like to dismantle India's caste system, it is still deeply embedded in society. There are four major castes—*Brahmins* are the priestly caste; *Kshatriyas*, the warriors class; *Vaishyas*, the merchants; and *Shudras*, the workers—but there are also many others, and every caste has sub-castes. There are also those who are considered to be lower than *Shudras* or without a caste. They are, from the point of view of the government, all lumped together as *Dalits*, with the exception of the tribal peoples. *Dalit* ("Oppressed") is the politically correct name at the moment; they were formerly called *Harijans*, ("Children of God"). The most politically incorrect name, one that you should never use, is "Untouchable." Most *Dalits* belong to the so-called "Scheduled Castes." The many tribal peoples of India, who are also called *Adivasis*, are allotted "Scheduled Tribe" status.

Ironically, the government of India continues to propagate the caste system by making "reservations" for the Scheduled Castes and Scheduled Tribes (which are considered to be disadvantaged and backward) in education and government, as well as allotting them special welfare benefits. This policy has caused much divisiveness and disharmony, but there's no end in sight.

There are many rules of conduct specific to each particular caste and sub-caste. The highest *Brahmin* castes have the most complex and stringent rules, which not only determine who one can marry, which foods are allowed, what work one can do, etc., but also include very rigid rules relating to contact with people of lower castes. Strict rituals of purification are prescribed in case one has become polluted by contact with something or someone forbidden.

It's possible that you'll meet people whose caste rules affect you in some way. You may be entertained outside someone's house because caste rules won't allow you to be inside, or in certain parts of the house, or in contact with certain items. Although you may be served food, the host may not partake with you. When you come up against such behavior, accept it gracefully. It may be because of caste rules, but you probably won't be told the reasons behind it because your host wouldn't want to make you uncomfortable. Even though Westerners generally feel more comfortable knowing what's going on behind the scenes, it wouldn't occur to most Indians to explain. The reasons are usually obvious to other Indians, and stating them could create an awkward situation. Don't take it personally.

The caste system was originally about a person's work and family *dharma*. It wasn't until later that it became the abusive system that it is today. The idea was that when a family has been doing the same kind of work for many generations, then that activity comes easily and most successfully to them and to their descendants, and it was thus felt to be the most evolutionary activity. This aspect of the concept of caste—the family duty or *dharma*—is still a practical reality for many Indians, right along with the oppression and abuse that they may suffer as a result of that *dharma*.

For the more than 800 million Indians who earn less than Rs.100 a day, mere survival is a challenge. Nevertheless, Indians are often incredibly optimistic even in the face of extreme adversity, continuing to harbor hopes that somehow their life will improve, or at least that their children will be better off than they are. They place a high priority on providing for their families, and getting their children married and settled. If following the family *dharma* provides the means to accomplish these goals, they tend to be pretty satisfied. What they do is simply what they have to do, and there is not much to think about. People from cultures that place a higher value on the individual than on society find this concept difficult to understand, but India is a collective society and the values are different.

Racial Discrimination

Racial discrimination based on the color of one's skin exists in India as it does elsewhere. Indians strongly prefer light skin to dark. You only have to look at matrimonial ads and the popularity of "fairness" creams that supposedly lighten the skin with regular use to see the reverence for fair complexions.

One aspect of this racial discrimination is that white foreigners are often singled out for preferential treatment, although they are generally expected to pay for it in one way or another. There are also some people who still seem to feel resentment toward the British (or maybe it's towards foreigners in general), and such people may vent their bitterness on any white person they encounter. In any case, virtually all foreigners experience economic discrimination in India, though Caucasians seem to bear the brunt of it.

Blacks tend to be discriminated against almost everywhere in India except where the locals also have dark complexions (most notably, Kerala). Even dark-skinned Indians suffer harassment because of their coloring when they travel to parts of India where the locals are fairer. Non-Indian Asians from certain countries may also be subjected to discrimination. Latin Americans, who blend in fairly well color-wise, seem to have fewer problems.

About Beggars

Avoid giving money to beggars. It just encourages them to keep living that way. Don't even look. Just pretend you don't see them.

Any reaction, even a negative one, encourages them to keep trying. People sometimes give money to get them to go away, but this is a mistake. It will only encourage them to ask for more. If beggars can't get any reaction from you, they usually give up pretty quickly and move on to the next person. But if you give anything to one, you'll instantly be mobbed by others. Moreover, they often continue to demand more, unsatisfied even if you give everything you have.

Beggars tend to congregate in large cities, tourist areas and pilgrimage places. You don't see as many beggars elsewhere, at least not professional ones. When Indians give to beggars, they usually do so for the purpose of gaining *punya*, religious merit, and not necessarily out of compassion for the beggars' condition.

Many visitors have a hard time coming to terms with all the beggars in India. It is hardest to ignore the children, which is why professional beggars often use them to do their begging, though there are also quite a few street children on their own. Stories of children who have been purchased from poor families or kidnapped and then forced to beg are true, unfortunately. But by far the worst thing is that many of the children are deliberately mutilated to make them more effective beggars. Women begging with babies sometimes even borrow other people's babies to get more sympathy.

On the other hand, you'll often find school children begging for a pen or chocolate or a few rupees. They aren't destitute street kids, and you are doing them no favors in encouraging this behavior. In some tourist areas, parents complain that their children are leaving school to pester tourists. Don't encourage them!

People beg for different reasons. For many of the beggars that you are likely to see hanging around the tourist areas, begging is an inherited "profession." They beg because their parents did. Widows who have been turned out of their homes after losing their husbands with no means to fend for themselves are among the most truly destitute people of India, but they are, sadly, often the least successful beggars. Others may have been cast out of their homes because they became sick with leprosy or AIDS; or they may have lost their home and livelihood due to some trickery or just bad luck. And there are some for whom begging may be a one-time venture. Perhaps they were robbed while traveling and need money to get home.

But some people, strange as it may seem, just see begging as an easy way to earn a living. Once I was pestered by a couple of strong, healthy-looking, rag-clad young men, so I told them in Hindi that they should do some work. One of them replied in excellent English that if they wanted to work they wouldn't be begging!

While many beggars are genuinely destitute, many aren't. Some professional beggars (especially in the tourist areas) are far more affluent or healthy than they appear. You may hear stories of beggars who go to a comfortable home at the end of the day. This is assuredly not the case for the majority of beggars, but one can hardly doubt that some make a fairly good living by begging.

Obviously, many people in India have become beggars out of dire necessity, but it is often not possible to tell the professional beggars from the truly impoverished who have fallen on hard times, though habitual beggars typically have a certain characteristic whine. The wretched appearance and woeful expression on the face of the habitual beggar is often greatly exaggerated. If you watch the change of expression once money has been given and the beggar turns in search of the next donor (especially if he thinks you aren't looking), you can often catch a fleeting glimpse behind the mask. Apparent deformities may be faked as well, though many are so skillfully done that it's nearly impossible to tell.

I never give anything to beggars in tourist areas, because they are virtually all controlled by a boss, which means some wealthy criminal will end up taking whatever they receive. Beggar bosses do tend to be very rich. Once in a while, I'll find my heart so torn by some extremely emaciated child, wretched leper or old lady that

I have to give them something. But I make sure it's something they can't turn around and resell.

How beggars receive whatever you give will tell you if they are as genuinely wretched as they look. Some will throw it on the ground in disgust and demand money instead. Others will receive it gratefully. If their eyes light up with gratitude when given a *chapati* or a piece of fruit, you can assume that they are truly destitute.

There are many poor and wretched people in India, but if you really want to do something for them, find a better way than giving money to beggars, which is like trying to fill a bottomless pit. For instance, you might donate to or even join one of the NGOs that exist to help street children.

Religious beggars are in a different category altogether. It's traditional in India for ascetics, monks and *sadhus* (holy men) to go door to door begging for their food, and you still see many who do, though these days more often you will find them sitting on the ground outside temples and tourists places begging for money. Giving alms to such people is regarded as a meritorious act that is deeply rooted in Indian culture. However, the tradition is to give them food (rice, *dal*, *chapatis*, fruit, etc.) or sometimes clothing, not money or other items except in extraordinary circumstances. These days, many are just ordinary beggars in disguise.

Environmental Issues

Environmental awareness is slowly dawning in India, but it has a long way to go. You will surely notice, for instance, that littering is a huge problem in India. Almost everyone does it, but middle- and upper-class Indians are the worst because they expect someone else to pick up after them—this is, incidentally, a central aspect of the whole social hierarchy—and they also simply have more to throw away than the poor.

Plastic packaging has only become common in the last 20 or 30 years, and Indians are just beginning to wake up to the fact that throwing it away as casually as they would a banana peel or apple core is creating a major problem in their environment. But there is still little awareness that there is anything wrong with throwing a soft-drink bottle or candy wrapper out the window, even in the most pristine environment.

In most towns and cities, the usual practice is to throw trash on the street, where someone will eventually come along to sweep everything aside, and cart it away now and then—at least, that's the expectation. And many people do make a living by collecting paper, cardboard, clothes, and anything else that is somehow usable to recycle or resell, though there is very little systematic plastic recycling so these items typically end up in huge rubbish piles.

One bright note is that many cities are banning polythene bags, especially the very thin ones, and they are encouraging people to carry reusable shopping bags.

The government has recognized that clear-cutting the forests is a bad move, however, and efforts have been made to stop illegal tree cutting, though, of course, quite a lot of it still goes on. Also, wildlife conservation is improving, though it is often linked to tourism, and is not so much valued for its own sake.

So can we as visitors do? Don't litter. Try to be less wasteful. Avoid buying bottled water and packaged goods. Take bottles, etc. to recycling places where there are any. Carry reusable shopping bags. Refrain from buying tiger skins, *shahtush* shawls, ivory or anything else that comes from endangered species.

• • •

Spirituality & Religion

Religious Diversity

RELIGION PLAYS A MAJOR ROLE in the lives of most Indians. Those who are considered Hindu make up more than 80% of the population. However, rather than being a single religion, Hinduism actually encompasses myriad different religions, all of which have their roots in the ancient Vedic tradition—as also do, to varying degrees, Sikhism, Jainism, Buddhism and Zoroastrianism—for which reason India has been called the "Land of the Veda."

Although the words *Hindu* and *Hinduism* have come into common use, they are not indigenous. The English were confused by the religious practices they saw and simply lumped many different religions under the single category, *Hindu*. Those who we call *Hindus* refer to their religion not as *Hinduism* but as *Sanatana Dharma*, which means "eternal law" or "eternal way of life." Of the rest of the population, Muslims make up about 12%, while Sikhs, Buddhists, Jains and Christians each comprise 2–3%. Jews and Parsis together account for less than 1% of the population. In addition, India is also home to numerous tribal religions.

In order to feel most comfortable in a country with such immense religious diversity, it is necessary to be tolerant of all religions, no matter what your private feelings about them may be. Spending time in other cultures gives you a superb opportunity to realize that people naturally don't all think alike and that forcing them to do so is impossible. But instead of focusing on the differences, try focusing on the similarities. You may be surprised at how many parallels there are between all religions.

In India, there are literally thousands of names for God, many of which are shared by more than one religion. As Mark Twain so delightfully put it, "India has 2,000,000 gods and worships them all. In religion, other countries are paupers; India is the only million-naire."[7] However, the "2,000,000 gods" of which he speaks are actually different names for different personified aspects of the one supreme God, rather than different gods. Hindus (as well as Jains and Buddhists) generally understand that one ultimate Reality, one supreme God, underlies all these diverse aspects. Although some may be vehemently attached to a particular aspect that they consider primary, most people revere them all.

There is God (with many names) and there are *devas*, who are gods with a small *g*. *Devas* are merely the personifications of the forces of Nature, which are seen as aspects of God. God, on the other hand is One, Unbounded, Eternal, without a second and without a form. This is stated beautifully in the Veda: "Truth is One, but the wise call it by many names."[8] However, as it is difficult to worship the formless God, *Brahman*, people take whatever aspect they like and worship that as a means to approach God. "For Hindus, God is effectively in every living thing, in every drop of the Ganges [India's holiest river] and every molecule of the atmosphere. For them, Divinity pervades everything and can be seen in daily life—if you only know where (and how) to look." [9]

Hindus generally recognize that different people have differ-ent spiritual needs that can change as they grows older. Although traditionally one inherits the religion of one's father, it is commonly acceptable for any family member to favor a different aspect of God according to his or her own inclinations. Religion is a personal thing for Hindus. It is not canonized in any way.

People who have attained the state of enlightenment see God as infinite and unbounded, and they recognize that boundaries belong to humans. Enlightened people also have certain boundaries, which are inherent in a physical body since living in the world is impossible otherwise; but on the level of consciousness, they are free and unbounded. The more limited a person's consciousness, the more the boundaries predominate.

Roger Housden gives a lucid account of how Christians and Muslims came to misunderstand Hinduism as worship of the physical idols (which it isn't): "Christian missionaries, and Muslim invaders even more so, were naturally shocked at the profusion of 'idols' they found in every town and village in the country. Their distaste, however, was caused more by their own literalist manner of thinking than by any intrinsic inadequacy in the Hindu religion. The three religions of the Near East [Christianity, Judaism and Islam] are all religions of the book. The word, which they all must depend on, tends inevitably towards concretization: this is the truth, so that must be false. Once cast in stone, the truth has no freedom of movement. It becomes linear, set down for all time, and casts a shadow as dark as its words are bright. Hinduism had no founder, and no single book, foundation, or organization to set uniform standards and rules. As in life, all the subtle variations of light and dark thrive there, and are indeed encouraged to do so."[10]

Because so much of Indian thought is rooted in the ancient Vedic tradition, which is all encompassing, Indians are innately disinclined to embrace more limited viewpoints. Even when Hindus convert to Christianity, for instance, you may see a picture of Christ sitting on the family altar along with Ganesh or Lakshmi or Buddha or Guru Nanak, or all of them and more. And you may also see Christian pictures in the homes of non-Christians. The concept of an underlying unity makes most Indians naturally inclined to be tolerant.

What about the conflicts between Muslims and Hindus? And the Sikhs? And the Christians? There are conflicts, but they are usually instigated by greed for power, money or land. It's rare that they are only about beliefs. It is well known that the original scriptures of the various religions, including Islam, give little or no basis for the conflicts they have been misconstrued to justify.

Religion is a powerful motivator since most Indians actively practice one religion or another, which is why leaders use religious motives to manipulate the people. Politicians routinely stir up trouble over religious issues in order to further their own selfish interests (often for the purpose of discrediting the ruling party so as to get their own party into power).

Indians are by nature easy-going, pragmatic and adaptable people who are typically not inclined to violence. However, even though violence is generally against their nature and religious values, once they get stirred up, mob consciousness often takes over and they simply go wild. Some people have theorized that it is precisely because it is so much against their temperament and code of behavior that they become so hysterical when provoked to violence.

There are countless stories of villages where Muslims and Hindus lived and worked side by side as friends until the Partition (the political division of India, Pakistan and Bangladesh along religious lines in 1947) or other destructive political manipulations made them enemies, and in some places they still do.

Some religious conflicts arise over the issue of forced conversions (including situations where people are persuaded to convert by being offered jobs or other incentives), but again, these conflicts can be attributed to the machinations of religious and political leaders and not to the religions themselves. Christ won people over through love. It was later leaders of the church who were responsible for the aggressive expansion of Christianity by any means. And although some fanatical Muslim leaders and their followers in certain countries are extremely intolerant, this is generally not the situation in India where most Muslims are peace-loving people who are generally fairly tolerant of non-Muslims.

Most Indians feel that religion is personal and that what a person believes is his or her own business. Because they cherish the freedom to worship God as they wish in keeping with their own traditions, it's hardly surprising that proselytizers aren't welcomed. Missionaries have been violently attacked for proselytizing, even though they may also have been doing desperately needed humanitarian works. But it's not usually that the assailants have anything against Christ. They simply don't want anyone telling them what to believe and how to live their lives.

The issue of religious conflicts in India is, obviously, far more complex than a simple summary can even begin to describe. If you are interested in understanding the situation better, I recommend that you read the insightful writings of William Dalrymple, who has been studying these issues for many years.

Karma and Reincarnation

Most Indians have a deeply ingrained belief in reincarnation and *karma*. Reincarnation means that one has taken birth many times before and will continue to do so again in the future until *moksha*, liberation, is attained. *Karma* simply means "action," and the idea behind the law of *karma* is that whatever action you do eventually comes back to you—if not in this life, then in some future life. It's ultimately the same principle that is embodied in the Golden Rule of Christianity ("Do unto others as you would have them do unto you"[11]) and which is expressed in one form or another in every religion.

Since the *karma* that one has done in previous lifetimes determines to a large extent how one's present lifetime will play out (though one has the free will to change it to a certain extent), many Indians are somewhat fatalistic. Those who don't fully understand how the law of *karma* works often blame *karma* for their misfortunes while ignoring the fact that they are merely suffering the consequences of their own past actions.

Spirituality & Enlightenment

The best thing about India is its spirituality, so if you have any spiritual inclinations, letting your mind be attuned to this level of life will be rewarding. The knowledge of higher states of consciousness is still available in India, though there is much confusion and mixing of traditions, which has greatly reduced the efficacy of many paths to enlightenment. Nevertheless, the underlying spirituality that permeates the whole of society is beautiful, and letting your attention go to that aspect of life can greatly enhance your enjoyment of India.

Many people see religion primarily as a means for attaining their worldly aspirations—and almost all religious performances in India are done with materialistic aims in mind, such as having children or gaining wealth—while knowing God or attaining enlightenment are vague and distant goals. Nonetheless, India has a history of spirituality that can't be denied. It has been home to many great saints, and spirituality is a natural part of the culture—a spirituality that coexists with and sometimes transcends the materialistic tendencies that predominate in India as in the rest of the world. Even today you will find that many Indians are genuinely spiritual in their outlook and aims in life.

One aspect of that spirituality is that most Indians rely heavily on God for everything in their lives, no matter how small or mundane, and that there is a certain recognition of God in everything. Roger Housden tells a delightful story that illustrates this. An American visitor wanted to see what "God means for the ordinary person," so his friend took the man to meet a farmer, and after a little discussion the American "picked up a handful of the earth at his feet. 'This,' he said, 'is dead matter, the material world.' Then, pointing to the sky, he asked again, 'Where is God to be found? If this is earth, what is spirit?' He was on the point of throwing the handful of earth to the ground, when the farmer grasped his hand and took the earth from him. 'You call my Mother dead?' he said. He was on the verge of tears. He kissed the earth, then knelt to return it to the ground. The visitor was silenced. With some embarrassment, he thanked the farmer, and returned to the car, his question answered. For the time being, the majority of Indians still live in a sacred world." [12]

Ultimately, who you are determines whether you see more of the spiritual side of India or the materialistic. "The world is as you are" [13], so if you are a materialistic person, you may see only the materialistic side of India, whereas if your inclination is more spiritual, you will also see the spiritual side.

Many foreigners come to India as spiritual seekers. They are on a spiritual quest—for God, for enlightenment, to find meaning in their life, to gain self-knowledge, peace of mind, or all of the above. According to certain traditions, especially the ancient Vedic tradition, the true purpose of life is to gain enlightenment, the direct experience of ultimate reality in higher states of consciousness. This experience has nothing to do with any particular religion. It is available to people of all religions.

In modern times, it is not so easy to find truly enlightened souls, genuine saints, though they do exist. India is home to countless spiritual masters, gurus, saints and teachers. Some are wise and deeply sincere, though only very few among them are fully enlightened. Some have been given techniques by enlightened masters and are able to teach them effectively, even though they may not yet be fully enlightened themselves. Of those who are enlightened, a few have the ability to effectively impart their knowledge. Others have no idea how they came to be enlightened and are therefore unable to lead anyone else to that state. Many are sincere enough but with little to give, and, sad to say, quite a few others are frauds.

Some people adopt the outward appearance of a holy man while having no real substance inside. Others like to show off their "powers," but they are almost always the tricks of a magician. These show-offs usually don't have any genuine yogic powers, which are known as *siddhis*.

Even many sincere spiritual seekers are confused about the difference between higher states of consciousness, which are spiritual, and artificially induced altered states of consciousness, which have little to do with genuine spirituality. This confusion has been compounded by the romanticization of *chillum*-smoking *sadhus* who claim that the use of drugs (usually *cannabis* in one form or another) is their *sadhana* or spiritual practice. But while there may be legitimate spiritual uses for certain drugs, none of the great enlightened masters of India have endorsed the use of drugs as a means to gaining enlightenment.[14]

Religious Etiquette

Because religion is an important part of most Indians' lives, you will probably be invited to some religious celebrations or places of worship during your stay in India. No matter what the religion, take care to be respectful and not to cause offense when attending a religious place or event. You may not be allowed into certain parts of some temples, especially the sanctum sanctorum. Remember that all temples, monasteries, *gurudwaras* (Sikh temples), mosques, etc., including the most famous ones that attract many tourists, are places of worship and not mere tourist attractions.

In any place of religious worship, refrain from smoking, talking loudly, holding hands or even touching a member of the opposite sex, spitting, and drinking alcohol. Turn off your cell phone or put it on silent mode before entering. Don't disturb monks, nuns and other worshippers during prayer. Remember that religious festivals are important rituals.

Shoes must be removed before entering a holy place, so it is best to wear inexpensive rubber sandals (*chappals*) that can be easily slipped off at the entrance. Sometimes even socks are not allowed in temples. Often there is a place for washing the feet outside the temple, in which case you should wash them before going in. If you wear good shoes to the temple, leave them in the care of a shoe-keeper or in the car.

There are some temples where ladies will not be admitted unless they are wearing a *sari*, though even Western clothes are acceptable in most temples as long as they are modest. A few temples require men to take off their shirts; and sometimes a *dhoti* is required as well. A *dhoti* is a length of cotton cloth wrapped around the waist and tied into sort of a skirt. You can put it on over your pants and take it off as soon as you leave.

Everyone is required to cover his or her head before entering a mosque or Sikh *gurudwara*.

When visiting temples and *gurudwaras*, you may be offered some holy water or other forms of *prasad* (offerings blessed in the temple, usually some form of sweets), which you should not refuse. Always accept *prasad* with both hands together, with the right a little on top of left. However, in the interest of health, you may want to do as many Indians do, which is to touch the water to your lips and then put it on top of your head. You can also do this with milk, though of course the result is a bit messy. Unfortunately, drinking either of these can be enough to cause a severe bout of Delhi Belly.

You may also be offered *prasad* consisting of sweets. Don't refuse it, but be discriminating about whether it is safe for you to eat. Food that is hot and fresh is usually OK, depending on how it is served. If in doubt, receive it respectfully and take it with you to share with others. Most Indians will be delighted to have some, and it is not likely to have the same effect on them. *Prasad* should always be shared, but any *prasad* that hasn't been given away may be put in a river or stream. It shouldn't be thrown on the ground or even fed to animals.

Refrain from touching any religious statues or holy pictures even if they are just crammed into a corner with other items, which is often the case, and never put anything on someone's personal altar, even an offering, without permission. Don't touch any other sacred items, including books, without asking first.

You should also refrain from putting any religious books or images of any kind (photos, statues, drawings, etc.) on the floor because people may take offense.

When walking around a temple or shrine, always go around it in a clockwise direction, keeping it to your right.

Leather items are offensive to traditional Jains and Hindus, and pigskin is particularly offensive to Muslims. Leave all leather items in your room whenever you are going to any religious shrine or ceremony. The easiest thing is to use only non-leather items (wallet, luggage, briefcase, purse, belt, shoes, etc.) while in India, so you never have to think about it. Don't make the mistake of assuming that people automatically condone the use of leather just because they seem cosmopolitan.

Swastika as a Sacred Symbol

Many visitors to India are initially shocked and horrified to see that the swastika is used extensively all over the country. Although in the West and many other parts of the world, the swastika is a symbol that is hated because of its association with Hitler and the Nazis, in India it retains its original sacred meaning and is greatly revered. Hitler chose the swastika because it is an auspicious symbol of great power, but he inverted it and thereby made his version extremely inauspicious. Any negative associations you may have with this symbol should be kept to yourself, as they do not apply here.

• • •

Money, Bargaining & Shopping

THE INDIAN CURRENCY is the *rupee* (abbreviated *Rs.* or *INR*), which can be exchanged for any other currency within India. There's a new rupee symbol, ₹, but most people still write *Rs*.

The rupee (worth around 2 US cents at this writing) is subdivided into 100 *paise*. Denominations of paper money are 5, 10, 20, 50, 100, 500 and 1,000 rupees. Most coins are 1, 2, 5, and 10 rupees, though occasionally you will see 10, 25 or 50 *paise* coins. Indians mostly use *paise* these days to give to beggars sitting in rows outside of temples or other pilgrimage places where there will usually be someone making change for that purpose. Large denomination notes are not always available, so you may receive huge quantities of Rs.50 and Rs.100 notes if you are changing a lot of money. Whenever you change a significant amount of currency, or get it from the ATM, take a bag or case to put it in that will adequately conceal the contents. Don't casually put it in your pocket.

Don't rely on only one way of getting money. And always carry some cash along with whatever travelers' checks, credit cards and/ or an ATM card you have, because very often cash is all you can use. It's possible to have money wired to you through Western Union, or through American Express or Thomas Cook, but it's expensive.

Changing Money

It's best to change money only at banks and authorized foreign exchange ("forex") agencies. They will give you an encashment certificate to prove that you have changed money legally. You should keep these—along with any ATM receipts—because you may need them from time to time. There are instances where foreigners are expected to pay in foreign currency, but if you have the exchange receipts, you can use rupees.

The other reason to deal with banks and authorized forex agents is that counterfeiting has become fairly common in India. Changing money unofficially is risky. If you somehow do get any counterfeit notes, having sufficient receipts to account for all the rupees in your possession is essential.

Changing money at a bank—especially the government-run ones like State Bank of India—can sometimes take as much as an hour or two, so don't rush in right before their lunch break or at closing time.

Banknotes are commonly stapled together in bundles of 100 with a signed and sealed piece of paper that certifies the amount and the number of banknotes stapled onto the bundle. The bundles usually have several staples, which can really be a pain to remove without tearing the banknotes. There is an art to doing this, so have someone show you, or else get a staple remover.

Always count your money before leaving the counter. If you get a stapled bundle with the stamped paper missing, you should definitely count it because someone could have removed some notes and simply re-stapled the bundle. Sometimes a clerk will hand you a pile of notes that is less than the correct amount. Usually the rest will be forthcoming if you just wait patiently, but occasionally you have to point out the error. Do it politely without making accusations. Always assume it's an honest error, which it may well be. The same goes for shops, hotels, restaurants, etc.

Many people will not accept torn banknotes, even if they have been repaired with tape, so try not to accept them. Even a tiny tear is unacceptable to many people. You can change old notes for new ones at most banks, but it's scarcely worth the effort.

In small towns, Rs.500 and Rs.1,000 notes can be hard to spend, either because no one has change for them or because merchants are worried that they could be counterfeit—which they sometimes are—so it is often better to have smaller denominations, anyway. Ask someone at the bank to show you the security features of the various notes so you know what to look for. Counterfeiters have managed to replicate virtually all the features, so the government is planning to introduce polymer currency notes, which are considerably harder to duplicate. Always check Rs.1,000 and Rs.500 notes for obvious defects when you get them.

If you are going to a remote area, you may have to rely exclusively on cash for all your needs. If you can't find out in advance what resources are available before you go, assume the worst and take quite a bit more cash than you expect to need—but not too many big bills, especially Rs.1,000 notes. Note that most rural banks have no foreign exchange facilities, their ATMs may not be international ATMs, and it may be difficult to get a bank wire sent to them within any reasonable amount of time. You wouldn't want to have to travel several hours to get money, especially if you're faced with an emergency. In the cities, it's easy to find an international ATM.

Credit cards are often accepted in major shops, hotels and restaurants in Indian cities and larger towns, but are of no use in more remote areas. Also, merchants add as much as 7% for using a credit card. In many places, you can also get cash advances (in rupees) from your MasterCard, Visa, American Express or Diners Club card, again with a substantial commission tacked on. If you bring more than one card, keep the second one in a safe place separate from the one you are using.

Don't forget to tell your bank and credit card companies that you are coming to India. If you neglect to do this, you'll have access problems. Keep the phone numbers and account numbers in a safe place separate from the cards in case of loss.

The Change Game

Small change is a chronic problem in India. You'll quickly notice that due to the shortage of small banknotes and coins, Indians engage in a perennial game to try to get the other person to come up with the change. You always want to have enough small change so it is available when you really need it, which you often do. The idea is that each person pretends not to have any change, and makes a show of looking. When you buy a bottle of water, for instance, you might offer a Rs.100 note, shrugging helplessly when asked if you have exact change, perhaps making some vague comment about how change is always a problem while you make a show of searching your pocket or bag, but without finding it at first. The shopkeeper may deny having any change, but you can continue your own search for a few seconds to see if some materializes when he searches his pockets, etc. If he really doesn't have change, bystanders will be asked for change or someone may be sent across the street to another shop, which could take several minutes. It's usually not worth having someone go out for change if you actually have it.

Merchants will often ask for exact change even if they have a whole drawer full, but first thing in the morning most businesses really don't have any change. If you have only large notes, especially 500s or 1,000s, you will be really stuck if you suddenly have to pay for a rickshaw or a bottle of water.

And, of course, whenever you are paying for anything, always count your money before giving it, and count your change as well. If it happens to be short, holding the money up with a questioning look will usually bring forth whatever is due. If it doesn't, then firmly insist on the rest.

Tipping and the Local Economy

Indians are more inclined to tip for the purpose of ensuring good service or getting something done rather than as a reward for service already rendered. Most Indians don't tip as we do in the West, though it has come to be expected of foreigners. Nevertheless, even if you are extremely wealthy, do try to respect the local economy and refrain from tipping ridiculous amounts, which not only makes it harder for the locals and raises the expectations of the people you are tipping to unreasonable levels. Over-tipping often results in people following you around looking for ways to get even more money out of you. Ignore demands for outrageous tips, and keep lots of small change on hand so that you don't end up giving huge tips simply because you don't happen to have anything smaller with you.

Tourist restaurants often add a 10–12% service charge to the bill, in which case a tip is not necessary, though if you wish to leave something extra, a few rupees will generally suffice. It's hard to give guidelines for tipping, because the usual is different in different places and no one really agrees on what is appropriate, anyway.

When you hire drivers for a full day or longer, it is customary to give a tip at the end. It's not necessary to tip prepaid taxi drivers or drivers who have just dropped you across town.

Giving tips as you go ensures good service, especially in the case of hotel maids or porters, so it is often better than waiting to tip until you leave, although the latter is a bit more graceful. Certain places have strict rules about tipping, though, and it is best to comply. Sometimes restaurants and hotels have a box near the cashier's desk where you can put tips for distribution among all the staff, including the people in the background that you may never see. If there is a box like this, you should use it. Otherwise, try to give tips in person. Ashrams and religious institutions normally don't allow tipping.

If you want to give someone some special appreciation for a job well done, write a letter of commendation. This will be deeply appreciated and in the long run may be worth much more to the person than the extra rupees would be. Also, the person will be sure to remember you and give you a warm welcome if you come back.

There are many situations where a little *bakshish* will get some-one to bend the rules a little, e.g., to let you into some place that doesn't allow outsiders in order to use the toilet, and that may be

OK. However, many cases that may seem quite harmless (giving *bakshish* to get you onto a full train, or to get some official to get your work done a little faster, for instance) are viewed by the government as bribery, which is best avoided.

At times you may encounter someone who is determined to fool or intimidate you into using his or her services. Ignore such people or firmly tell them *no* and walk away. Often people will insist on helping you (e.g., pushing your trolley at the airport) even when you don't want or need their help. If you accept their help, don't allow yourself to be bullied into giving them too much.

Bargaining is Expected

Bargaining is an essential skill in India, especially in the North. In the South, bargaining is not always necessary. Most shopping involves bargaining, although government shops and other fixed-price shops don't allow it. If possible, try to observe what locals are paying for the type of item you want, or ask someone reliable before you start.

When bargaining, smile, laugh and be friendly in order to keep the process as enjoyable as possible for yourself as well as the person you are bargaining with. The ideal is to arrive at a price that is fair for you while also allowing the seller a reasonable profit. It's not just to get the lowest possible price. For Indians, bargaining is also a means of establishing a relationship and mutual respect. In the North, if you don't bargain, you may lose the respect of the merchant who will think that you're a fool for wasting your money.

Don't forget that many of the people you may be bargaining with are poor and are struggling just to survive. Often at the end of the day, people who earn a hand-to-mouth living by selling their wares are so desperate for enough money to feed their families that they may let go of something for virtually their cost, or sometimes even less. It's not good to haggle these people down to the bone. You should always let them have some profit.

Vendors who come in from the villages and spread their goods out on the ground are invariably poor. You won't usually want what the poorest of them have, but if for some reason you do, try to be a little generous. You should remember that the majority of Indians are poor and struggling to survive, and, being particularly vulnerable, they are frequently exploited and harassed by greedy bosses, hoodlums, cops, loan sharks, etc.

On the other hand, don't feel guilty about bargaining hard with more prosperous merchants and aggressive street hawkers, especially in tourist areas. In any case, you'll probably never succeed in taking advantage of any hawkers or prosperous merchants, although they will often try to convince you otherwise. Many people you are bargaining with will tell you all sorts of stories about their starving families, etc. Sometimes the stories are true, of course; but often they are just stories, especially with people you meet in the tourist areas.

It's not always easy to determine what a fair price should be, so you often need to ask. Even in fixed-price shops, if you are buying in large quantities, you should be able to strike a deal. A good way to open negotiations is to ask for a discount, unless you are shopping for special items like carpets, where prolonged bargaining is expected.

Foreigners are generally considered fair game, especially in the tourist areas. With aggressive hawkers, you should bargain hard. Don't even look at their goods if you aren't interested, because if you show even the slightest interest, they will continue to follow you and harass you until you give in.

In tourist areas, and sometimes other places, the opening price stated by the shopkeeper or street vendor is often much higher for foreigners than it would be for locals. If the price seems almost reasonable, counter-offer a quarter of the amount and settle for half or two-thirds of the asking price. If the asking price seems totally outrageous, offer maybe a tenth or even a twentieth of the amount, and go back and forth several times before settling. If the item is an expensive one, accept the merchant's second or third offer of tea and intersperse your offers with questions about his family and other idle chitchat. The longer you take to conclude the deal, the more likely it is that you will get a good price. This process is part of the game and shows them that you are more knowledgeable than the average tourist. You'll always pay too much if you are in a hurry.

If you're looking to buy something expensive, such as a fine carpet, you would do well to come back several times over the course of a few days. Take the time to shop around, learning as much as you can about carpets in the process. Once you have found what you want, ask the price in an offhand way and immediately start looking at something else to distract the seller from your interest, coming back to it casually and then, after a few cups of tea, offering maybe 20% of the asking price. Shrug when the merchant pretends to be outraged and act as if you don't care. Never let him see that you really want what he is offering, and don't let your impatience show. Hide your feelings. Pretend that you are more interested in something else.

Walking away is an essential tactic, too, and will often lower the price dramatically. If walking away doesn't inspire a more reasonable offer, you could come back later with a slightly higher offer. If you really don't have a clear idea what the price should be, ask around before you come back. Take your time, though; buyers often come back several times before settling on a price. If the merchant won't give you a reasonable price, try to find the same item elsewhere. Incidentally, carpets which are sold as pure silk often aren't, especially the less expensive ones, so try to verify what you are getting before you buy.

Never start bargaining for something you don't intend to buy, and never offer an amount that you aren't prepared to pay. If a merchant asks how much you would pay for something, don't give an amount unless you really want to buy it. Just say you aren't interested. A friend of mine accidentally bought a fine carpet that he didn't particularly want when he casually offered half of what the vendor was asking, assuming the offer wouldn't be accepted. The man quickly accepted his offer, so my friend ended up with the carpet. This immediate acceptance by the vendor indicated that he could have bought the carpet for a much lower price. In any case, the carpet dealer was astute enough to see that he really wasn't interested, so he figured he should take whatever he could get, which was no doubt a handsome profit for him.

Be careful when you are shopping for gems or carpets or other high-priced items, as many dealers will not hesitate to swear that their goods are of a much higher quality than they really are. If you buy gems, or jewelry with gemstones, always insist on taking them to the nearest government gem-testing laboratory to verify what you are getting (you can do this in Jaipur, Delhi, Mumbai and several other cities). You should also get gold tested for purity if you are buying gold jewelry.

If you are having goods sent from a shop, have the items packed in front of you and make sure you have all the paperwork. If possible, take photos of the items you are having sent, preferably with the invoice in the photo, and the shop owner as well. Your photos may deter an unscrupulous shop owner from succumbing to the temptation to cheat you in some way, but they will also provide solid evidence in case of problems, including shipping loss or damage. Pay for expensive items with credit cards, if possible, as they provide some hope of redress in case of problems.

Bargaining for accommodations is normal as well. It's customary to ask for a discount at hotels, etc., except for government tourist bungalows, where the prices are fixed. Except during the high tourist season, you can often get a reduction. You don't necessarily have to accept the first discount price offered, however. It's OK to press a little for a better discount, especially at more expensive places. "Can you do a little better?" is a good way to ask for a deeper discount.

Make sure that you have a definite agreement for services (including taxis, rickshaws, tourist guides, etc.) in advance. Find out the going rate in advance and negotiate from there—then stick to what you agree on, even when they ask for more at the end, which is not unusual.

You can and should always bargain with non-metered taxi and auto drivers—before getting in—though if they're already busy they may not be interested in negotiating. Getting a few drivers to compete against each other is the most effective way to negotiate.

It's usually necessary to bargain with cycle-rickshaw drivers, but don't overdo it as they are always poor. For a short ride, i.e., less than a kilometer, a typical rate is Rs.10. You can negotiate an hourly rate for sightseeing, which should be at least Rs.50–60, though in some areas it may be much higher. Fairly often, the cycle-rickshaw-*walas* will try to avoid bargaining and just say, "As you like." Almost invariably, your idea of an appropriate fare will be met with dismay and derision even if your offer is generous, and they will demand more. They are counting on the guilt factor to get more out of you.

Coolies at railway stations in tourist towns often demand many times the going rate. In Delhi, it's not unusual for porters to ask Rs.500 or more, which is many times the official rate of Rs.40. When they demand such an amount, the best strategy is simply to start laughing as if this is the funniest thing you have ever heard. Usually, they will start laughing, too, and then you should be able to negotiate a reasonable rate without much trouble. The official rate, incidentally, varies from place to place, but it is usually less than the actual going rate. You can ask other passengers what you should pay, but many will try to help the porters by quoting an inflated rate. Rs.40 per head-load (40 kilos, which they do carry on their heads) is typical, depending on where you are. The official rate may be much less in smaller stations. Rs.60–70 is about the most you should pay a single porter, unless your luggage is extremely heavy or if he has to carry it for an exceptionally long distance. Some porters will claim that a distance of 100 meters is really half a kilometer to try to get more money out of you, but you can ignore this, since 100 meters (109 yards) isn't all that far.

Hill stations usually have porters available for carrying luggage and goods up and down the hills, especially to hotels that are off the road. Rates are usually similar to what you would pay railway porters, though hill station porters work a lot harder because of the hills, and the distances are often much farther.

Enjoy bargaining, but keep your perspective. While bargaining is normal, and many people will think you are foolish if you don't, it's silly to carry it to extremes. Is it worth haggling for half an hour to get the price down by a few rupees?

Many Westerners get worked up about being overcharged. Unfortunately, the Indian government fosters overcharging in a big way by charging foreigners exorbitant prices for entry to major tourist attractions (usually 20–25 times what Indians are charged), so merchants then feel it is their right to charge foreigners more than locals. Unfortunately, the government doesn't realize that this atti-tude—especially because it is taken to such extremes—really puts people off, and it actually hurts the economy more than it helps in the long run. The government tends to think of nothing but short-term gains in this matter. At any rate, merchants etc. are often reluctant to give foreigners the local price because of it, particularly in tourist areas. However, if you have some idea of the correct price, you can often bargain them down. Or you can ask an Indian friend to help. Often a local can talk a merchant into adjusting the price.

Some tourists will pay whatever price is asked because they feel that bargaining is somehow demeaning, but this is not the case in India. Bargaining is simply part of life here. Sometimes you can bargain without haggling by maintaining silence when the price is mentioned, looking at the merchant knowingly, and then waiting expectantly. If the price really is too high, this can occasionally work to bring the price down without having to say a word.

By doing as the locals do as much as possible, you're respecting the local economy and helping to keep it balanced. Paying too much artificially inflates the going rates and thereby creates hardships for local residents who cannot afford to pay as much as you can. It also fosters greed, envy and corruption.

If you don't bargain, you may end up paying as much as 10–20 times the going rate, or even more, since prices escalate if people notice that you are an easy mark. However, if you refuse to bargain, you should expect to be seriously overcharged and put up with it gracefully. Indians haggle constantly, although even they may be taken advantage of when they are away from their home area.

A Shopper's Paradise

India is a fabulous place to shop. Roaming the local bazaars can be a delightful experience. They are colorful, noisy, and filled to over-flowing with wonderful items and fascinating people. The local bazaars where Indians shop are usually more interesting and con-siderably cheaper than the tourist markets. You can get just about anything you can imagine, and many more things besides. It's just a matter of knowing where to look.

At the other extreme are high-end shopping malls where you'll typically pay Western prices (or more) for imported goods or foreign brands. Many of the foreign brands are actually made in India, so you can sometimes buy the same items at a fraction of the price in the local markets. Export rejects can be found in certain local mar-kets (e.g., Sarojini Nagar in Delhi) for almost nothing—and since sometimes the only reason these items were rejected was because the delivery was too late or the color was a little off, it is possible to get designer goods at far less than discount store prices. Really good Western-style clothes are otherwise a bit hard to come by.

Sometimes, if a merchant doesn't have what you want, he may tell you the item is "unavailable anywhere" or that it is "impossible." Most often, if you continue asking around, you will find what you need somewhere, especially if you are in a big city. Small towns are another matter altogether. In some cases, of course, you may need to do quite a lot of asking.

Most cities, towns and villages (or clusters of villages) have a weekly or monthly street market where you can buy fruits, vegetables, spices, house-wares, clothes, etc. The weekly markets are always held on the day the regular shops are closed. Usually they are most crowded later in the evening. Just ask anyone where and when the markets are held in your area. Small towns and villages also have an annual *mela* (festival) that is a much larger outdoor market that is usually set up in a big field in or near town. The local markets and *melas* are where you will find the cheapest prices available anywhere, so there's often not much leeway for bargaining.

In the Himalayas you can buy any woolens you will need if you are there during the cold season, and the prices are incredibly cheap. Kashmir is famous for *pashmina*, which is another name for cashmere. Be aware, however, that fine wool or other fibers are often passed off as *pashmina*. *Shahtush* is much finer even than *pashmina*, but it comes from the Himalayan Ibex, an endangered species, and the animal is killed to obtain it, so buying it in India or importing it into most countries is illegal unless you have proof that it was produced before the ban. The penalty for smuggling it into the US is 10 years in prison and a $10,000 fine, and other countries have similar penalties.

Many merchants claim to offer the required proof, but there are so many *shahtush* shawls on the market these days that were "woven before it was banned" that it's safe to assume that many of the certificates are forged, or else the shawls aren't genuine *shahtush*. Most of what is now sold as *shahtush* is not genuine *shahtush*. *Shahtush* is the fabric used in the original "ring shawls," i.e., shawls that can pass through a wedding ring, but *pashmina* and even wool can be spun so finely now that the expression "ring shawl" means nothing.

The finest *pashmina* is exceptionally soft and light and is a good alternative to genuine *shahtush*. It's also a much better buy. Similar names such as *shamina* and *pashtush* have been coined as marketing ploys. Some of these fabrics are honestly marketed for what they are (which is usually extremely finely woven *pashmina*, though it may be mixed with some other fiber), but many aren't. If you are determined to own a genuine *shahtush*, insist on a written guarantee that it is old and that it is genuine *shahtush*. Even so, you may be fooled into paying extremely high prices (many thousands of dollars) for a relatively cheap imitation.

Antiquities can't be taken out of India if they are over 100 years old without an export clearance certificate from the Archaeological Survey of India. Antiques will be confiscated if you are caught taking or sending them out of India, and you could be fined or even jailed for smuggling as well, so you should insist that the merchant get the export clearance certificate on anything that looks like it could be an antique before you pay for it.

Export of endangered plants or animals, or any items obtained from them—including ivory, hides, furs, antlers, claws, potions made from rhino horns, etc.—is also prohibited. There are also restrictions on exporting firearms, gold, gold jewelry and certain other items. You'll find complete information on the website of the Indian Central Board of Excise and Customs <www.cbec.gov.in/cae1-english.htm>.

Avoid buying counterfeit and pirated goods, which are widely available. These goods include books, electronics, designer clothing, sporting goods, watches, DVDs, luggage, etc. Counterfeits are usually pretty easy to spot by the misspellings and generally unpolished look or blurry printing on tags; poor quality of the item; shoddy packaging, etc.—in other words, there is almost always something about them that looks or feels cheap. Bringing these items back to the United States or other countries could result in confiscation of the goods as well as fines.

Getting Clothes Made

It's fun to have clothes custom made, and you can really get creative if you find a good tailor. If you have ever had any desire to try your hand at fashion designing, India provides the perfect opportunity to do it. Just be sure to make your drawings clear and detailed. And be sure to ask the tailor to leave really wide margins (seams) so that you can compensate for any errors or miscommunications. Adjustments are often necessary.

If you have difficulty finding your size or something that appeals to you, just buy some fabric and take it to a tailor. Beautiful fabrics abound, and clothes can be tailor-made cheaply in India. Most any tailor can do an adequate job of copying simple clothes or making *kurtas*, *cholis* and pajamas. Finding a really good tailor can take some doing, though. Try to get a recommendation from someone whose clothes you like. Otherwise, go from shop to shop and examine the clothes the tailors have made to see if the quality is up to your standards.

Taking measurements can be a bit awkward for women if the tailor is a man. Most tailors behave honorably enough, but there are always a few who will get a little groping in if given the chance. If a tailor brushes against your breasts as if by accident, for instance, you can assume that it's deliberate. Indian men are brought up to scrupulously avoid such "accidents." In case the tailor tries to surreptitiously feel you up, grab the measuring tape indignantly and do the measurements yourself or have a friend do them for you—or find another tailor.

A *choli* (*sari* blouse) can usually be made in about half an hour, while a whole ladies' suit takes a few hours. Many tailors will take on "urgent" jobs, in which case you can get your clothes the same evening or the next day, but there are also many who won't unless you offer them some extra money.

Some tailors can also make fine Western clothes, including suits. But in this case you should definitely ask around and check the tailor's work carefully, because most tailors can't make suits properly, and you don't want to end up with something that is unwearable back home. Tailors at fine hotels and some London-trained tailors who advertise in the city magazines in the big cities, especially Delhi and Mumbai, are the best bets.

Most competent tailors can do pretty well if you give them a garment to copy, especially if it fits you perfectly, while some tailors are geniuses at recreating a design from a picture. Ask for wide margins so that if the finished item doesn't fit properly, there is room for adjustment.

Bear in mind that tailors have their own ideas about how to make clothes, so even if you have given them detailed instructions, they may do something the way they are used to doing it or even decide to "improve" on your design rather than doing what you have asked for. Sometimes their improvements help, but quite often their good intentions spoil the effect you were hoping for. You need to be specific about what you want as well as what you don't want, but at the same time you should try to keep your instructions as simple as possible to avoid confusion. If you give too many instructions, your tailor may focus on just one thing you said and ignore the rest. But don't get too upset if it doesn't come out right. Often the tailor can fix it while you wait, or after a fitting or two. Otherwise, try to see if it is wearable anyway. If not, try again or look for a different tailor.

• • •

Doing Business

Positioning Yourself for Success

POSITIONING YOURSELF is all about helping your associates figure out how you fit into their world. It's not about trying to present a false image, but the best true image that you can.

Indian society and Indian business are both extremely hierarchical, so a person's *auqat* (status or position in society) is of major importance in all interactions. For this reason, when doing business in India, it is essential to present yourself at as high a level as possible. Your power to get things done depends a lot on how your counterparts perceive your *auqat*, your status. Let your connections and accomplishments be known. Everything matters: your family, your education, any awards you have won, and any other accomplishments you may have.

Ultimately, the most important aspect of positioning yourself is building relationships. Business relationships have everything to do with one's position in society, for which reason it is essential to learn as much about the people you are doing business with as possible while at the same time allowing them to learn about you. Your associates will naturally ask you many questions that you may consider intrusive because they need to know who you are, and whether you are sincere. They are also trying to find out how much power and influence you have and where you can wield it. You are also expected to reciprocate and ask the same kinds of questions of them that they ask of you. Pavan K. Varma observes, "To meet someone without knowing the coordinates of his status is like entering a pool without knowing its depth. Everything—response, behavior, body language, social niceties, form of address, receptivity—depends on an assessment of where the other person stands on the scale of power and influence."[15]

Who you know is crucial in Indian business, so you need to make your connections known. In many businesses, it is impossible to get anywhere if you are unconnected. Direct connections with powerful politicians and business people are by far the best, but don't underestimate the value of acquaintance with any relatives or close associates of such people. If you happen to know someone who works in the Prime Minister's office, or a close relative of such a person, don't hesitate to say so.

Naturally, connections with influential people abroad can be as important as those with Indians, and often more so. If, for instance, you have met President Obama or Bill Gates at some time, mention it. Even if there is no personal relationship, the fact of having met such top people implies power and influence. But even other sorts of associations can be advantageous. If you know a cricket star or you are friendly with the family of a well-known Bollywood actor, for instance, then be sure to mention it if the subject of cricket or Bollywood comes up. Any connection with a prominent person will add something to how you are regarded by your associates.

Friends and acquaintances can be enormously helpful in getting appointments with top people and convincing them that you are someone worth listening to, so don't hesitate to ask your well-connected Indian contacts for help. A good third-party introduction can really boost your credibility, and sometimes there is simply no other way to get an appointment. Networking is essential in Indian business, so take the time to get to know as many key people as you can.

Always dress well and use your most polished manners, even if some of the people you are dealing with are a little less refined. Being too casual in speech or dress or mannerisms can undermine your position. Respect is an essential element of successful business dealings in India. You have to show respect for the people you are working with, and you also have to show that you are worthy of receiving their respect, as well.

Hierarchy in business is well defined: the boss makes all the important decisions, while employees defer to the boss and do whatever they are told without questioning anything. Indian employees address their superiors formally and are often rather obsequious. They know their place in the hierarchy.

Although Indian women are joining the workforce in ever-increasing numbers, there are still many men who are opposed to women working outside the home. India is mostly a male-dominated society, and you will often encounter attitudes that are a bit shocking to those of us from the West, but not only in business. In any area of life where men are used to being in charge but are now being challenged by women, there will inevitably be some resistance on their part. If a woman happens to be in charge of a company or delegation, there may be some men who insist on addressing a man instead, even if he is lower in the hierarchy. This tendency is changing, especially in multinational corporations, but you are still likely to encounter it from time to time.

If you are a woman used to giving orders or generally being assertive, try to tone it down a bit. Indian women are usually not so outspoken, and you will do well to follow their lead. Even the most powerful Indian women know how to use soft, sweet words get what they want. Being too bold is likely inspire some resistance on the part of male colleagues, and it may, as mentioned elsewhere, also encourage unwanted sexual advances.

When a man and women are dining together in a restaurant, the waiter will usually look to the man for the order. If there is a question about the woman's order, it may also be asked to the man. In this case, the waiter might even expect the man to ask her and convey her response to him even though he can hear it perfectly well himself. You'll find many situations like this. For instance, if a man and woman are riding together in a taxi, the man is generally expected to give the directions even if it's the woman who knows the way. It's not comfortable for Western women who are used to speaking out and taking charge of situations, but that's how it is, so the best thing is simply to learn to operate as Indian women do in such situations. It's often much more effective in this environment.

When you are doing business, refrain from socializing with those who are lower in the hierarchy than the people you are dealing with. Being too friendly with subordinates can undermine your position. Always respect the hierarchical structure of the organization.

Business Etiquette

In order to get along well in India, you need to understand how Indians perceive time. Unlike Americans and Northern Europeans, who like fixed schedules and are disinclined to mix business and pleasure, Indians regard schedules as general guidelines that are constantly adjusted to accommodate the needs of the moment. They also don't tend to make a rigid division between their business and personal lives.

Most Indians keep their schedules flexible. The idea of fixed time slots is unusual. If people need more time for something, then they take more time, without worrying overmuch about the next person waiting to see them. This behavior isn't usually a sign of disrespect, however. It's just a different style of functioning. In the West, a person will customarily drop whatever he is in the middle of doing, whether or not he is finished, in order to meet the next person on time, but in India this behavior would usually be considered rude. It's important to recognize these cultural differences and adjust accordingly.

Nonetheless, punctuality is important within many big corporations, so you should show up on time for business appointments. It is, however, a good idea to call to reconfirm before you come to be sure your meeting is still on. Always leave plenty of time between appointments—think in terms of hours here—and don't schedule too many in one day.

Don't show up without an appointment. Schedule important appointments well in advance—if possible, several weeks in advance—especially if you will only be in town for a short time. Call and reconfirm a few days ahead of time to make sure your appointment is still on. Take a flexible attitude in the case of some last-minute change or even a cancellation.

Early morning appointments are pretty unusual in India. Late morning or early afternoon is preferred for important business meetings. Don't push for morning appointments; your contacts may feel you are impatient. Even if they agree to your request because they don't want to say *no* to you, they may be hours late because it just isn't possible for them to come as early as you would like—or you may arrive only to find that they aren't able to come at all.

Don't be surprised or offended if your meeting gets canceled or rescheduled at the last minute. This happens fairly often in India, and it doesn't necessarily mean anything. If the person you are negotiating with is the head of a large joint family, for instance, he may have to drop everything in order to deal with some family emergency. If there is a death in the family of someone among the top management, everything will come to a standstill for at least a day or two because tradition demands it. Nevertheless, if your meeting gets canceled or rescheduled again and again, or if you are kept waiting for several hours, it may be that the person you are trying to meet doesn't want to meet you for some reason. Or it could be that he doesn't feel he can help you but doesn't want to hurt your feelings by telling you so.

Business meals are usually held in high-class restaurants, with five-star hotels being the preferred venue. Most businesspeople want to be home with their families for dinner, so they generally prefer business lunches to meetings over dinner. However, in some places, dinner and breakfast meetings are becoming common. Traditionally, mixing food and business is not done, so business meals are more about building relationships than negotiating. Let the Indians lead the conversation.

If you are hosting a meal, be sure to make advance reservations to avoid possible embarrassment. It's normal to arrive a few minutes late unless you are the host. If you are a woman, it is acceptable to host a meal for businessmen; however, your male guests are likely to insist on paying for the meal. In fact, men are generally expected to make such an offer. You may politely decline, but if they continue to insist, give in gracefully.

Always present a business card (with your right hand, of course, positioned so the person can read it) whenever you introduce yourself or are introduced to someone. Indians always list their degrees, titles, and honors on their business cards (which are referred to more commonly as *visiting* cards), so you should do likewise. Men should refrain from introducing themselves to women who are alone. It's better to wait for someone else to make the introduction.

Always address the people you are dealing with formally, and expect them to address you in the same manner. Even if they invite you to use their given names, avoid doing so in the presence of subordinates. Likewise, don't ask business associates to address you by your first name unless they are really insistent on a first-name basis. Refer to male business contacts by their surname rather than by their given name.

In establishing business relationships, a lot of time is spent in small talk over countless cups of tea or coffee. (Incidentally, when tea, etc. is offered, it is customary to refuse the first offer and then to accept the second or third offer; but it is important to accept something or the person making the offer will feel insulted.) Indians always want to know you before getting around to serious business, and this process can easily take days or weeks. In getting to know you, they are gauging your trustworthiness and credibility. Once they feel good about you, then they will be ready to get down to business.

Business is transacted slowly in India. Never try to rush the process. Doing so will be seen as an insult, and you will be perceived as a greedy, uncultured person who is only interested in money. Don't be aggressive. If you start to feel impatient with the people you are dealing with, don't allow it to show. Getting angry or impatient may cause your associates to doubt whether you are someone they want to do business with. Trying to hurry the process will work against your interests in the end, and if you push to get things moving, your associates may just cancel the whole deal. As a rule, the bigger the deal, the longer it takes, and that time frame can be many months, or even years in some cases.

When you do get down to serious business, don't rush in with a rigid offer, and minimize the legalese. Tradeoffs always need to be made, so you should come to the negotiations with a flexible attitude. If you have any disagreements with anyone involved in the negotiations, on either side, deal with those individuals privately, one-on-one, rather than in an open meeting where there is a risk of losing face.

Most businesses are family businesses, so various family members are usually involved in any important decision. Indians are brought up to respect their parents and to look to them for guidance, and they often continue to consult them on important matters as adults. The head of the family typically has a lot of influence on his or her children, no matter how successful and powerful they become. Family consultations often slow down the decision-making process because many family members may be involved behind the scenes, and this may bring many unseen factors into a business deal, so if some obstacle suddenly arises just when negotiations seem to be going along beautifully, family influences may be the reason.

This is not by any means an exhaustive guide to doing business in India. Many subtle (and sometimes not-so subtle) differences and practices exist from one place to another. If your company is making its first venture into India, you would do well to hire a cross-cultural trainer or consultant to help you understand the process and to keep you from derailing the proceedings with your ignorance. The bigger the deal, the more important this is. I also highly recommend Craig Storti's excellent book, *Speaking of India*, which goes into great depth on how to communicate successfully in a business environment.

Coping with Bureaucracy

If you stay in India for some time, you will inevitably have to deal with the bureaucracy. Anything that brings you anywhere near government regulations is likely to be a little frustrating, and often much more than a little frustrating. Banks, utility companies, phone and Internet service providers are all highly regulated, whether they are government owned or privately owned. Employees of these companies are trained to go absolutely by the book and not to think logically or creatively. If anything about your request is unusual or outside the rules, they tend to just keep repeating the same irrelevant thing as if they aren't hearing what you are saying.

The best way to accomplish anything is to know someone who knows the person in charge and get him or her to help you. If you don't have connections, bringing an Indian friend who has some understanding of the procedures can also help. If you are on your own and the process seems like it could drag out over many days or weeks or even longer, you may need to try some different strategies. If the first person you approach can't or won't help, try to see his or her superior. Find out who the top authority is and try to see that person. You may first need to establish a friendly relationship with someone in the office. Naturally, he or she should be as high in the pecking order as possible as people in low positions won't be able to help at all. People with power but no status are prone to being corrupt, and they are also prone to abusing their power in other ways as a way to make up for the lack of status. For this reason, lower-level bureaucrats are often more difficult to deal with than their superiors.

Remember that in order to deal successfully with Indians you have to be patient and soft. If you make accusations, if you get upset, if you are too critical, or if you are too harsh in your expressions, you'll meet with resistance. Getting angry almost invariably makes matters worse, and those who do have the ability to help you are likely to turn their backs on you if you are rude. Always be polite, especially when dealing with powerful people, no matter how angry you feel inside. If you aren't getting what you need, just keep asking patiently but firmly how you can accomplish what you need to accomplish, and who is the best person to help you.

People in positions of power—even relatively minor ones—need to be given the amount of esteem they feel is their due in order to get them to do anything for you. If they feel slighted, you will have a difficult time getting anything out of them. On the other hand, don't give too much esteem to an official while in the presence of someone higher up in the hierarchy. It's hard to know what they expect, so you may need to ask someone.

Indians respect power, so if you are a person of some importance in government, business, or any other field, let your status be known. If possible, have a third party with you who has contacts in the right places and who can quietly whisper this essential information into the appropriate ears. Even if you have no position or connections to speak of, if you can project a powerful image, many people, especially lower-level bureaucrats and clerks, will take you at face value and will not want to take a chance that you aren't a powerful person. If you have connections that could have any bearing on the task at hand, flaunt them. If you don't have any, try to make some. It's easier than you may think.

Acknowledging a person's position can also help to put that person in the mood to help you. You could approach an official by saying something to this effect: "Sir, I know you are a busy and important person, but so am I, and I need this now. Kindly see what you can do for me." Then persist until he makes some concession towards helping you. Usually he will do so eventually.

Sometimes the only way to accomplish anything is to be imperious. Nevertheless, it is essential to remain calm and courteous at the same time. Don't just march in and shout, "I am [whatever your position is], and I demand that you. . . ." This extremely crude tactic is frequently used by pompous politicians, and you'll do much better by not imitating them. Anyway, it would probably backfire, especially since you are a non-Indian. Declare your status, but be polite and firm rather than dictatorial and rude. To get things done most effectively, you need to establish a relationship, and rudeness will not achieve that.

Usually someone will be more than happy to bend the rules for a little *bakshish*, but giving bribes is never a good idea as it can land you in trouble later. When a new political party takes power, the bribes that have been given and accepted during the previous administration may suddenly come under scrutiny. If you have paid bribes to buy land that you were technically not allowed to buy, for instance, you could lose it all. [Note: *Bakshish* is a word that has several meanings. It can mean money given to a beggar, or a tip, or an out-and-out bribe. In many circumstances, giving *bakshish* in the form of a tip is either appropriate or necessary, but it's always best to avoid giving actual bribes. And just because *bakshish* is expected doesn't mean you have to give it.]

As already noted, respect and honor are of prime importance, and any insinuation that a person isn't doing his job properly will be taken as an insult. Even if a person really isn't doing his job, avoid saying so. It's better to take a more oblique angle. Try positioning yourself on the same side: "We have this little problem. What can we do about it?" Even when the problem is serious, it needs to be stated simply and calmly. If you insult someone, they are more likely to sabotage your agenda than to help you.

Because you need to vary your approach according to the status of the person you are addressing, try to find out his or her place in the hierarchy in advance. In any case, you should use extra polite language when dealing with bureaucrats if you want to get things done smoothly. If you are dealing with a top official, you're really not overdoing it to say something like: "Madam, I am a guest in your country and I don't understand how this should be done. Since you are knowledgeable and occupying such an important position, I am sure you can help me. Kindly explain it to me." Because the majority of Indians consider it a sacred duty to take care of guests, this approach may inspire them to help if they are able to do so. Positioning yourself as a guest is also a good way to deflect rudeness if someone is behaving badly towards you.

Threats—even subtle, softly phrased ones—should be avoided, especially with people in important positions. Instead, try getting them to ask themselves what can be done to avoid a more serious problem. Instead of demanding a particular solution, it is better to let them come up with one, or perhaps feed one to them in a way that allows them to feel it is their idea so they can take credit for it. If you push them against the wall by the wrong approach, they may stubbornly refuse to do anything. Indian bureaucrats are master stonewallers.

If all else fails and no one is willing to help you, ask for the complaint book. Find out the name and position of the person who has been stonewalling you or whatever so that you can complain to his superior. Sometimes people will decide to help just to avoid having a complaint lodged against them. If they still won't help you, you can go ahead and put your grievances in writing. Complaint books are also available in buses, taxis, hotels, etc., and you have every right to demand to use them, though they are often "unavailable" for some reason, and you may be encouraged to write your complaint on a plain piece of paper to be forwarded to the right person. Not likely.

India has the most complex and bogged-down bureaucracy in the world. One thing that keeps it going is the fact that planned inefficiency allows more people to have jobs. Often you will find four or five people doing a job that could be done by one. This is accomplished by dividing the job into small tasks, and hardly anyone would think of doing someone else's job. Efficiency is actually regarded as being antisocial in many contexts, especially in the government. It is astounding how many different people have to sign and stamp every document that is subject to government regulation, no matter how insignificant. Red tape is inescapable when dealing with Indian bureaucracy, so always allow plenty of extra time to deal with it.

Business Hours

Government offices are open Monday to Friday between 9 A.M. and 5 P.M. However, the Post Office, which is usually open on Saturday as well, may have variable hours, especially in small towns, where it may be open for only two or three hours a day. There are usually limited hours for certain services (e.g., 10 A.M. to 2 P.M.), such as booking Speed Post or insured parcels, though there are some 24-hour Post Offices in the metropolitan areas.

Large stores are usually open until at least 7 P.M., but small shops often keep longer hours, especially in the summer. Different towns in a region and different areas within a city will usually have different market closing days, so you can usually find someplace to go within a reasonable distance to buy things you need. In some areas, shops don't open until 10 or 11 A.M.

Restaurants may be open all day or only for lunch and/or dinner. Those that are open in the evening will usually stay open until 10 or 11 P.M. Restaurants with bars stay open later in many places, and many five-star hotels have cafes that are open 24 hours.

Most banks are open from 10 A.M. until 4 P.M. and for half a day on Saturday, although some banks have different hours.

Railway booking offices in small towns and stations typically have limited hours, e.g., from 10 A.M. to 2 P.M., though in major stations they are commonly open from 8 A.M. to 8 P.M.

A surprising number of holidays are observed by government offices and banks—sometimes as many as two or three in the same week. Most of these holidays, and a few more, are observed by local businesses. Since most holidays are related to one religion or another, the religion of the owners plays a significant part in which holidays are observed, although in many communities, people may celebrate holidays from other religions as well as those of their own. In addition, there are numerous other reasons why offices and businesses may be closed on any given day—or why servants may not turn up—many of which are not obvious to foreigners.

Strikes are common, though most of them last no more than a day, and sometimes only half a day, as most people cannot afford not to work every day. If they last more than three days, the situation gets very tense and sometimes leads to riots. A strike *(bandh)* can be about anything: wages, working conditions, poor phone service, corruption, accidents, police brutality, terrorist attacks, etc. Most strikes seem to be due to political manipulations.

• • •

Safety & Security

INDIA IS NOT AN ESPECIALLY DANGEROUS country, but as with most places in the world today, you have to exercise a certain amount of care and vigilance. Fortunately, violent crime against foreigners is unusual, though it does happen occasionally. On the other hand, petty theft, including bag snatching and pickpocketing, is common. There have also been cases of unsuspecting tourists being given drugged food or drink and then robbed. Although terrorist attacks have become more common in India, most of them haven't been directed at non-Indians, and the likelihood of being a casualty of such an attack is so much less than the risk of getting hit by a car when you are walking down the road that it is practically negligible as long as you stay away from the trouble spots.

You aren't likely to run into most of these problems (aside from unscrupulous taxi and/or auto-rickshaw drivers, which is practically inevitable), but being aware will help you avoid them. And it's also good to know what to do if something unfortunate does happen.

Avoiding Scams

At major airports, railway stations, and tourist sites, many taxi and auto-rickshaw drivers, touts, and porters solicit travelers with offers of cheap transportation, tours, and hotels. Avoid these offers. You will almost always end up with a bad deal at a much higher price than you would have paid on your own.

At railway stations, many taxi and auto-rickshaw drivers come onto the platform to solicit customers. They often operate illegally, having bribed the local police. They are invariably persistent, and even if there is a booth for prepaid rides, they may tell you there isn't or that it is closed. They may offer low rates and then demand much more once you are in the car. They look for foreigners because they know they can often get away with charging far more than they charge the locals.

If a driver offers you a suspiciously low price to take you somewhere, you can be sure that he has a hidden agenda—often in the form of expected commissions from hotels or shops—and that he will do everything he can to get you to those places rather than to where you want to go. Never let a driver take you somewhere you don't want to go. If you get a taxi at the airport and ask for a specific hotel, the driver may tell you it is full or closed for repairs. This line is virtually always a lie. He just wants to take you to a hotel where he will get a fat commission. In such a case, tell him that you know he is mistaken because you have a reservation (even if you don't). Insist on going where you want to go, and if he won't take you, get out and get another taxi, but don't pay the first driver. This will result in a dispute, but you can usually shut him up by writing down the car number and the driver's name and threatening to report him to the Traffic Police or Tourist Police.

Taxis and auto-rickshaws usually have a fare chart (either from the government or the local union), but if the rates seem too high or it looks homemade, it may be a fake. Check with someone in the know if you suspect that there is a problem.

Touts and taxi or auto-rickshaw drivers will often use aggressive and shady tactics to try to manipulate you into taking tours you don't want, etc. A recent scam reported in Delhi is where the driver claims that every Delhi hotel is full and your only option is to stay on a houseboat in Srinagar—which is in Kashmir, many hours drive from Delhi. This results in an extremely expensive trip for the victims. Despite initial claims to the contrary, these drivers invariably charge a ridiculous amount for both the car trip and the houseboat, and there are inevitably many undisclosed extra fees. There are many variations of this scam where the drivers want to take you to Jaipur, Agra, or other destinations.

Another ploy drivers use is to try to get you to stop and check out their "uncle's" or "brother's" shop. The usual refrain is, "just looking, only looking." The promised "bargain" prices are virtually always higher than you would normally pay, since the shopkeepers always pay a commission to the drivers and pass the extra expense right along to the customers.

Any time you ask a driver to take you shopping and leave it up to him where to go, you can assume that a commission will be involved and that the prices will be high. If it's worth it to you because you have no idea where to go, be sure to use your best bargaining skills. Whenever a driver follows you into a hotel or shop, he does so for the purpose of getting a commission. On the other hand, although the commission business can certainly be an out-and-out scam— when prices are much higher than normal—it isn't always. Drivers typically receive pitifully low salaries so they depend on getting a substantial portion of their income from commissions, which means that to them it's just business as usual.

Ask the locals and other travelers what the latest scams are, so you can protect yourself from them. Thieves often work in teams, with one person creating a distraction while the other snatches your bag. If someone squirts something on you, or suddenly points out a mess on your shoes (which he put there just a moment earlier), hold onto your bags and valuables and get away. Get someone to clean up the mess who is not standing conveniently nearby.

Scam artists often operate by befriending unsuspecting travelers, often over the course of a few days or even weeks. They may start out by saying they just want to practice their English, but at some point, "because you are such a good friend," they will offer you an opportunity to make some money. The offer always sounds like a really easy way to make money, and no doubt it is—for the scam artist, not you.

If the offer sounds too good to be true, assume that it is. Often it involves transporting gems or gold (which means smuggling, a serious offense if the goods are real, which they never are); or transporting drugs (even riskier); or taking delivery of expensive goods once you get back home (with some scheme to avoid customs duties, but of course the goods never arrive); or selling these items to you at "wholesale" so you can supposedly make money selling them back home (which you can't because you have paid way too much). A deposit is always required, and the goods are usually fake or inferior, or else they don't get sent. Phony customs agents may call demanding bribes. Young travelers in Goa, Jaipur, Varanasi, and Agra are the most common targets for this sort of scam, and those who fall for such schemes end up losing a lot of money.

Be alert for credit card fraud. Don't let merchants take your card out of your sight to process a transaction. They may run off duplicate forms in order to bill your account for phony transactions. If the machine is in another room or another location, go along with them. This is most common in tourist areas.

Protecting Your Belongings

For security in India, you need to take the same precautions as you would in LA or Paris or New York, with a few enhancements. While there may be more risk of petty theft and scams, India is much safer for visitors in terms of violent crime.

Tourists tend to meet up with more than their share of pickpockets, con artists, and thieves because they flock to tourist attractions such as Taj Mahal in Agra and the Red Fort in Delhi in search of easy prey. Consequently, you may hear many stories of people being robbed or cheated. But don't judge India on this basis! If you get even a little off the beaten path, you'll find that most people in India will receive you with sincere warmth and are delighted to help you in whatever way they can.

To avoid trouble, do your best to blend in. It's best to wear clothes that are neat, clean and conservative, and not ragged or torn. Incidentally, hippie garb marks you as a tourist just as obviously as shorts and Taj Mahal T-shirts. Con artists, thieves, and other scoundrels are more likely to target tourists, so it's safer not to dress like one. But it's not a matter of trying to disguise the fact that you are a foreigner. Most people couldn't do so, anyway.

Expensive or flashy jewelry attracts too much attention of the wrong kind. Leave the good stuff at home. "Chain-snatching," which means stealing a woman's necklace, is a common crime in India. The usual modus operandi is for a boy or two on a motor scooter to swoop by and make a grab. When riding in a taxi with open windows or an auto-rickshaw, or when meditating in a temple, keep your arm through the strap of your day bag so no one can snatch it.

Money pouches or belts worn inside your clothing are the best place to keep your passport, plane ticket, and money, but don't keep all your money in one place. Arrange your money so that you can get at it easily (and modestly, if you are a woman), but try to avoid letting people see you take it out. When you aren't carrying these items, keep them in a hotel safe or securely locked in your luggage, in which case you should carry a photocopy of your passport and visa with you. Always take your actual passport when traveling, as airlines and hotels won't accept a photocopy, and you will need it to change money. When you carry your passport, leave the photocopy in your luggage.

Pickpockets prefer to go for the easy mark, so work at making it hard for them. I like to keep my passport, money, etc. in a wallet that not only zips all the way around, but has a chain to attach it to my bag, which I also keep zipped up. Reinforced bags of any kind are helpful.

Keep your luggage locked even in your room. Even in a family home, especially where there are servants or people coming and going, you should keep your valuables locked up. Sturdy combination locks—the four-digit kind—are best, but don't let anyone see your combination. Always lock the lock, even when the suitcase is open. Otherwise, if an observant person comes into your room while your suitcase is open, he could make note of the combination and come back later to pilfer while you are out. And always keep your hotel room locked. Even if you step out for only a minute or two, lock the door. If you are staying in budget places, you'll need to carry your own padlock.

Pickpockets and luggage-snatchers commonly lurk around train stations and tourist areas; they are extremely adept and fast. Don't walk away from your luggage in a public place or turn your back on it, and never leave your luggage in the care of a stranger. Keep it in sight and/or touch at all times. If you have to leave it for a few minutes to use the toilet or something, chain it to a post or some other immoveable object. When standing in line to buy your ticket, keep your bags in front of you, and be especially wary of anyone pushing up against you. Don't keep valuables in a soft bag or backpack that can be easily opened or cut open from behind you without your noticing. Never keep your wallet in your back pocket or the outside pocket of your jacket. Luggage and day bags should be sturdy and hard to cut open.

Be extra careful in crowds or avoid them altogether. Sometimes a group of children will surround and jostle a tourist so that he doesn't notice his camera or wallet being stolen until they've run off. Another ruse is to hold a piece of cardboard or something else in front of a person while nimble little fingers go after the purse or camera bag, but you'll only see this kind of thing in crowded, touristy places such as Agra and Jaipur. Away from the big cities and tourist areas, this kind of crime is virtually unknown, but it is always better to be on the safe side. If you make a habit of being careful, then it will become so automatic that you will hardly think about it, and you won't get careless just at the wrong moment.

Even if you feel certain that your driver is honest, don't put temptation in his way. Never leave a camera or laptop or an unlocked bag containing valuables sitting on the seat when you leave the car. If something disappears, the driver will claim it was stolen. But when anything gets stolen from a taxi, the driver is usually involved. Supervise the loading and unloading of the car, and check at both ends that nothing is missing.

If you leave your bag in a storeroom for any length of time, you should use some sort of tamperproof seal, such as a plastic zip-tie that can only be removed by being cut. This precaution is also good for checking luggage on an airline, etc.

If you have a laptop, it's much better to carry it in something discreet, especially if you are traveling a lot or staying in places where the security is not so good. A nice laptop will always attract attention, so be careful about showing your laptop in public—especially on the street, railway stations, trains or buses—to prevent any observers from following you with the intent to snatch it later. Some places are quite safe, of course; computer security is usually not a problem in the lobby of a five-star hotel, a good private guesthouse, or the 1AC compartment of a train, though you should still be careful and alert. In any case, never turn your back on your laptop in a public place where someone could grab it easily.

If you lose your passport, report it to the police immediately. They will give you a form that will enable you to check into hotels, etc., although it won't work for changing money. You also have to contact your embassy about getting a replacement or else an Exit Visa.

Personal Safety

From the point of view of violent crime, India is safer than most Western countries, especially for non-Indians. Personally, I feel much safer here than in the US. Though of course there can be problems, as there can be anywhere—especially in tourist areas—common sense, alertness and respect for the culture will keep you safe in most circumstances.

The number one hazard is traffic, not crime or disease. When contending with the traffic here, you need your full attention. A moment's distraction can spell disaster. For this reason, one of the riskiest things you can do is to walk around or drive while talking or sending text messages on a cell phone, which is the cause of a huge number of accidents in India. If you have to answer a call, or make one, get off the road before you do.

Whenever you are riding in a car, keep the doors locked, especially at night. Keep your handbag and other valuables away from open windows, and roll the windows up if you stop at a light where there are beggars or itinerant vendors (unless you actually want to buy something), or tough-looking guys on motorbikes who are taking too much interest in you.

Carry a flashlight when you go out at night, for safety as well as to avoid stepping in undesirable substances or tripping over hidden obstacles that may litter the path. Power outages are a daily occurrence all over India, and you don't want to be caught outside without a light. When walking along the road at night, even if the road is fairly well lit, carry your flashlight by your side so vehicles can see you easily. A lot of drivers still resist using their headlights at night, which results in many accidents. A small keychain flashlight is convenient because you can keep it with you all the time, so if you return home unexpectedly late in the evening, you at least have that much light. In many places, walking around at night is not safe, especially for women. Ask the locals what the situation is.

Never accept food or drink from strangers, especially on trains or buses or around major tourist sites. Instances of travelers being drugged and robbed are not uncommon. When people offer, it is better to thank them while politely and firmly declining. A smile and simple hand gesture are sufficient. Most people understand and are not offended. However, if someone has ill intentions, he or she may pretend to feel hurt by your refusal and your lack of trust. This is just an act. You're not declining their hospitality while at their own house, and you certainly have no obligation to trust someone you just met. Even if they offer something that appears unopened, or if they take a cookie from a package before offering some to you, politely decline.

After sharing a compartment with someone for many hours or days, you may feel that you know them enough to trust them, but remember that you are seeing them completely out of context so it is unwise to let your guard down. While most of the people you meet will be sincere, there is always the risk that they aren't. Don't forget that con artists usually have charming personalities.

Always lock your door at night. In hotels, etc., you should keep it locked all the time, even when you are there during the day. An open door is an invitation for anyone to come in.

Avoid protests, demonstrations, and big, disorderly crowds. Demonstrations are especially hazardous because the police tend to be brutal in their control tactics. If you find yourself in a pushing, shoving crowd, get out as quickly as you can, without drawing attention to yourself by stopping to take photos or even asking someone what's going on. A crush like that can turn into a stampede or riot in seconds. It just takes a shout or an incident of some sort. If someone goes down, then others start falling on top of them and people panic. Even if they stay on their feet, children and small adults can get smothered in a packed, seething crowd.

If you attend a major religious festival where the crowds are dense, get up and out of the action to a place where you can observe from a safe distance. Look around for a vantage point such as a balcony, a rooftop, or a stairway. Don't be shy about asking the locals if you can join them there. Usually, they will be delighted if you do. Not only can you see better than from the midst of the crowd, but also it is much safer. Besides, even if you are in the front row for a major procession, you may not be able to see well because of a line of policemen standing in front of you. And up front is not the place to be if they start swinging their *lathis* (sticks) at an unruly crowd. Religious stampedes happen fairly often in India, and a number of people get killed or seriously injured in them every year.

During the *Kumbha Melas*, the world's largest gatherings, there are auspicious times when several million people want to bathe in the same place in the river at the same time. At the *Kumbha Mela*—or even the smaller annual *Magh Mela* in Allahabad, which also attracts a few million people, though the crowds are not nearly on the same scale—the safest plan is to hire a boat to go out on the important bathing days.

If you will arrive at an airport or train station late at night, pre-arrange a ride, especially if you are alone. Prepaid taxis are usually OK, but not always. Don't let the driver bring a friend or "brother" along, especially if you are alone and it's nighttime.

If the driver gets lost getting to your destination, he may demand more money from you even though he isn't entitled to it. If he does, don't argue. Just say something vague but noncommittal like, "OK, let's go." Whether you actually give him some extra money once you get inside with your luggage is up to you. If you are uncertain, ask someone at your destination whether paying seems appropriate. Don't pay if he is clearly trying to cheat you. You can also report him later if doing so seems worth the hassle. Taking his name and license number and threatening to report him will often solve the problem.

If your driver suddenly stops on a dark, deserted road for no apparent reason, tell him in no uncertain terms to keep moving. In case there is a mechanical problem or flat tire, stay in car with the doors locked while he deals with it.

If an armed robber approaches you, it's recommended to hand over your wallet, your money, your jewelry, etc. without argument. These are all less important than your life. If you keep your real valuables well hidden with just enough money in an accessible wallet for your daily needs, you run much less risk of a significant loss in this and other situations.

Keep people informed of your whereabouts. If you have a pre-planned itinerary, write it down and include telephone numbers where you can be reached. Leave a copy or two with family members or a trusted friend. If you are traveling without any fixed plan, try to keep in touch with someone by e-mail at least once or twice a week.

Safety Tips for Women

Personal safety is naturally a much bigger issue for women than men, although it is possible for even single woman to travel around India alone without being constantly harassed. I know because I have been doing this for many years with little trouble. You must be careful and security-conscious, of course, as is absolutely essential for a woman living or traveling alone anywhere. Safety in India is mainly a matter of the right demeanor (friendly and confident, yet aloof with men), modest behavior, modest dress and alertness. All four elements are essential, no matter who you are with. Respecting the culture will give you more protection from sexual harassment than anything else can.

Indian men are mostly brought up to respect women. However, there is a widespread belief in India that foreign women are readily available for sex with anyone, as a result of which rather a lot of men think it's OK to treat foreign women like prostitutes, especially when their dress and demeanor are indecent by Indian standards. This attitude has a lot to do with the extremely sexy way foreign women are portrayed in the media and movies. Most Indians know nothing else about us, so they assume foreign women are all as eager to jump into bed with anyone as many of the women featured prominently in the media appear to be. The situation is not helped by the immodest way many foreign women dress in India, as from the usual Indian point of view, only prostitutes dress that way. Of course, some women do come to India looking for sex, and that contributes to the impression that all foreign women are like that.

Ultimately, whether you like it or not, it is necessary for you as a woman to respect the standards of the Indian culture if you don't want to suffer some degree of sexual harassment or abuse. In order to be safe in India you have to work at it by dressing, speaking and behaving much more modestly than you would at home. The way you dress and behave has a significant influence on how successfully you interact with the locals and how they perceive you. If you dress like a prostitute according to Indian standards, you are sure to be treated like one—and that can be more than you bargained for even if you happen to have an especially casual attitude about sex. Rape is a growing problem in India[16], as is *Eve-teasing*. *Eve-teasing* is the innocent-sounding euphemism that covers everything from the mildest sexual harassment to any physical assault short of actual rape.

Instead of taking responsibility for their own behavior, men who are lacking in self-control often put forth the specious, self-serving excuse that women are weak because they can't resist trying to seduce men. This is an absurd argument, yet it is accepted by much of Indian society. In any case, however unfair it is that men blame women for their own weaknesses, the reality is that men do get easily aroused, and they don't always manage to control their urges. Since in India there are few legitimate opportunities for sex outside of marriage, men often feel extreme sexual pressure and frustration, so it's foolish to do anything that will inflame these feelings. Because the society is so conservative, Indian men are easily aroused by modes of dress and behaviors that are not considered even slightly provocative in the West. The trouble is that if a man gets aroused by the way you dress or act, it's not just *his* problem. It's *your* problem if he treats you like a prostitute because he thinks you're inviting sex when you aren't.

In India the cultural norm is for women to keep a safe distance from men, especially strange men. Most Indian men wouldn't approach Indian women as casually as they may approach foreign women. Unfortunately, it's necessary to be on your guard with Indian men, no matter how nice they seem. Sometimes the most charming ones are the worst con artists. And of course there are always some who are out to get whatever they can. Men of this sort tend to view foreign women as a source of "safe" sex (in the sense that foreign women can easily be kept away from family and friends who disapprove of sex outside marriage), money or a ticket to another country.

Naturally, you have to use your judgment. But in general, try not to invite too much familiarity with Indian men, and refrain from saying exactly where you are staying unless you want them knocking on your door—or maybe climbing in the window. Do as the Indians do in order to avoid problems.

Women traveling in India need to be generally reserved with men, while at the same time radiating a feeling of universal friendliness. In fact, this attitude is a much better protection than being wary and tense, which can attract the wrong kind of attention because it makes you look weak and vulnerable. Smile at the world, but at the same time, be confidently aloof with respect to men. Pretend that you don't even notice them when you are passing them on the street, especially groups of young or rough-looking men.

If you are alone, it's often best not to admit it. Be evasive and avoid answering overly personal questions.

Try not to look men in the eye, even when you are talking to them, as this is seen as an invitation to greater intimacy. And don't flirt with a man unless you really want to end up in bed with him.

Flirting is not taken as innocent fun in India as it is in some other countries. It's seen as a definite invitation for sex.

Avoid situations where you will be alone with an Indian man unless you want to get intimate with him. Your willingness to be alone with a man even in innocent situations may be interpreted as an open invitation for greater intimacy.

If you behave intimately with your partner in public (hugging, kissing, or fondling each other), you are unwittingly sending a message to passersby that you are a sex-starved woman who may be available to anyone, even if you really have no eyes for anyone else. So save your intimacies for when you are alone. Indians traditionally do not touch members of the opposite sex in public. Even holding hands in public is often too much.

You see many foreign women running around India in unacceptable clothes. However, it's important to realize that dressing immodestly is not only insulting the culture but also inviting unnecessary harassment.[17] Even if it seems like "everyone" is dressing like that (which is almost never the case if you look a little more carefully), this still applies. For the vast majority of Indians, the basic standards of modesty are compulsory.

Sexy, revealing attire is typically seen as an open invitation India is not a country where flirting and wearing sexy clothes is a normal part of the culture and of the way men and women relate to each other. Dressing and acting in a way that is designed to be as sexually attractive to men as possible—which almost everything we see in the media tells us we are supposed to do—is unintentionally inviting trouble. If you dress or act in a sexually provocative manner, don't be surprised if men grab you and fondle you or worse. You'll be regarded as fair game. Dressing provocatively and flirting indiscriminately is simply not safe.

Indian men generally prefer to see modestly dressed women, because such attire shows respect for the culture and doesn't put unnecessary strain on their self-control. Most Indians, including women, are embarrassed to see women wearing clothes that are considered indecent. To my surprise, on two or three occasions men have come up to me and actually thanked me for dressing modestly! This was, as you might expect, in an area where many female tourists dress inappropriately by local standards—and some even by most Western standards.

If you are in a cosmopolitan environment where you have little direct contact with traditional Indians, you may feel that you can safely relax your dress code, but I would still advise you to dress fairly conservatively. In addition to the men you are interacting with socially, there are many men present in the background that one tends to not notice—servants, drivers, etc.—and they typically come from traditional backgrounds, even in the most rarified environment. Moreover, they are often from distant villages, so they only see their wives only once or twice a year. This cultural context makes a huge difference and you can't ignore it, even if your cosmopolitan friends and associates like to believe that they are completely disassociated from traditional Indian life. Many upper class Indians simply do not include Indians of lower classes (i.e., the vast majority) in their thinking. They go about their lives without really seeing them. This is only an illusion, and all illusions come to an end eventually.

Simply being in a cosmopolitan environment will not necessarily protect you. Rape is the fastest growing violent crime in India, cutting across all classes and economic brackets. A case in point: a few years ago, after a gala event in Delhi, a Swiss diplomat was kidnapped in her own car from a crowded parking lot and raped by a man who was evidently a well-educated man from quite a high level of society. It was reported that the rapist told her that she should "respect our traditions." As is often the case with rapists, he blamed *her* for his lack of control, and he attempted to vindicate his evil actions on the grounds that he was teaching her a lesson. The knowledge that this kind of thinking is only a self-serving excuse that is intended to justify weakness and bad behavior is absolutely no consolation if you get assaulted.

Although the law theoretically protects rape victims, in practice the courts tend to favor men, and conviction of rapists is relatively rare. This is because Indian society tends to put the blame on women. It's not only religious extremists who think that men shouldn't be held responsible for their own actions if women "tempt" them in the slightest way, no matter if it's completely unintentional. Many other people hold the same view, including a surprising number of women from conservative families. Ironically, it's always the woman who is regarded as weak, and if a man has an affair or abducts a woman, often it's only the woman who is punished, while the man may go free with hardly a reprimand to continue his licentious behavior with other women.

Because of the tendency to blame women, as well as the extreme pressure on them to remain silent, there are easily dozens of unreported rapes for every one that gets reported. All too often the police refuse to register a case even when a woman does get up the courage to report the crime.

If a man's behavior is inappropriate by Indian standards—if he is making suggestive remarks or uninvited physical contact—then firmly tell him to stop. If he doesn't get the message, slap him. Don't wait until the situation is out of hand. If he doesn't respond appropriately, make a commotion and appeal to other people nearby for assistance.

You can do quite a lot to protect yourself so that you don't make yourself an obvious target. You can't change the culture, so you will be safer and more comfortable if you simply adapt.

Avoid taking taxis or public transportation alone at night. Also, be discriminating about where you go for evening entertainment and who you go with. Don't walk alone at night, and avoid walking alone in isolated or bad areas even in the daytime. If you must do so, then at least carry some pepper spray in a way that you can use it quickly if need be. Any time you are out walking alone, no matter where you are at any time, try to act confident, as if you know exactly where you are going, even if you haven't a clue. Standing around looking lost and vulnerable may attract thieves, con artists and other scoundrels. If you really are lost, go into a decent-looking shop and ask for directions, or else ask any woman who is passing by.

If you need to hire a taxi, especially when you are alone at night, it's better to get one from a hotel or a taxi stand, or else call a radio taxi, if the service is available, rather than flagging one down on the street (which isn't always possible, anyway).

When you are staying in a hotel, check the windows to make sure they can be closed and locked securely. If the doors and windows are not secure, get a different room. Always keep your door locked even when you are in the room.

It's good to keep a cell phone with you in case of emergency. India now has a universal emergency number (108) that you can call for any kind of emergency.

Public Safety

Other considerations often take precedence over public safety. For instance, when the bridge near my summer home in Ladakh was being rebuilt, it meant a detour of a couple of kilometers to get to town by road. For a few weeks the bridge was nothing but a framework of steel girders set on a concrete frame a couple of feet above a rough mess of dirt, scrap steel, and large rocks resting on a concrete base. It was still open for foot traffic, but officially closed to vehicles. In spite of this, along with the pedestrians, many motorbikes were carefully walked across the steel girders, which were only about 4" wide. The situation was fairly dangerous, but the authorities didn't want to close the bridge to foot traffic during the season because the guesthouses on the other side would have lost too much money.

Indian Law & Law Enforcement

Indian law allows the police to arrest anyone accused of a crime for any reason. Although this rarely happens to non-Indians, there have been reports of foreign men being arrested on trumped-up charges on account of their inability to get a visa for their Indian wives. In such cases, the Indian families consent to the marriage in expectation of deriving some financial or other advantage from their daughters living abroad with their husbands—and if this doesn't happen right away, they come up with spurious criminal charges.

India has laws covering most of the usual crimes, plus a few more. You can be arrested for behavior that wouldn't be a crime in many countries, e.g., saying derogatory things about any religion, or about a woman, or even, as I already mentioned, kissing in public. It's possible to be accused of spying and thrown in jail for photographing bridges, airports, train stations or military bases; for hanging around military installations; for trespassing in restricted areas; for hanging out in the border regions without a permit; for making unauthorized maps; or for asking too many questions about the military. You can be imprisoned for up to five years for maiming or killing a cow. Sex with minors can also land you in jail. As in other countries, ignorance of the law is no excuse. For all that, it is extremely unlikely that you will get arrested, of course, so long as you make a reasonable effort to behave well and stay out of trouble.

It's against the law in India to sell anything that you brought to the country, even for your personal use. When you leave, you are expected to take back to your country everything that didn't get used up. If you have declared some expensive equipment and it gets stolen while you are in India, you will need to get a police report in case customs demands to see it when you leave the country.

Unfortunately, the police in India are sometimes more dangerous than the people they are supposed to be protecting you from. Moreover, it's common for police officers to ask for bribes.

If you have to deal with an unhelpful officer, try positioning yourself as a guest in their country or their city, e.g., you could say something like, "but sir, I am a guest here and I need your help." Remain calm and keep your voice soft. Getting angry or hysterical will invariably make matters worse. As in most places, police in India are touchy about such behavior, especially if they think you are being disrespectful.

Bribery and Corruption

Corruption is common in India and most Indians are accustomed to paying bribes as a matter of course, especially to government officials and police officers. However, you should try not to resort to bribery for any reason, whether to get someone to bend the rules or just to get them to do their job. Bribery only perpetuates all that is corrupt in India.

There is a big movement on to end corruption, so the situation is changing. It's certainly not going to happen overnight, but at least things are finally moving in the right direction. The government has been talking about fighting corruption for decades, and they often make a show of cracking down on officials who take bribes. But many of the top people in the government are themselves corrupt, and the worst offenders usually go free. On the other hand, they often go after inconsequential people just for show.

If an official or police officer demands a bribe, pretend not to understand. If it's too much trouble, they will often just give up. If that doesn't work, try to talk them out of it on whatever grounds occur to you. Insisting on a receipt is a good strategy that works pretty often. No one will give an official receipt for money that is going into his own pocket.

Saying you're not carrying much money is another reasonable strategy. In this case, however, the official is likely to ask how much you have with you so he can adjust his demands accordingly. If you are expecting demands for *bakshish,* don't take any money with you or else keep your money hidden so you can show an empty wallet.

If someone demands a huge bribe, find out the person's name and position in case you decide to contact the Central Bureau of Investigation (CBI), the government body that deals with corruption. If it is clear that nothing will happen without a bribe, you could say that you don't have the money with you and then arrange a time to come back. Refrain from making any hints about the CBI. If you do report the incident to the CBI, the agents may set up a sting to try to catch the person red-handed. A list of CBI offices can be found at <www.cbi.gov.in—default.php>. Avoid making threats, as they are likely to backfire.

If you are involved in a major deal such as buying land, setting up a business, or even just getting equipment out of customs, prepare your strategy in advance, since many people along the way will want a sizable cut. Whatever tactics you adopt, try to remain calm.

Bribes are frequently extorted from the unwary in the form of a fake toll or tax of some sort. In these cases, demanding a receipt seems to have a relatively high success rate.

When police officers stop drivers for traffic violations, they often offer the option of taking care of it on the spot at a "reduced" penalty. This "offer" is nothing but a bribe.

If You Are the Victim of a Crime

In the unlikely event that you have to report a crime, the first step is to file an FIR (First Information Report) at the nearest police station, but try to avoid going alone, especially if you are a woman. Often the police are reluctant to register an FIR, either because the officers on duty are lazy and they expect a bribe for doing their duty or because someone is leaning on them to keep the crime statistics low. Note that merely recording the details in a journal is *not* the same as filing an FIR. When an FIR is filed, the police must start an investigation. If they are unhelpful, remind them that the Supreme Court recently ruled that police officers turning away a person without registering a complaint may face contempt of court charges and jail if they fail to justify their non-registration of the FIR. They can also be charged if they fail to follow up on the FIR within a reasonable time. This approach should get some action, but if you are still stonewalled by the officers on duty (who may try to bluff you into believing that the ruling has been overturned), notify your embassy and let the police know that you have contacted them. Then go to the Superintendent of Police and emphatically remind him of the ruling.

If the police begin an investigation, and then it suddenly comes to a grinding halt, it has either been suppressed from above—typically because the suspects are closely connected to someone in the department, politicians in power, the local mafia, or other wealthy and influential people—or a considerable amount of *bakshish* has changed hands. In such a case, you can go to the CBI and demand an investigation.

Travel Warnings and Advisories

Although India is on the whole a pretty safe country, especially if you take a few simple precautions and respect the culture and religions, certain areas should be avoided.

The U.S. State Department has a website with security and political information for every country: <www.travel.state.gov>. The reports include current travel advisories and warnings about terrorist activity, epidemics, and certain problems frequently faced by foreigners in specific places. You should take the travel advisories seriously, but you can read between the lines and make enquiries on your own, since these warnings don't always mean you shouldn't visit a place at all. Sometimes the warnings are left in place long after a situation has settled down.

If you want to go to a location where a travel warning is in effect, you should find out what the situation is from people who are there or who have been there recently, preferably within the last couple of months. Ask a few different people, but not anyone who has a vested interest in your visit, such as a travel agent or hotel owner, as they will usually tell you that everything is just fine even if it's not. You should also take the time to do a web search of the local media for the area you are hoping to visit to see if there have been any recent incidents that you should know about over the last few months or so. Local incidents, even when they are fairly serious, don't always make it into the national and international news.

A terrorist attack can come any place at any time without warning, but if you avoid the hotspots, the chances of getting caught in one are practically nil.

About the Drug Scene

Many foreigners have heard that drugs are cheap and easily available in India, which is true enough. However, it's not true that there is little risk in obtaining and using them. Those telling such tales may have been lucky enough to avoid problems so far or they may have an ulterior motive for lying, maybe because they are selling drugs or because they are looking to set people up for a swindle or an arrest.

Aside from places where there is considerable unrest and terrorist activity, areas where the drug scene is active are the least safe places for foreign visitors due to a huge rise in violent crime associated with out-of-control drug use. There is also a high incidence of AIDS among drug users. Drug overdoses are the leading cause of death among foreigners.

Designer drugs have become increasingly popular in India, but you should know that they are manufactured with little concern for the welfare of those who take them. Drugs of all kinds are commonly mixed with other substances that may look similar but are not necessarily edible, and that may be extremely toxic. In India, these risks are greater than in most other places. Certain drugs are routinely adulterated with any cheap and similar substance the dealers can come up with, including rat poison.

According to reports, drug dealers have taken to giving free cocaine and Ecstasy to young foreign women and then sexually assaulting them when they are high.[18] Thefts and muggings are also common, as is the case in any location where drug use is widespread.

Cannabis has been used medicinally in India for millenia, but while it is widely available, it is (with certain exceptions) illegal, and being convicted even for simple possession can mean years in jail—and there are many foreigners wasting away in Indian jails for drug-related crimes.

Penalties for possession of other drugs or for drug trafficking are more severe. They include long mandatory sentences or even the death penalty. If you are caught, your embassy and friends can do nothing to help you. You may languish in jail for years just waiting for your trial because India's court system is seriously over-burdened. Chances of conviction are high, and once convicted, you will be in jail for a long time. Indian prisons are brutal, hellish places and many inmates die before completing their sentence.

Drug dealers are always on the lookout for people to carry their goods abroad, whether knowingly or unknowingly. They never smuggle their drugs personally, even though the payoff would be extremely high, because of the high risk involved. If a stranger asks you to take a package back home to mail, even though he may assure you that you have nothing to worry about and that the package doesn't contain drugs or anything else that could get you arrested, don't do it. The person may in fact be honest, but is it worth the risk?

• • •

Accommodation

MOST OF THE BEST PLACES TO STAY come through the recommendations of friends and acquaintances. Networking is really important in India. So many wonderful opportunities can come your way just by talking with people. I always ask people I meet about their favorite places because their recommendations are usually more reliable than any guidebooks. Even the best guidebooks are filled with inaccuracies because conditions can change quickly.

Another good way to find a place to stay is to head out for a long walk in the area you want to be in, stopping to talk to people along the way. It's easier if you aren't carrying your bags with you, of course, and the station Cloak Room (where you can check your bags) is a good option if you have just arrived.

Even better than travelers' recommendations are personal references. In India, being the friend of a friend really means something. They'll almost always receive you as an honored guest and invite you to tea, or maybe to a meal; and if they don't offer to put you up in their own home (which they often will), they will usually help you find a place to stay and maybe show you around.

If you are an unmarried couple traveling together, many places will not allow you to share a room. If you don't like their policy, it is better to go somewhere else than to make an issue of it. Where there is such a policy, the owners usually won't give in.

If you want an attached bath, always ask for one when making a reservation, since many places have shared baths. In budget places, you'll want to ask about the availability of hot water, too. Upscale hotels virtually all have Western-style bathrooms and 24-hour hot water. However, the farther down the price scale you get, the more likely you are to find Indian-style bathrooms and sporadic or nonexistent hot water—or hot water available by bucket only after 7 a.m., etc. Some places have a variety of rooms with both Western and Indian-style bathrooms.

In many places, the lack of infrastructure produces special challenges. Electricity is often available only at certain times of the day. Sometimes there may not be any for a few days. Power cuts are common. Often load-shedding is scheduled, but there may be unscheduled power cuts as well. Water is also not always available.

You'll rarely get heat in places that are less than luxurious even though the temperatures may be down to freezing. If you are in a place like that, you may want to get a hot water bottle. Even if the temperature isn't that low, it can seem like it if you are never able to get warm. Northern India feels really cold in the winter, and not just in the mountains.

Hotels & Guesthouses

Hotels in India range from among the most luxurious in the world to the most spartan. Many hotels have a star rating, but sometimes the ratings are self-proclaimed, and those are often misleading. The Indian Government has recently revised the standards for star category hotels. However, these standards are related only to the type of facilities offered by the hotels—how many rooms with attached bath, how many restaurants, whether there is a swimming pool or shopping arcade, etc.—and not their quality. So you may encounter four-star hotels that are dumps, and starless hotels that are superb. There are a few hotels that advertise themselves as "seven-star resorts," though the highest rating on the government scale is five-star deluxe.

If you haven't prepaid, try to see a room or two before you commit. You really can't judge a hotel by its lobby. A hotel with a nice lobby may have grubby, unacceptable rooms.

There are really no clear indicators to distinguish budget from mid-range hotels. Price doesn't always have much relationship with the quality of the facilities. You may find a comfortable room for Rs.150 (but not in big cities like Delhi or Mumbai), or you may pay several times as much for a room that is really terrible. Generally, Rs.400–500 is about the lowest rate for mid-range hotels outside of the big cities. However, depending on where you are, you can find AC (air-conditioned) rooms for as little as Rs.250, though the cost might be as much as Rs.1,000 even for the most basic AC room in other places. Mid-range hotels usually provide a phone and TV. They often provide 24-hour hot water, a Western-style toilet and a shower as well. Sometimes the more expensive places are worth the extra money and sometimes they aren't.

Heritage hotels are often delightful places to stay—they are hotels and guest houses that have been converted from palaces, forts, stately ancestral homes and other interesting old buildings. There are, of course, new hotels made to look old, which lack the heritage ambiance.

Many budget and moderate hotels aspire to enhance their images with names that include words like "deluxe" or "palace" or "international." A name like that is a cue to look a little closer. While some of them may live up to the names, most don't. Overly cutesy names are another bad sign.

Some places offer "Swiss tents," which are permanent tents that may have attached bathrooms and even AC. They can be nice for a change, though they often have more mosquitoes and creepy crawlies than other sorts of accommodations, and you can hear everything that is going on in the surrounding tents. "Log huts" are rustic cabins, but they usually aren't made of logs.

Five-star hotels and resorts may have an Ayurvedic spa along with the usual amenities. Havens for wealthy people who want to feel pampered and protected, they are also good places to go for a short break if you are suffering from culture shock or homesickness. You can take refuge in one for an hour or two as a break from shopping or sightseeing, even if you aren't staying there. They usually have good restaurants, and even a tea break in such a place can really lift your spirits if you are feeling homesick.

In many areas of India, there is a luxury tax (10–20%) on hotels over a certain price. Most places don't include service in the price of the room.

Many people prefer guesthouses to hotels because they are smaller and more personal. You are also much more likely to meet interesting people. Guesthouses are often like staying with a family but with considerably more privacy. They tend to be much cheaper than hotels, also.

Checkout times vary, so you should always ask when booking or before checking in. Although many hotels have checkout times around noon, there is no standard. Some hotels have 24-hour checkout, which can be convenient if you don't arrive too early. However, if you arrive early in the morning and stay until a little later the next morning, you may be charged for two full days. In some places checkout times can be as early as 7 a.m., while other places may let you stay until 4 p.m. Checkout times can often be extended simply by asking (especially if you say you will stay elsewhere if you really have to leave at the prescribed hour), but some hotels refuse to give any concession.

Ashrams & Monasteries

The word *ashram* is often understood to mean a place with a guru who teaches some form of meditation or yoga to everyone who stays there. However, there are different types of *ashrams*, and many of them have nothing to do with gurus or yoga. Some *ashrams*—and these virtually always have a guru, though he or she may not be in residence—are only for people doing a specific program or taking classes. Others are simply a quiet haven for anyone engaged in any sort of *sadhana* (spiritual practice). There are some that, although supposedly spiritual in intent, in no way resemble a quiet haven due to constant propaganda assailing the ears over loudspeakers. There are also *ashrams* where pilgrims can stay for a day or two while visiting holy places. An *ashram* can even just be a place where one or two hermits live in silent meditation. *Sevashrams* are *ashrams* where everyone is dedicated to public service of one sort or another, such as running a school or hospital, working with the poor, etc.

Although many *ashrams* are particular about who may stay there (and they don't all take foreigners), others don't mind who you are as long as you don't disturb the environment with inappropriate behavior. *Ashrams* are not hotels, and they shouldn't be treated as such. Usually they have rules that include no smoking, no drinking, no drugs, quiet hours, and a curfew. *Ashram* food is virtually always vegetarian, and usually extremely simple.

Accommodation is typically given on a donation basis (Rs.200-400 or so a night is usual, unless you are staying for a long time, in which case it can be much, much less). Some *ashrams* have fixed charges. Others will let you stay for free, but unless you have just lost everything you own, you really must give something. Or you may exchange work for room and board.

Some Buddhist monasteries and nunneries have guesthouses where you can stay, as do some of the Sikh *gurudwaras*. These range from extremely austere to quite comfortable. Accommodation may be either by donation or a fixed rate. As with *ashrams*, these facilities have strict rules about smoking, drinking, drugs, etc. All of these places typically offer simple vegetarian food.

Renting an Apartment

Service apartments can be a good deal if you will be staying in one place for several weeks or months, depending on where they are located and the level of luxury you require. They come fully furnished, with linens, pots and pans, etc., as well as maid service, and there is no lease. You can usually find these in the large cities through the local city guides.

On the other hand, if you are planning to stay for a longer time, it's much cheaper to lease an apartment or house. This is a pretty involved process, however, so you are advised to get an Indian friend or an agent to help. In the expat enclaves of Bangalore, Hyderabad, Gurgaon and Delhi, especially where there are many multinational corporations, the rents are often astronomically high, but most other places, they range from reasonable to incredibly cheap.

Other Options

Government Guesthouses and Bungalows are usually spartan but acceptable for a night or two. They vary quite a lot from state to state. In some states they tend to be poorly maintained, while in others they can be clean and comfortable. Prices are usually quite reasonable. Forest Rest Houses are mostly reserved for government personnel, so don't count on staying at one just because it happens to be listed in a guidebook. Always make enquiries in advance. They are generally very rustic, and you have to bring your own food.

In Srinagar and Kerala you can rent houseboats, either by the room or the whole boat. Houseboats range from practically palatial to dumpy. If you can, look at several before settling on one, and negotiate hard. Never book a Srinagar houseboat package from touts. The package may seem like a good deal, but even if it supposed to be an "all-inclusive" package, they are likely to charge extra for every little thing—heat, hot water, meals, *shikara* (the small boat you need to get around the lakes), airport transfer, etc.—which can end up being expensive. Get recommendations from people who have been satisfied with their stay, if possible. Otherwise, go through a reliable travel agent, or else go to a hotel the first night and then shop around.

Many tourists complain that they have been harassed constantly to buy one thing or another.

Problems have also been reported with houseboats in Kerala, though not nearly as many as in Kashmir. Nevertheless, in both places single women are advised not to stay alone, especially in isolated situations.

Homestays, where you take a room with a family, are becoming increasingly popular, especially in Ladakh and Kerala. Several cities, including Delhi and Jaipur, now have homestay programs. Make inquiries at the central tourist office or look online. The price varies according to the accommodations, which range from spartan to downright luxurious. In any case, homestays are an excellent way to get to know local people and learn more about the culture.

There are also several non-profit hospitality organizations, such as Servas and CouchSurfing. These organizations have volunteer hosts throughout India and all over the world who are interested in having foreign visitors for a couple of nights or so. Their purpose is to promote international peace and understanding through getting to know people from different cultures and countries on a person-to-person basis, so plan to spend time with your hosts. You have to join in advance and there is usually a procedure for screening or verifying applicants that takes time. People who open their homes in this way are usually nice people, and many have fascinating stories to tell. Although accommodation is free, it's often appropriate to offer some little donation, especially if they feed you. It's a wonderful way to meet local people and to enhance your understanding of the culture.

When you stay at a homestay, especially with members of any of the various hospitality organizations, it is expected that you will spend time getting to know your hosts. Don't treat them like hotels that are just places to sleep. Your hosts won't appreciate it if you stay out late. If you must arrive late, be sure to ask them in advance whether it will be OK.

On the other hand, there are some bed-and-breakfast places that are run as impersonally as hotels, where you never even see the owners, though I would say that these are quite rare. You would only find such places in big cities like Delhi. Most Indians would be ashamed to provide such inadequate hospitality in their own homes.

Tips for Budget Travelers

Even if you are on a very tight budget, you can almost always find a place to stay that won't be too much of a stretch financially, but sometimes you have to really ask around. A budget hotel is not always called a *hotel*. It could also be called a *lodge, boarding house, guesthouse,* or even *café.* The word *hotel* more commonly refers to a simple eating place than to lodging. Youth hostels, YMCAs and *dharmashalas* (pilgrims' lodges) are available in various places as well. *Dharmashalas* offer extremely basic accommodation for pilgrims, usually in dorms, but they don't always take foreigners.

Most budget places offer simple rooms furnished with beds that have mattresses made of foam or coir (fiber from the outer husk of the coconut), a fluorescent light, maybe a chair and table, and sometimes a ceiling fan. Some rock-bottom budget places may provide only a bare wooden platform bed or a cot with no mattress at all. If you can't bear rock-hard beds, bring a camp pad. Bathrooms may be attached or common, but they tend to be basic. The cheapest budget places often have dormitories (separate for men and women, of course) with common baths.

Baths are usually of the bucket kind. Hot water can often be ordered during the cold season for Rs.5–10 a bucket, but otherwise it may not be available, especially in the South. Sometimes there may be a geyser (hot water heater), but if it doesn't come on when you press the switch, there is probably a master switch that is turned on only at certain hours or for a short time on request.

There may be no sheets, or perhaps a single sheet plus a blanket or bedspread. Traveling on a budget means that you will inevitably encounter places where the sheets are unsavory and the blankets are never washed, so it is recommended to use a sheet sleeping bag. You can buy one before you come or else have one made in India. All you need is about five meters of fabric (depending on your size), folded so that the bottom is a couple of feet longer than the top and stitched most of the way up one side and maybe a foot or two up the other, with a kind of pocket at the top folded under and stitched so that you can insert a pillow. Silk sheet sleeping bags are the lightest and easiest to carry, while pure cotton bags are the coolest. Or you could have one made with silk on the bottom and lightweight cotton on top.

Low-budget places don't provide towels, so you have to bring your own. If they supply drinking water, it is generally not adequately purified, so avoid it.

Budget rooms almost always have a bolt-and-hasp type of lock. A padlock and key is usually provided, but you are much safer using your own, since you don't know who else might have a copy of the key. A cable lock and steel-mesh cover for your backpack is highly recommended if you are carrying anything valuable. Dormitories often have a steel closet where you can lock up your things, but you need to provide your own lock.

The cheapest places can be downright seedy, though some are spotlessly clean and altogether delightful, especially in the more remote areas. Check the room before taking it and ask to see a few rooms, if possible. Check for cleanliness, bedbugs, security, a working fan (and whether it is really noisy, if that would bother you), the bathroom and hot water situation, etc.

Bedbugs, lice and fleas tend to harbor in unwashed linens and old mattresses, which is why it is good to have a sheet sleeping bag. If you see little bloody spots on the sheets, you can assume that there are bedbugs.

Window screens are not the norm in budget places, and mosquitoes are, so you should carry a mosquito net.

Camping is not a realistic option most places in India unless you are trekking or rafting in the mountains. There are no campgrounds in India like there are in Western countries. Some hotels and guesthouses provide space for tents on their property, but these are mostly in the mountains along the major trekking routes. Sometimes you can arrange with private families to camp on their property. It would be rude to set up your tent on someone's property without asking in advance. Offering the family between, say, 50–100 rupees would be appropriate, depending on the circumstances, and if they were initially reluctant, it might change their mind.

This is a delicate point, but it must be mentioned, although it may not apply to most of you: Indians appreciate clothing that is neat, clean, and conservative, and they are appalled by foreigners who make a point of looking impoverished—wearing grubby, ragged clothing, with dirty or matted hair, going barefoot on the streets, etc. This appearance is considered to be far beneath the dignity of someone who was able to afford the price of a ticket to India. Some foreigners regard this style of dress as a show of solidarity with the Indian masses, but even India's poorest people don't see it like that. In fact, many people find it offensive—though, of course, the majority of Indians are too polite to say so even if you ask. No matter how tight a budget you are on, it is best to be as well groomed as you can. If you feel you have no time to wash your clothes, it's time to slow down.

• • •

India by Train

TRAINS ARE A POPULAR WAY to get around India, and for good reason: they provide an easy way to immerse yourself in the local culture, and they bring you face to face with an India that package tourists, isolated in their well-protected groups, never get to see. You can meet people from all walks of life and see many things you have never even imagined.

India has an extensive and surprisingly efficient train system, but the trains themselves vary greatly. Some are good; others are really terrible. Some nearly always run on time; others are usually late. Some are well kept; others are really dirty. There are regional differences also: the trains in the South tend to be cleaner and safer than in the North.

Understanding Timetables

If you aren't at a major train station with an International Tourist Bureau, it can sometimes be confusing and frustrating to try to figure out the trains, especially if you are planning a complex itinerary. At most big stations you can buy a timetable called *Trains at a Glance*, which lists all of the major trains with reasonable accuracy, though it doesn't list many local trains and many small stations. If you will be doing a lot of train travel, it is almost essential. There are many regional versions of *Trains at a Glance*, some better than others, but they are all laid out about the same. There is also a more complete version, called the *Indian Bradshaw*, although it is not as readily available.

The main station in some cities is listed under a different name than you might expect: for instance, in Hyderabad, the main station is Secunderabad, while Howrah is the name of the main station in Kolkata (Calcutta). Some cities have several stations, which are often far apart, so you need to know which one you want.

While schedules for some of the major long-haul trains are listed on a single timetable, for many trains you have to look at two or three timetables. Every train has a number as well as a name, and these are listed at the top of the page. The following row shows which days of the week the train operates. Not all trains are daily, and some trains to remote destinations only go once a week. In the next row, you will see that some columns have numbers and others don't. If there is no number, the train is starting out from the first station listed. If there is a number, then the train is coming from somewhere else and the number indicates which timetable you have to consult to get that information. A corresponding row at the bottom of the page gives the number of the timetable you have to look up to see the next part of the train's route. Consequently, one train can appear on several timetables. Except for some of the less important routes, which may list "up" and "down" trains on the same page, most schedules will show train routes in only one direction. Distances are shown in kilometers. Some timetables include alternate routes.

Many trains are overnight trains, and some take as long as three or four days, so if you are taking a long journey, check the departure and arrival days carefully so you don't mess up your connections. It takes time to figure out a long or complex journey using these timetables, especially if there are many places where you have to change trains.

If you look closely at a timetable that lists many trains, you'll notice that the trains don't all start and stop at the same places even though they are on the same timetable, and many trains may not be going where you want. However, with careful reading you can easily come up with some interesting itineraries. Unless you simply want to get to your destination as quickly as possible, you'll may want to see what interesting places lie along the way, or not too far off of it, and plan a few stops accordingly. It's worth the effort to spend an hour or two going through *Trains at a Glance* with a guidebook and map in hand. Even if you are going to the Tourist Bureau to book your ticket, it's easier if you have already come up with at least a tentative itinerary to work with, and perhaps with some alternate possibilities, as well.

Categories of Trains

There are different categories of trains and different classes of accommodation on the trains, and usually several options are available for any given route. There are eight classes in all (with a few variations according to the type of train, etc.), but not all classes are available on all trains. Unless there is no other choice, you will probably want to avoid the slow local passenger trains, which stop at every little station and usually have only extremely crowded, second-class, non-AC carriages. With few exceptions, it is essential to book reservations in advance for overnight trains if you want to be sure of a berth to sleep in.

The fastest, safest, most reliable and most luxurious trains are the classes of trains known as *Rajdhani* and *Shatabdi*. They have the fewest stops and are generally on time. They are more expensive than other trains, and reservations are required. *Shatabdi* trains are short-haul day trains with sitting accommodations only. *Rajdhani* trains are long-haul trains, consisting of only air-conditioned (AC) first, second and third class coaches. Non-AC classes are not available. The mail and express trains are a little slower and make more stops. Ordinary trains or passenger trains are the cheapest, slowest, and most uncomfortable—and there is no AC. *Trains at a Glance* doesn't list ordinary trains except in a few cases where there is nothing else available. There are also special trains: the mountain trains such as the "toy trains" (i.e., narrow gauge) of the Nilgiris, Shimla, Kangra Valley and

Darjeeling, all of which are slow, but exceptionally scenic, cheap and delightful; and an increasing number of special tourist trains which are expensive and luxurious, such as the *Palace on Wheels* and the *Deccan Queen*.

Once a train gets behind schedule for any reason, it will keep getting delayed further, except, usually, for the *Rajdhani* and *Shatabdi*, which have priority over all the others. In many places there is only one set of tracks, so a train often has to wait while trains coming in the opposite direction pass by. Therefore, if one train is late, it will delay many other trains as well. If there is a major accident, trains may have to be rerouted, and this process can result in delays of many hours. In the winter, fog delays many trains by several hours, especially in the North.

Many of the metropolitan areas (e.g., Delhi, Kolkata, Mumbai, Chennai) have local commuter trains, and Delhi has a new metro rail system, which is clean, safe, efficient, and which rivals any metro system in the world. Mumbai, on the other hand, has possibly the most over-crowded and miserable commuter rail system that you will find anywhere.

Classes of Accommodation

The various classes of accommodation differ in terms of passenger density, comfort and the toilets. The cheaper the ticket, the more crowded the carriage, the harder the seats/berths, and the dirtier the toilets.

In every passenger-carrying train, one compartment of the lowest class of accommodation is supposed to be reserved for ladies. However, in many cases the ladies' compartment has hard wooden seats even when the other carriages of the same class have nice padded ones, so this choice isn't always a pleasant one.

A word about the toilets: there is usually at least one Western toilet in each AC carriage, though most are of the Indian squat type.

The cleanliness of the toilets decreases rapidly in the more crowded classes, and they are apt to be increasingly wet and slippery. The Western ones in 1A or 2A tend to be OK, but otherwise you are usually better off with the Indian style ones. Using them is a bit of an art, however, due to the wobbling and lurching of the train and the slippery floor, and you'll really need to hold on to the handrail. Don't use these toilets with your wallet, glasses or other valuables in your pocket because if anything falls out, it's gone for good. The toilet is definitely not the place to fuss with contact lenses, either. The toilets empty directly onto the tracks, so avoid using them while the train is stopped at a station.

AC Chair Car (CC). AC Chair Car class is available on short-haul daytime trains (particularly the *Shatabdi* and *Jan Shatabdi trains)*. The seats, which are arranged three on one side of the aisle and two on the other, are fairly comfortable, and they recline. Tea, coffee, meals and mineral water are included on the *Shatabdi* trains. Sometimes there is loud music, but they'll often lower the volume if you ask. The *Jan Shatabdi* is similar to the *Shatabdi,* except that there is a little less legroom and meals are not served, so the tickets are considerably cheaper. Also, instead of ECC, the *Jan Shatabdi* has a non-AC chair car that is cheap and has non-reclining seats. The *Jan Shatabdi* is often more convenient for people on a relaxed schedule, as the *Shatabdi* is scheduled to accommodate business travelers.

Executive Class AC Chair Car (ECC). *Shatabdi* trains have an ECC class, which has wider, plusher seats (2x2 instead of 3x2) that recline much farther, with more legroom and fancier meals.

First AC (1A or 1AC). First AC is the most expensive class and is available only on important long-haul trains. Reservations are mandatory. Compartments have either two berths (up and down) or four (two up and two down). They are pretty comfortable and often have carpeting on the floors. The berths are wider, longer and softer than those of other classes (so they are especially good for larger people) and mostly have cloth upholstery instead of vinyl. There is usually a sink in the cabin as well. Sheets, towels, pillows and blankets are provided. The compartments have doors that can be locked from the inside. On many trains, the doors can also be locked with a padlock from the outside, so you could all get off at a long stop without worrying about your luggage if your party is occupying the whole compartment.

1AC is an excellent option for women traveling alone because it is the most secure. You're traveling with a higher class of people in general so you are much less likely to have problems. Also, there are attendants in the car that you can call in case of need. Berths are not assigned until a few hours before the train departs, though you can indicate your preference on the reservation form. When boarding, women can ask the TTE (conductor) to be in a compartment with other ladies or a family. The TTE will usually be quite accommodating, as the culture traditionally protects women in this way. If you do get in with all men, an upper berth is safest. If the train is not crowded, the TTE may sometimes give you a coupe (two-berth compartment) all to yourself.

On some trains, meals and bottled water are provided, but on others there is nothing. Sometimes there are even showers, though these aren't particularly convenient and they don't come with hot water, except, perhaps, on a few special trains.

First Class (FC). First Class is being phased out in favor of 2AC. On mail/express trains, First Class is similar to 1AC, but without the AC, and it costs about the same as 2AC. No pillow, linen or blankets are provided unless you order them in advance. FC is fairly comfortable, but less so than 1AC. There are compartments with two or four berths and they have lockable doors. Local daytime passenger trains sometimes have a First Class Ordinary section that is just for sitting. It's not exactly luxurious, the main differences from Unreserved Second Sitting being that the bench seats are padded and that it is much less crowded because it is so much more expensive.

Second AC Sleeper Class (2A or 2AC). 2AC is also called AC 2-Tier and sometimes just AC Class. Reservations are required. This class is a two-tier arrangement where the lower berths are used for sitting in the daytime. You should request an upper berth if you want to rest during the daytime. The berths are a little shorter and narrower than 1AC and not quite as well padded. On most trains they are arranged bunk-style, four to a compartment along one side of the train, with bunks arranged above and below the windows running along the corridor on the other side, with curtains for privacy. The berths along the side of the carriage offer more privacy but not so much space to put your bags—which is a concern because since they're right on the corridor, theft is a greater risk. Avoid the berths at the end of the car, where the door opens and closes all night. Sometimes the TTE can shift your berth if an empty one is available once you are on the train. Blanket, pillow and sheets are provided. As with all the AC coaches, the windows are dirty and tinted, so you don't get to see much of the countryside. 2AC coaches typically have four toilets, with one Western-style and one Indian-style toilet at one end of the carriage and two Indian-style toilets at the other.

3-Tier AC Sleeper Class (3A OR 3AC). 3A, or AC 3-Tier, has a middle berth that is folded up during the day so people can sit on the lower berth, and extra people may be squeezed in, though you have your berth to yourself at night. Berths in this class are also harder and narrower. Berths are also available along the corridor on the other side. There are no curtains for privacy. Bedrolls are available for a small fee, but they have to be booked before the journey.

Sleeper Class (SL). Sleeper Class on mail/express trains is a three-tier arrangement like 3AC but without the AC. The windows open and there are roll-down metal louvered shades to keep out the rain. In good weather, it is delightful to have fresh air blowing through the car, but in cold weather, you need something to bundle up in as there is no heat. No bedroll is provided, so you have to bring your own bedding. Sleeper class is extremely cheap, and vast numbers of Indians use it to travel from one end of the country to the other. However, you need a certain fortitude and determination to stay in one of these for really long journeys that can last up to three days or even more as conditions are cramped. At night you have your own berth, assuming you have reserved one (which you must), but during the day they squeeze many more people in, and the berths can become quite crowded. Sleeper Class Ordinary on passenger trains is a rougher version, which has hard, unpadded bunks.

It is strongly recommended that women not take overnight journeys in Sleeper Class unaccompanied by a man. Women who can't afford anything more expensive could ride in the women's compartment, take day trains or team up with other travelers (including, if possible, a man or two). At the very least, make sure you are in with families or couples. And go for upper berths, if possible.

Trains heading for holy places typically have lots of families on board and are usually safer than trains between business centers, which often have a predominance of men. Although in Sleeper Class you can meet up with people from any class, there may be some rough characters from a low stratum of society. Moreover, since foreign women are perceived as being sexually available, those traveling in such circumstances are frequently regarded as offering an open invitation. While violent assault is rare, harassment of some sort (vulgar comments, groping, etc.) is unfortunately quite common. Even if you are with your partner, you may suffer harassment, especially if you don't take care to respect the culture. Avoiding even the slightest physical contact is particularly important.

Unreserved (II). Unreserved carriages are normally crowded, but sometimes they are packed to such an extreme that most people will be standing with about as much space as sardines in a can. In the most extreme cases, such as during the Kumbha Mela, where literally millions of people are heading to the same destination at the same time, those with seats will have other people sitting on or under them. Others will be hanging out the doors three or four bodies deep, sitting on the roofs, hanging onto the front and the sides of the engine, etc. In such cases, the trains may move at no more than walking speed for fear of accidents.

Many Indians do not like to see foreigners—especially those from developed countries—in the unreserved carriages, except on commuter trains or passenger trains where there isn't any alternative. It comes across as a pretense of poverty, which is incomprehensible to Indians.

Making Reservations

You can buy train tickets at a station or reservation center (which may be somewhere at a distance from the station itself), or through a travel agent who will charge maybe Rs.100 for the service, or over the Internet at <www.indianrail.gov.in>. To book directly through their site, you need an Indian credit or debit card. It's easier to book online through ClearTrip.com or MakeMyTrip.com, both of which are authorized to sell train tickets online.

Senior citizens get a substantial discount on train tickets—50% for women 58 and older, and 40% for men 60 and older. This doesn't apply to *tatkal* (emergency quota) tickets.

To alleviate the need for buying individual tickets for each journey, you can get an IndRail Pass, which is valid for periods ranging from half a day to 3 months for unlimited travel on the Indian Railways network; these are available for 1AC, 2AC or IInd Class. Pass holders don't have to pay any reservation fees, superfast charges, or surcharges for their journey. With the IndRail Pass you can reserve everything in advance, though it's likely to be more expensive than buying point-to-point tickets unless you are traveling almost every day. Nevertheless, it's quite convenient because it allows for maximum flexibility within its specified validity, so getting one may be worthwhile if you are planning to do a lot of traveling during that time. The pass doesn't guarantee a reservation. You still have to book reservations at a small extra charge. If you don't have reservations, the IndRail Pass allows you to board the train and to ride in the designated class or a lower one, and to get a seat or berth if one is available. However, if there is no open seat or berth, the situation can be tricky. You can't even stay in the 1AC compartment if there is no room. In 2AC, 3AC or sleeper class, you may be given sitting accommodation if no berth is available. In Unreserved class, you'll be squeezed in somewhere.

If you go in person to make your train reservations, you have to fill out a reservation form. If there is a special desk or counter for foreign tourists, the agents there will help you figure out the schedules, etc. Otherwise, you can usually find an Enquiry Counter where you can get some assistance. If the specific train you need is not available, see below for tips on getting tickets.

You can request an upper or lower berth and also whether you want an inside or aisle berth on the Accommodation Preference space of the booking form. If you are going by *Shatabdi* or *Rajdhani*, you can also request a vegetarian or non-vegetarian meal.

When you get your ticket, check the train name and number, coach, and berth number, to make sure they are correct. Also make sure that your age and sex are correct and that your name is at least recognizable, even if it isn't spelled correctly.

A few stations have International Tourist Bureaus where you can get reserved tickets by paying in US dollars or British Pounds. You can also pay in rupees if you have an ATM receipt or an encashment certificate (which banks and money-changers are supposed to give you to show that you have exchanged money legally). In any case, you have to show your passport and Tourist Visa. You can also get Indrail Passes at the Tourist Bureaus. Some of the larger stations let you pay with MasterCard or Visa.

When you buy a ticket for a destination that is more than 500 km away, you are allowed to break your journey once at any station beyond 500 km from the starting station, and you can stop over for up to two days. For journeys of more than 1000 km, you get to stop twice. Each stop has to be specified when you buy the ticket, not en route. You have to get your ticket endorsed by the Station Master at the stopover station or you will be fined and required to buy a new ticket when you get back on board. Sometimes you can get a refund for the remaining portion if you decide not to resume your journey after a particular stop. You can't break your journey on *Rajdhani* and *Shatabdi* trains. If you want to stop over, you have to buy two separate tickets.

If you have a reservation but decide to board at a different station, you have to make the request in writing at least 24 hours before the scheduled departure of the train from the originating station. However, you won't get a refund for the unused portion.

Getting Tickets for a Fully-Booked Train

Many trains are booked up days or weeks in advance, but even when reservations for a train are fully booked, it is usually still possible to get them by one means or another.

There are a number of quotas that set aside reserved space for various needs, although many of the quotas are not available to nonresidents. If you have a Tourist Visa, you can usually get a ticket on the Foreign Tourist Quota, which is available between major stations. Even if you have a different visa, sometimes you can sweet-talk the ticket agents into giving you a ticket if the Foreign Tourist Quota is available (but they will usually do so only within 24 hours before departure, and some places won't do it at all). If the Foreign Tourist Quota is unavailable, ask about other Quotas. The Station Master (or one of the other officers) has the discretion to give you a seat reserved under any quota (e.g., the VIP Quota) if the quota is still unfilled shortly before departure.

Most stations don't have a Foreign Tourist Quota or a special counter for tourists. In this case you should ask to see the person in charge—usually the Chief Reservation Supervisor—who can, if he is inspired to do so, allocate you a ticket from unused quotas. By asking for an unused VIP Quota slot at the right time, you may be able to circumvent the waiting list. Most quotas are allocated at the time of charting, but it seems that the VIP Quota is held until an hour before departure.

If you've purchased your waitlisted or RAC ticket more than 24 or 48 hours ahead of the train's departure from the originating station (depending on whether or not it's a major station), you can apply in writing to have your reservation confirmed. If you are on a Tourist Visa, you'll usually get it. Otherwise, you need to give some reason for the request that sounds sufficiently urgent.

Once a train has been fully booked, a certain number of seats are allotted for Reservation Against Cancellation (RAC). RAC is essentially a provision for using a berth as two seats. Getting an RAC ticket means you have a confirmed reservation for a seat with the provision that you'll get a berth if one becomes available. Even if there are no free berths at the start of the journey, some may open up as the train proceeds to other stations due to cancellations, unfilled quotas or no-shows. Although you can board the reserved coach for an overnight journey, you have no guarantee of a berth. RAC holders are generally allotted the side lower berths, which convert to two separate seats in the daytime. If no berth becomes available, you may have to share one with another RAC ticket holder and remain sitting all night.

Next in priority after RAC is the waiting list. Once all the RAC ticket holders have berths, waitlisted passengers are promoted to RAC seats. Berths freed up by canceled reservations, unfilled quotas, no-shows, etc. are then allotted to passengers based on their position on the list. Usually, the RAC passengers get berths, as do those who are high on the waiting list. In some cases, you could start out at WL/50 and still end up with a berth, and you would almost certainly get one if you were WL/2, even in 1AC, which has a very limited number of berths.

If a passenger with a reserved ticket does not turn up within 10 minutes of the scheduled departure of the train, that reservation can, according to the published rules, be canceled and allotted to a passenger on the RAC list or waiting list. In practice, they rarely seem to do it.

If you are on the waiting list, you can find out whether your reservation has been confirmed by calling the Railway Enquiry number, which is listed on your ticket. Otherwise, you can arrive early for the train and check the reservation board, which has a list of all the passengers on the train. This board is usually located near the station entrance or else on the platform from which the train departs. If you have a reservation but can't find your name on the lists, you should ask the Station Master for assistance.

If you are boarding at a station towards the end of the run of a long-haul train, you may not always need a reservation, even for 2AC. For example, if you want to board the Mumbai to Kanyakumari Express at Cochin heading for Trivandrum, you will rarely have any problem finding a berth or a seat, even if you have only a journey ticket without a reservation; but you couldn't be sure of the same result with a train originating in Cochin. Some trains almost always have seats for portions of their route, and you can often find out the likelihood of this by checking with the Station Master if you are leaving from the same station where you are buying the ticket.

When buying a journey ticket, you need to specify whether you want AC or non-AC. If you specify air-conditioning, the ticket will only be issued for 3AC or AC Chair Car, but you can upgrade to 2AC or even 1AC if berths are available. Unreserved ordinary tickets can only be upgraded to non-AC sleeper class.

If you want to buy a ticket for a train that is scheduled to depart within four hours, you have to go to the Current Reservations Counter. These tickets are unreserved only and they do not guarantee a seat. The reservation charts are written up four hours prior to the train's departure from the originating station, so no reservations are issued after that time.

The Tatkal Quota is another option for booking tickets on certain long-distance trains that are otherwise fully booked. This quota is intended for people with urgent needs. It becomes available only one day prior to the departure of the train, and you have to get the Tatkal reservation before the preparation of the charts. If the train is popular and you really need the ticket, you should arrive at the station before the counter opens at 8:00 am (or be logged on to the IRCTC site ready to book, having already pulled up the right train). In busy stations, there are often many people already waiting when the Tatkal counter opens, so getting the ticket can be a bit of a hassle. Tatkal tickets for popular trains often sell out within minutes.

Tatkal can't be booked through travel agents between 8-9 AM. These tickets are only available between certain major stations and there is a surcharge of 10% to 30% of the basic fare, depending on the class. They are also non-refundable. However, you can get a full refund if the train is delayed more than three hours, if it's rerouted, or if you have been downgraded to a different class and don't want to travel. The rules have already been changed twice in the past year, so more changes could be ahead.

Even in the normal scheme of things, you may have difficulty getting a reservation if you want to board or get off at an intermediate station, whereas it might be easy to get a seat on the same train between major stations. When you buy a ticket, you can indicate that you will be boarding at a different station. While some intermediate stations have station quotas, many do not. If you want to board at an intermediate station that has no quotas, you may be able to buy a ticket from a previous station that has a quota. Otherwise, you can buy an RAC ticket or else an unreserved journey ticket that you can try to upgrade on the train. If you are at a small station that doesn't have a computerized reservation facility, you have to submit your request to the Station Master at least 72 hours before the train is scheduled to depart from that station in order to get a reservation for a berth.

If the above strategies don't get you a reservation, or if you don't want the uncertainty of RAC or waitlisted tickets or of trying to upgrade a journey ticket on the train, consider traveling in a higher class. The cheaper the class of travel, the more quickly the tickets get sold out. Berths are often available in 2AC when the waiting list for 3AC is closed, and sometimes 1AC will be nearly empty even when there is nothing available in 2AC.

Your last-ditch strategy if you absolutely have to travel on a certain day is to buy a journey ticket and then go to the TTE (Traveling Ticket Examiner) once the train reaches the platform. If there are no-shows, he may be able to get you a seat. You could even get on the train with your journey ticket and hope for the best. You may not get a seat, of course, so you have to be willing to chance an uncomfortable journey.

If you jump on a train without a ticket, you'll have to pay a few hundred rupees fine. The TTE may try to find you a seat or he might tell you to get off at the next station if he doesn't see you until the train is moving, but you'll have to pay the fine in any case.

At the Station

Arrive at least 20–30 minutes early for your train to allow plenty of time to get to it. A coolie (the Hindi name for railway porters) is useful not only to carry your bags, but also to get you to the right car on the right train. If you get to the station only a few minutes before your train, he can keep you from missing it. If you are traveling in unreserved class, a good coolie can wriggle through the crowd and (usually) get you a seat while you follow comfortably behind. This is extremely helpful because many people traveling in unreserved class don't get seats, and they may end up sitting on the floor or even standing the whole way.

Reservation lists for each long-distance train are posted on the notice board at each station 2–4 hours before departure, showing the name, age and sex of each passenger along with the coach and berth numbers. If your reservation is not confirmed, your ticket will have "W/L" and a number, which indicates your position on the waiting list. To find out whether your reservation is confirmed, call the railway enquiry number. The reservation list will also be posted on each coach of the train.

The departure time printed on the ticket is not absolute. Check the correct departure time on the day of the journey (at the station or through the railway enquiry number printed on your ticket). Tickets are printed up to 60 days in advance, so schedules can change; and, of course, the train may simply be late, sometimes by as much as 18–20 hours if there has been a serious accident.

Food for the Journey

If you are traveling by *Rajdhani* or *Shatabdi* (except the *Jan Shatabdi*), meals are included. On other trains, itinerant vendors board the trains at many stations with food and beverages for sale. The kitchens in which these meals are prepared often have very questionable hygiene, however, so it's safer to pack your own meals. You just need to do a bit of advance planning. If you are taking an overnight train, you can often have dinner before you leave and breakfast after you arrive, eliminating the need to bring anything but water and a snack or two. Restaurants can usually pack a meal for you. Just refrain from ordering wet preparations that may leak all over everything. At long stops, you can get off and buy snacks, etc. on the platform. If you do get off, of course, be sure your luggage is secure so it doesn't disappear in your absence.

If your journey is very long, be sure to bring extra food. Bananas and oranges are good, as are biscuits, dried fruits, nuts, juices that don't need refrigeration, etc. Never accept food or drink from strangers, no matter how nice they seem. Instances of passengers being drugged and robbed are not uncommon.

Security on Board

The more expensive classes are more secure, especially 1AC, which has attendants and lockable compartments. Don't rely on other passengers to watch your bags. If you are traveling in unreserved or sleeper class, you have to be extra careful.

Always secure your luggage to the racks or luggage loops below the berths with a good lock, especially if you are going to sleep or if you will be leaving your baggage unattended for any reason. And do lock all the pockets and zippers. While securing your luggage, keep your day bag and valuables on your person or right in front of you, not on the seat where someone could snatch them as they walk by, which happens fairly often, especially in the lower classes of travel.

Other Points

Keep your ticket until you leave the station at the end of the journey, in case a ticket examiner asks to see it on the way out. If you are asked for your ticket and you can't produce it, you may be charged the maximum fare for the train.

You will also need your ticket if you want to leave your luggage in the Cloak Room (left luggage) or if you want to stay in the Retiring Rooms.

You aren't allowed to transfer or resell train tickets. The TTEs (conductors) don't always ask for ID, but if they do and if the information on the ticket doesn't match the ID, you'll be fined and either told to get off or to buy a new ticket.

If you are seeing someone off at a train station, you are supposed to buy a platform ticket for a couple of rupees. You could be fined for being on the platform without one.

Smoking and drinking are not allowed on trains or in stations.

The air-conditioning on trains is often much too cold, so you'll want to have something warm to wrap up in, even if the weather is hot outside. In the winter, AC carriages should have heat, but the temperature is almost always inconsistent and in the middle of the night is likely to get cold. You can ask the attendant to turn the heat up or down, though you'll have to wait a while to notice a change. If the air-conditioning is not working, you can get a partial refund, but this is little consolation if you're miserable. You can ask to be shifted to another carriage; but you should do it as soon as you realize there is a problem, as everyone else will want to move, too, if the weather is really hot. The air-conditioning is supposed to be switched on immediately upon departure, but it may be turned off during long stops.

Information on getting refunds is available in the back of *Trains at a Glance* or on the IndianRail website.

If you are carrying more than the free allowance of luggage, you are supposed to book it on the baggage car. Forms need to be filled out two hours before the train departs at the luggage booking office, which is usually in the Cloak Room. Bicycles and motor scooters are accepted (usually wrapped in burlap), as well as just about anything that is well packed. There are packers at the major stations, so you shouldn't have to do it yourself.

The charge for booked luggage is determined by a combination of distance and weight. It's really cheap, but because there is a charge, most people try to get away with carrying all their luggage with them, even if they have way too much.

Station Amenities

Most train stations, with the exception of small local stations, have at least one kiosk selling mineral water, snacks, etc. Larger stations also have bookstalls or newsstands—though almost all their offerings will be in the local language, except in the metropolitan areas—and vendors selling snacks, fruit, locks and chains for securing luggage in the trains, and an assortment of other items.

You can check your luggage in the Cloak Room, which provides short-term storage of luggage for up to a month (though it gets more expensive after the first day). Cloak Rooms are available at all major and mid-sized stations, as well as some of the smaller ones. If you don't have a room lined up when you arrive, or if you just want to go sightseeing between trains, the Cloak Room is a real boon because you'll be able to look around much more easily without a heavy bag in tow. It's also convenient if you have to check out of a hotel many hours before your next train, or if you are taking an excursion for a few days, but don't want to take all your luggage.

The Cloak Room is usually quite secure, though you have to protect your bags from pilferage. Luggage must be fully locked, or it won't be accepted. Make sure your bags don't indicate the contents. Cloak Rooms won't be responsible for valuables. Don't leave food in your bags, since rats will inevitably try to chew right through the material to get it.

In order to use the Cloak Room, you are supposed to produce a train ticket either for arrival or departure, but often just showing your passport is good enough. If necessary, you could just buy the cheapest journey ticket for the next station.

If you are planning to leave luggage in the Cloak Room to pick up for a later train, be sure to check the timings. In small stations, the Cloak Room may only be open for 15 minutes before and after each train. When you leave luggage in the Cloak Room, be sure to allow plenty of time to retrieve your bags before the train leaves. In a really big station, as much as half an hour might be needed. Be sure you don't lose your receipt. If you do, you're likely to miss your train for all the running around you'll have to do.

Most important stations have an Upper Class Waiting Room, which is intended for holders of 1AC, 2AC or 3AC tickets. In addition, there may be a Ladies' Waiting Room. The waiting rooms typically have a toilet and sometimes a shower, as well. For the vast majority of the Indian public, however, the "waiting rooms" are the floors of the station and the platforms. People expecting long waits generally bring some kind of blanket or cloth or even just a newspaper, which they spread out on the floor to lie down on, using their bag for a pillow; and they often bring their own meals as well. The waits between trains can be extremely long for those going to obscure destinations, and it is easy to get the impression that some travelers have been camping in the station for several days—as may indeed be the case.

Many stations have Retiring Rooms, which may be either dormitories or hotel-style rooms. The rooms frequently have attached bathrooms, and sometimes you can get rooms with air-conditioning. The quality varies a lot. Some stations have nice, spotless, comfortable Retiring Rooms that are a great value, while other stations have really dirty or overpriced ones. Certain guidebooks include these rooms in their listings, and it is a good idea to check for them. They can be a great convenience if you are arriving on an evening train with an early morning connection. You always have to show your ticket in order to use the Retiring Rooms.

• • •

Other Ways to Get Around

THERE ARE MANY WAYS TO TRAVEL around India, some of which are scarcely seen elsewhere. Although traveling by train is the premier choice for many travelers because it is both cheap and interesting, there are, of course, many other options.

Air Travel

Several private airlines operate in India, in addition to the government-operated Indian Airlines (which is perpetually on the verge of going under), including some no-frills airlines that offer fairly inexpensive flights.

The easiest way to compare airline prices is to log on to a search engine that includes all the budget airlines. It's worth comparing prices, as the differences between one airline and another and between different flights even on the same day can be huge. The most popular times are usually more expensive, often by a quite a lot. Unless you have to fly on a particular day, you can often save a lot of money by checking on flights that leave a few days earlier or later. Usually, you have to book well in advance to get a good deal. Last-minute flights are usually considerably more expensive, as they are almost everywhere.

Many Indian airline websites and other travel sites don't accept foreign credit cards online, and some airlines may not accept them at all, so the easiest thing can be to decide which flight you want and then book the tickets through an accommodating travel agent. Travel agents typically charge a booking fee of Rs.100 or so, which is not much if it saves you wasting half the day sitting around in the airline's office. It's also convenient to use an agent if you need to make other arrangements at the same time. If you pay with a foreign credit or debit card, the price you have to pay may be significantly higher than the rupee price. If there is any chance that you might have to cancel the ticket, however, going through a travel agent may not be a good idea.

Try to call before heading to the airport as flights are often delayed. You aren't allowed in the terminal building too long before your flight (it's different for domestic and international flights), so verify what time you will be able to enter the terminal building before you get dropped off or you may have a long and uncomfortable wait.

When you enter the terminal building, you usually have to get your checked luggage x-rayed. Once they put a security sticker on the bags, you can go to the check-in counter.

The contents of carry-on baggage are restricted as in other countries, but batteries are a particular concern, so you need to put loose batteries and inexpensive battery-operated items in your checked baggage. Always carry laptops, cameras, cell phones, jewelry, money, credit cards and other valuables in your carry-on. When you check in, you get tags for your carry-on bags. These will be stamped when you go through security to show that your bags have been inspected, and then the stamps will be examined when you are boarding the plane.

Indian security checks are more thorough than in many other countries, and you'll be patted down, sometimes more than once. When going through airport security, keep a sharp eye on your belongings. If you are a woman, put your bags on the x-ray conveyer belt closest to the booth where they search ladies so that you are not too far from them. If there are two or more of you, one of you should go through a little ahead of the other, with the second person placing the items on the belt so that they are always within view. If you are alone, lock your valuables in your carry-on before putting it on the belt, leaving the lock just slightly off the right combination so it's easy to open if the security personnel want to look.

For flights to certain destinations such as Srinagar and other places where there is thought to be more risk of terrorist attacks, you may also have to go out to the baggage area and identify your luggage after passing through security. Also, they may want to see your boarding pass when you leave the plane, so you don't leave it on board.

Buses

Buses are incredibly cheap. Although most buses are pretty crowded and uncomfortable, they can still be fun for adventurous travelers. They are a great way to meet local people, although in some areas you may not find many people who speak English.

There are several different categories of buses. Ordinary government buses are the most basic, and these are dirt cheap (and often dirty as well). There are also some private buses in the same category. Semi-deluxe buses usually have slightly more comfortable seats, but they are not always a big step up in comfort. Deluxe buses are rather more comfortable, especially because they usually have reserved seating and no passengers standing. They may also have AC (air-conditioning). Long-distance sleeper buses, which are double-decker buses that give you space to lie down flat, always run at night, but they usually are non-AC. The private AC super deluxe buses are the best, especially the Volvo ones. They are typically quite comfortable. They are also cleaner, better maintained, with better suspension—which is important because many of the roads are terrible—and they almost always have better drivers than other classes of buses.

Some buses show Hindi (or Telugu, etc.) movies at top volume, so unless you love extremely loud music, you may want to ask whether the bus you will be taking is a video or DVD bus, or if there is music. In any case, the volume is generally sufficient to damage to your hearing, so earplugs are highly recommended.

Avoid the buses that are overloaded with people, animals and baggage on the roof, a common state of rural buses. While riding on the roof can be fun and romantic for the adventurous (and it's extremely cheap), the roof is not a good place to be unless you have excellent acrobatic skills. If there is an accident, passengers on the roof usually fare much worse than those inside. Unfortunately, there are a lot of bus accidents in India because the bus companies often give unreasonable deadlines, with financial consequences for the drivers, who therefore often drive much too fast, especially in the North. Buses seem to be generally safer and cleaner in the South, and the schedules are certainly more relaxed. Apart from Bihar and Uttar Pradesh, where drivers are most prone to driving fast and recklessly, the Garhwal region of the Himalayas is one of the worst places to ride the buses due to the narrow roads and steep precipices. Avoid night buses if you are traveling alone, especially if you are a woman. Incidentally, many buses have a few seats at the front reserved for women.

Usually you buy tickets right on the bus, though one company, whose website is <www.redbus.in>, has online booking. There are no reserved seats on the government buses; it's first come, first served. Deluxe and super-deluxe buses, on the other hand, are normally by reservation. Most buses except super-deluxe buses and private tour-ist buses can be flagged down, and they usually will stop if there is room or even if there isn't. Many buses lean to the left—an indica-tion that they are frequently overloaded with passengers hanging out the doors.

Obviously, you need to be extremely careful with your belong-ings. Always lock everything and keep valuables on your person. If your luggage goes on the roof, make sure it is well secured. Of course, it's much safer, but that may may mean paying for an extra seat if there's no place else to put it. Sometimes it's worth it. If someone puts it up on the roof for you, then it's appropriate to give him at least Rs.5 or 10 for the service.

Hiring a Car & Driver

Hiring a car and driver is a pleasant way to travel around, especially if you have a good car and a good driver. It's delightful to be able to take detours and stop whenever you want, because there is always something unexpected, and something often comes up that inspires you to change your plans a little—or a lot. If you will be going to many places in the course of a day, you're usually better off getting a private car than a taxi.

As of late 2011, the typical cost of a basic car (Indica, Maruti van or Ambassador) is between 600 and 900 rupees a day (8 hours/80 kilometers), depending on location, and Rs.150—300 more for air-conditioning, although in a few places the charges are quite a lot higher. Many other car models may be available at varying rates. The half-day rate (4 hours/40 kilometers) tends to be about 2/3 of the full-day rate. English-speaking drivers are fairly rare in most places, and many companies who do have them will have the English-speaking drivers only with their more expensive vehicles.

You should always bargain, especially if you are taking the car for a number of days. In the off season, drivers who usually take tourists on long distance trips may have little work and are sometimes willing to work for significantly less than the usual rate. Check around about the going rates and then negotiate. Many tourists end up paying three or four times the usual rate just because they have no idea what's appropriate.

Cars can be hired through hotels or travel services, as well as from local taxi stands. If you lease a car for a few months, the charges will be a lot less. However, if you need a car for more than a few months, it could be worthwhile to buy one and then sell it when you leave the country.

Licensed taxis and tourist vehicles are required to carry insurance, but private cars are often hired out unofficially, and these usually don't have the proper insurance. In a country with so many accidents, this is an important consideration.

If you get dropped off in a hill station or some other remote location, you may want to keep the driver's contact information in case you need to be picked up. While you can hire cars in all the hill stations, air-conditioned cars are generally not available, and local cars may be much more expensive because of the taxi unions. If you go to the union office, they won't negotiate. However, individual drivers are often willing to negotiate if you talk to them away from the office. If you say that the rates are so high you may have to take a bus, one or two drivers who are willing to negotiate will usually follow you.

If you are hiring a car for an extended trip, get a recommendation, or at least check out the company in person. Be sure the tires, spares, wipers and brakes are all in good condition. If you are going to be traveling to remote areas, make sure that vehicle has been thoroughly inspected before you leave.

It's not always possible to get an English-speaking driver, but you should always ask for one if you don't speak the local language. If the company sends a driver you don't like or a car that's falling apart, insist on a change. Problems with the car or driver can really spoil your trip. Look at the tires, ask to see the spare tire (which is called a *stepney*), check the odometer reading yourself, and insist on starting out with a full tank.

Always write down the driver's name, car number, and mobile number, if the driver has one. If the driver isn't his own boss, be sure to get contact numbers for the boss as well, preferably a mobile number or two along with office and residence numbers on a printed visiting card. Office numbers are no good if you have trouble in the middle of the night so it's essential to get the home number. If you get a driver who is really bad or a car that has serious problems, you should call the driver's boss and insist on a replacement. If he can't provide one, you may need to stop, find another vehicle, and pay some reasonable amount to the driver you are sending away.

There are a few bad areas where there are still *dacoits* (highway robbers) plying their nefarious trade, especially Bihar, Uttar Pradesh and adjacent areas of Madhya Pradesh and Rajasthan. Traveling by car in rural Orissa, Chattisgarh and Jharkhand, as well as the Northeast states, can also be risky, but most other places are safe from *dacoits*. If you are taking a trip out of the city, ask about the roads where you want to go and whether there might be any *dacoits*.

Get the terms of the rental in writing, even if it's just on the back of a business card, and be clear about whether you pay the driver or the agency. Avoid paying the entire amount before the end of the trip. Otherwise, the driver has no motivation to take good care of you, and you could even find yourself abandoned halfway. Pay half up front at most. You may have to pay for fuel as you go along, but that cost is deducted from the balance due at the end.

When you are hiring a car and driver for overnight trips, a standard additional charge *(bhat)* of Rs.100–200 a night is paid directly to the driver, who may sleep in the car or with other drivers somewhere or in a "drivers' room" of your hotel. Never give the *bhat* to the travel agent or the driver's boss. If you do, you can be sure that the money won't end up with the driver. It's for the driver's expenses and not for the car owner, so insist on paying it directly. Always give the agreed amount to the driver each day rather than all at once.

Don't forget that drivers have to eat, too. Around town, drivers often bring their own *tiffin* (snack). However, for longer trips, if you haven't pre-arranged a stopping place for lunch, the driver is likely to pull over at the cheapest *dhabba* he can find. The Indian version of a truck stop, a *dhabba* is typically a shed that's open at the front with an open-air stove, some rough tables and chairs, and sometimes a few *charpoys* (rope cots). If you eat in a *dhabba*, go for one that is crowded. The popular ones often have delicious food, and it's usually hot and fresh, though certainly nothing fancy. In the North, there is usually rice, *dal*, a few vegetable dishes, *rotis,* and *chai.* In the South you find *dosas* and *iddlis.* Just make sure your plate is clean and dry. Many *dhabbas* wash the dishes with cold water and little or no soap, sometimes in extremely dirty water. On some popular routes, you can find more upscale restaurants as well as *dhabbas.*

On extended trips, carry a good supply of water and snacks with you in case of a breakdown in the middle of nowhere.

In many cities, seat belts are now mandatory in the front seat, but they are often removed where they are not required, which includes nearly all back seats. If you are hiring a vehicle for a few days or longer, you could ask them to put in seat belts for everyone, if you like. Since seat belts increase the survival factor by a substantial amount, it makes good sense to use them.

Drivers are typically underpaid, so they depend on tips and commissions to make up the difference. Some drivers are always on the lookout for commissions—so much so that they may even follow you into shops and hotels. Make it clear right from the beginning if you are not willing to tolerate this kind of behavior. However, you should expect to give a good tip if they can't get any commissions from you.

You don't have to tip regular taxi drivers who have just taken you across town, though if you want to do so, Rs.10–15 is sufficient; but when you hire a car for one or more days, tipping is expected. You should give at least Rs.50/day unless the driver is really bad. You might give Rs.100–200/day to an excellent driver who works hard on your behalf, and not more than 10% of the rental fee for more expensive rentals. My Indian friends tell me that when foreigners tip too much, the drivers begin to have unreasonable expectations, which makes things more difficult for everyone concerned. Sometimes you might give a driver something other than cash or in addition to cash, if doing so feels appropriate. This will often be deeply appreciated, especially if it is something that you have brought from abroad, or something that the driver and his family can really use.

Taxis

Taxis, which are usually black and yellow, are available in most cities and large towns, and they range from dilapidated beyond belief to really nice. The fares are reasonable by Western standards, though many drivers will raise the prices for foreigners. In some cities taxis (and auto-rickshaws) have meters. However, many drivers try to avoid using them, in which case they usually claim their meter is broken. Sometimes if you insist and then start to walk away, the meter will be instantly "fixed." Unfortunately, it seems that even electronic meters can be rigged to run fast. If a meter is out of date, there will be a rate sheet that shows the increases, which you should insist on seeing.

In some places, the fares are always negotiated, while in other places the rates are posted and are fixed by a local union. Union rates are typically quite high; but if demand is low, they are usually negotiable. Getting drivers to compete against each other for your business is a good strategy.

Make it clear when you get into the taxi that you are only interested in going where you want to go and that the price is set. Checking with locals what the fare should be will help you to negotiate more effectively and so you don't end up paying ten or twenty times the going rate.

Whenever you hire a car, always write down the driver's name, cell phone number and car number. If he has to move the car while you are gone or there is some problem, you will be able to find him. If you happen to leave anything in the taxi, you may be able to retrieve it later.

Whenever you have to take a taxi, try to act like you are familiar with the area even if you aren't. Check where you are going on a map before you get in, hold the map prominently on your lap, and do your best to make sure your driver is not giving you an unwanted tour of the city. If he takes you where you don't want to go or deliberately takes you a long way in the wrong direction, it may be reasonable to deduct an appropriate amount from the fare. However, you should check whether or not genuine detours had to be made, which is often the case.

Unless you are going to a well-known place, always give the driver the name and address of your destination written out clearly on a piece of paper that you don't need to get back.

Most taxi drivers don't know how to read maps. Either they already know the place you want to go or they keep asking until they find someone who does. If you know how to get there, you can give directions; but if you are a woman, the driver may ignore you even when you know the way perfectly well. It's annoying, but that's the way the culture is.

Drivers always want to know your whole plan in advance. However, if you tell them more than one thing at a time, they tend to get confused, so it's easier to tell them as you go along. If you are planning a particularly long day, however, you should let the driver know before you leave.

Your driver may want to bring a friend or relative along, or pick up someone along the way, but in most cases you should not allow it, especially if you are alone or after dark. Drivers commonly give false excuses for taking on other passengers at your expense. On the other hand, policemen often flag down taxis for a free ride, and there's nothing you can do about it.

Many airports and railway stations in big cities have prepaid taxi stands with fixed rates. If you take a prepaid taxi, make sure the destination and the number of pieces of luggage is clearly stated on the payment slip. And verify that the car number matches. In major airports, there may be two or more prepaid taxi desks, so you will want to compare the rates and what they offer. The person at the desk records your name, car number and destination on a paper that can be traced in the event of some problem. Don't give the receipt to the driver until you have arrived at your destination and unloaded your luggage (it's how he gets paid). It's not necessary to tip prepaid taxi drivers, though of course they will appreciate it if you do. In any case, Rs.10 or so is enough unless they carry your bags for you, in which case you could give them a little more.

Shared Rides

In India you can often flag down taxis, auto-rickshaws and jeeps on the road even if they have other passengers. You can usually tell by the license plates and the color of the vehicle whether it is for hire, though this is something that differs from place to place, so you may have to ask someone. You can also find shared jeeps and taxis in the hills and rural areas at certain taxi stands. Typically, these shared vehicles don't go anywhere until they are completely full—but full means that an eight-passenger jeep may take twelve or more. Vehicles that are open in back may even have a few people standing on the back bumper. If you want more room, you can usually pay extra and get the whole front seat.

Many travel agents will arrange shared taxis to more distant destinations. Sometimes you can even specify which seat you will get in advance. If you use an agent, try to go to one who is known to you or your friends, if possible, or who has been recommended. It's a good idea to let someone know your travel plans, including the agent's contact information, as well as the car number and driver's name.

Driving Yourself

If you are a tourist wishing to drive in India, you need to get an International Driver's License through the automobile association of your own country before you come. If you are resident, you can get an Indian driver's license. But even though it's possible to rent self-drive cars, driving in India is not for the faint of heart. Traffic is intense and chaotic and will test your defensive driving skills and reflexes to the maximum. Lane driving is the exception rather than the rule. Traffic lights are frequently ignored, as are one-way signs. Signals are often not used when turning, and there are more obstacles in the road than you can possibly imagine. Unless you are well used to left-hand driving and wild conditions, you are probably better off hiring a driver.

A few major highways in India come up to international standards, but the vast majority of roads are much more challenging. Vehicles drive on the left side of the road, as in Great Britain. The number one rule of the road is that smaller vehicles move out of the way for bigger vehicles. Actually, cows have the ultimate right of way. They are often found wandering in the middle of the road, so you occasionally run into a cow jam where traffic comes to a standstill until the cows move over.

Except on the few restricted highways, there's always a lot of slow-moving traffic. There is no ban on any form of transportation on most highways, so you will see elephants, camel carts, horse-drawn carts, bullock carts, auto-rickshaws, cycle-rickshaws, push-carts, pedestrians, motor scooters, tractors, horses, donkeys, and bicycles—not to mention herds of buffaloes, cows, goats, yaks and camels—moving down the roads along with the cars and trucks and buses. Monkeys and dogs often join in as well.

It can be more than a little nerve-wracking when you see a bullock cart in front of you being passed by a bicycle being passed by a car being passed by a truck, without apparent regard for the oncoming bus passing a broken-down truck parked in the roadway. Even a bullock cart driver, if passing another cart going infinitesimally slower, will not want to "give side" (yield) to a faster vehicle because he won't want to lose momentum. No one wants to go onto the shoulder, which is invariably rough and frequently blocked by one thing or another.

Disabled vehicles are rarely moved to the side of the road. It's common to see a broken-down truck right in the road with a ring of stones around it, with the driver and helpers cooking lunch or napping under the truck as they wait for the needed parts to show up. Seldom do they bother to move the rocks when they move the truck. Buses, trucks and auto-rickshaws usually stop in the middle of the road to load and unload. In addition to obstacles such as wrecks and slow-moving vehicles, you may also encounter police barriers, speed bumps, potholes, sleeping dogs who won't budge until you are inches away, piles of gravel and barrels of tar used for repairing roads, the odd pedestrian lying on the edge of the road for a nap, and anything else you can (or can't) imagine. In addition, rural train crossings sometimes close long before trains are due and remain that way until the trains have passed, even if the trains happen to be extremely late, as they frequently are.

In parts of India, rural roadways are used for threshing rice during harvest time. The farmers spread the rice over the road surface and let all the passing cars, trucks, buses, bullock carts and anything else pound it as they drive by. Then the farmers sweep up the rice and winnow it to remove the chaff.

Indian drivers favor the middle of the road. On rural highways, especially, trucks and buses tend to stay in the center of the road in the face of oncoming traffic, swerving aside only at the last possible second. It's a deadly game of "chicken" in which there are a huge number of losers.

The unwritten rule of the road in India is that drivers are only responsible for what is in front of them. Everyone behind or next to them will have to accommodate whatever moves they make. Drivers never look behind them before making a move. The horn is just about the most important piece of equipment on an Indian vehicle, and other drivers, as well as cyclists, pedestrians, bullock-cart drivers, etc., expect that vehicles coming up from behind and passing by will make liberal use of their horns to announce their presence. This expectation is emphasized by the polite request painted on the back of many trucks: "Horn please" or "Blow horn." You could even be blamed for an accident that wasn't your fault if you failed to use the horn. Get into the habit of honking to let other drivers know you are there.

Indians never drive with their headlights on during daytime, and in fact, few people turn them on until it is quite dark. If you are in the habit of driving with your lights on during the daytime for safety—a common custom in some countries—people will constantly tell you about it because they can't imagine that you could be doing it deliberately.

Curiously, many drivers put on their high beams when another vehicle is approaching, rather than using their low beams—despite the fact that many trucks have a sign on the back that says "Use dipper (low beams) at night." Drivers who don't use their lights at night believe they are saving a significant amount of money. Obviously, this kind of thinking is penny-wise and pound-foolish, since it is the cause of many accidents.

Parking space is at a premium everywhere, so you'll often have difficulty finding a place. In some cities, the police issue fines and have vehicles towed—or they stand around ready to blow their whistles at anyone who dares to park in their zone.

Few drivers use the turn signals on their cars to indicate which direction they are turning. More often they are used to tell the vehicle behind that it is OK to pass. Hand signals are sometimes used to indicate the direction of the turn, although many drivers never bother to signal at all. Buses and trucks often have a helper along who signals left turns and stops.

Indian drivers don't pay much attention to road markings and traffic signs. In many places, lane lines are a waste of paint. A city road may have three lanes in each direction, but drivers still behave as if there were four or five, sometimes six. Small cars, mini-trucks and auto-rickshaws tend to drive right on the lines in the apparent belief that their vehicles are so narrow that traffic can easily zip by them on both sides. Motorbikes also drive on the lines when they aren't weaving in and out of traffic. Some cities have made a concerted effort to get drivers to drive in the lanes, but it's an uphill battle. Recently a newspaper reporting on unlicensed driving schools in Delhi found that most instructors tell their students that lane driving is unsafe!

Most cities have a steep fine for talking on your mobile while driving. Obviously, talking on the mobile while driving is the cause of many accidents. You need all your wits about you to drive safely, so pull over whenever you have to answer or make a call. Having an accident will make you much later than taking the time to stop while you talk or send a text message.

If you get in an accident, you can be in serious trouble, even if it's not your fault. If someone gets seriously hurt or killed, or if you hit a cow, you could be attacked by witnesses—even if you are only a passenger.[19] In case you have to leave the scene of an accident where someone is injured or killed, you must call or go to the police station to report the accident right away. If you hit a cow, buffalo, goat, camel, etc., you should find the owner and arrange for the appropriate compensation. Such an accident could easily destroy someone's whole livelihood.

Overloaded vehicles are the cause of many of the worst accidents in India, so keep your distance from them. Trucks are actually licensed to carry up to 50% more than their intended capacity, though they often carry much more than that. It's extremely common, for instance, to see a big truck with its back gate open and a huge load of grain wrapped in an enormous burlap bag hanging several feet off the back and extending several feet above the open top and out the sides. City buses often have people hanging out the doors and rural buses are even more overloaded, with people and animals riding on the roof, where the tickets are cheaper, or hanging onto the back, where they can escape paying altogether.

Gas stations in India are called "petrol pumps" or "petrol stations." If you ask where to buy gas, people will think you mean cooking gas.

Motorcycles & Motor Scooters

Motor scooters and motorcycles can be rented in many places. Enthusiasts can rent a classic Enfield Bullet in Delhi for touring in the Himachal area and other places. It's a fun way to tour around, and you will see many foreigners doing it. If you have never driven a motorcycle before, however, India is certainly not the ideal place to learn. And it's helpful if you know something about motorcycle maintenance, as they always seem to break down just when you are farthest from any repair shop.

While motorcycle helmets are commonly available, they are often of poor quality. Even where helmets are required, only the driver has to wear one. Women and children aren't required to do so, and neither are Sikh men who wear heavy turbans. You'll often see men riding with their helmets slung from their arms, ready to put them on if a policeman is sighted so that they can avoid the fine for not wearing a helmet. Sometimes men try to get away with wearing flimsy little hardhats rather than helmets. However, most deaths in scooter and bicycle accidents are due to head injuries that could have been avoided or reduced by wearing helmets, so it's foolish not to wear one.

Indian law forbids more than one passenger on a motorcycle or motor scooter although families with children seem to be exempt from the rule.

Auto-rickshaws & Tempos

Many cities have three-wheeled auto-rickshaw taxis for hire, which are usually referred to as "autos." They are much cheaper than a regular taxi. They may have a cloth top and no doors, with flaps to roll down in the monsoon season. In a few cities they have meters, which are usually "broken," so you may have to ask for the chart or just negotiate the fare.

For sightseeing in a city, you can hire an auto for the full day, but first check how much a taxi costs and negotiate hard, or you may end up paying nearly as much for a lot less comfort. The price should be significantly less than half the cost of a non-AC car. Compare rates for 8 hours/80 km or 4 hours/40 km.

Some places have larger versions of auto-rickshaws that are commonly known as "Tempos," "Vikrams," or "seven-seaters." Although they are designed for just seven passengers, in true Indian style, they are often packed far beyond their nominal capacity. These function as tiny buses that run along specific routes, picking up passengers anywhere along the way. The fare is usually just a few rupees to the end of the line within the same town. Just say the name of your destination before you get in and the driver will let you know if he is going there. Ask him to tell you when you should get off if you don't know the place.

Cycle-rickshaws

Cycle-rickshaws are slowly becoming less common in the big cities, though they still ply the roads in many places. Some are marvelously painted, worth a ride just for the photo. In some places, including parts of Varanasi and Old Delhi, they are the only means of transportation you can hire because the alleys are so narrow. In areas without a lot of trucks and buses or potholes, cycle-rickshaws can be downright delightful as they are so quiet and you can see much more than in a car. However, in areas with even little hills, they aren't much fun.

Some people balk at the idea of having another person doing that kind of work for them, but consider the *rickshaw-wala's* point of view. If you refuse to hire him because you feel the job is cruel and demeaning, he will have that much less to feed his family. It's an honest job, and it's actually easier than many other kinds of manual labor since they get to rest frequently.

Hand-Pulled Rickshaws

Kolkata is the only place in India where you can still find hand-pulled rickshaws. Because so many people feel that they are inhumane, the government decided to ban them as a politically correct move. Unfortunately, political correctness sometime harms those it is meant to help. In this case, the rickshaw pullers themselves protested for the excellent reason that they have no other means of income and it is extremely unlikely that the government will provide them with any. For now these rickshaws remain, though they are slowly disappearing, as the government is not issuing any new licenses. But don't feel bad about asking them to carry you. They'll welcome the opportunity.

Ironically, although hand-pulled carts are used for cargo all over India—and this is much harder work than pulling people—it doesn't seem that there is any move to ban them.

Political correctness notwithstanding, hand-pulled rickshaws are in great demand during the monsoon. They are the only way to move around the city without getting completely soaked because they sit so high off the ground.

Bicycle Touring

You can rent bicycles many places in India. Indian bikes are inexpensive to buy, but they may be much heavier and clumsier than what you are used to. If you bring your own bike from home, be sure to bring a good supply of spare parts as these can be hard to get. And don't forget your bike helmet. There's hardly any place to buy one in India. Bring your own cable lock from home, as well. And always lock your bike.

If you ride at night, you'll need a light for safety. Again, bring your own, even if you plan to rent. Almost no one uses them, so they are hard to find. A vast number of vehicles in India operate without any lights at all, which is one reason why there are so many accidents in India. Curiously, India's domestic elephants now have to wear taillights at night because of too many accidents. I'm not sure why bicycles (not to mention bullock carts, camels, etc.) are not required to have lights as well. After all, you would think that an elephant would be a whole lot easier to see than a person on a bicycle!

Bicycles can easily be taken on trains, though you have to pay a small extra fee to check them. On buses, they go on the roof.

Elephants, etc.

In certain places, elephants can be hired for special occasions or even for sightseeing. Riding on an elephant is fun, but if you are inclined to motion sickness, you may not want to go far. The ride is rather like being in a small boat in heavy seas.

Camel safaris are popular in Rajasthan. The whole adventure can be quite romantic, camping in the desert in big tents. But you might want to try one out for an hour before you sign up for a week-long safari. Some people find camels a little scary because they are so tall and skinny and have a strange gait. Also, they can be really uncomfortable, especially if you are on one for several hours.

Horses are available for hire in some places, especially along the mountain pilgrimage routes, though mostly they are hired out for weddings, a premium being placed on those that are all white. When not carrying bridegrooms, horses are usually pressed into service pulling carts of some sort. Horse-drawn carts (*tongas*) are still available in many places, and you can hire one to take you around. They are cheap and less than comfortable, but they can be fun for a change if you aren't in a hurry.

Bullock carts aren't likely to be anyone's choice of transportation. They are extremely slow and uncomfortable. However, if you are going to a remote village in the jungle, you could end up on one simply because the only other option is to walk.

In Kerala, Srinagar, Varanasi, and several other places, you can get around by boat, which can be a delightful experience in itself. If you stay in a houseboat in Srinagar, you will get around by *shikaras,* which are small boats that ply the lakes there. The beautiful backwaters of Kerala are quite extensive and you can spend many blissful, lazy days exploring them. You can get to the Andaman Islands and Lakshadweep by boat. Near Kolkata, the Sundarbans (the Hoogly delta region near Kolkata) is only accessible by boat.

Hitchhiking

Hitchhiking is not recommended. However, if you do hitchhike, don't stick your thumb out in the American fashion. Indians hitch rides by holding out their right hand, palm down, and making a patting motion towards the ground, sweeping slightly inwards. The same motion is used to flag down a taxi or bus.

Be discriminating who you accept a ride with. Don't just hop in blithely without looking carefully at the driver and other occupants as well as the vehicle's state of decrepitude. Of course, you also have to make sure they are going where you want to go, which isn't always easy if you don't speak the language.

Walking

Walking is the most delightful way to get around if you don't have far to go or else you have lots of time, because you can get to know a place much better than when you're zipping around in a car. Every village, town and city has many little lanes that you will never discover any other way. In those lanes is much of the real life of India, where nothing is on display for the tourists. You can stop to chat with anyone you meet, take photos at your leisure, drop in to the local tea stall for a cup of *chai*, join in a local cricket game with the local children or anything else that strikes your fancy. If you are in a car, you miss all that because it's so hard to break the momentum. Tramping around the countryside is another joy, but ask locally before getting too far off the beaten path.

Of course, you do need to be a bit careful. Walking is not always safe, especially in the cities and along busy roads anywhere. Be attentive and defensive when walking on or across a road. India has the world's highest incidence of traffic accidents. Injuries associated with motor vehicles pose a significant risk of serious disability or loss of life to both travelers and local residents. Traffic accidents, not any tropical disease, are the leading cause of death among travelers almost everywhere in India. But don't be paranoid about it. Just be alert and careful.

Given the lack of skill of the average Indian driver, the general disinclination to obey traffic laws, and the sheer density of people and vehicles weaving in and around each other, it's not surprising that India has a high accident rate. If any open place is available along the road, more than one person or vehicle is usually aiming for it. The incredible variety of vehicles sharing the same roadways makes for utter chaos.

It always feels like open season on pedestrians in India. The only saving grace is that the traffic moves relatively slowly. Drivers frequently ignore one-way designations of roads and divided highways because they don't like to go any farther than they have to (petrol is expensive), so you should never let your guard down. If you are crossing the road, always, always, always look both ways even on a supposedly one-way street. And if you are crossing at a corner, always look in all directions. Never assume that a one-way street is really only one way.

If there is a zebra crossing (i.e., a crosswalk), use it, but don't assume that all drivers will necessarily stop to let you cross. Subways and elevated walkways are sometimes available to get across some busy city roads, and it's certainly safer to use them than to make a mad dash through the traffic.

An assortment of people, vehicles and animals moving at different speeds can make it really difficult to time your dash to the other side of the road. Having found an opening in the traffic, you may get part way across the road when suddenly a beggar or tout or a boy selling toy ducks blocks your way to get your attention, or a bicycle veers in front of you, or an auto-rickshaw screeches to a halt in front of you to see if you want a ride—all completely unmindful of the bus bearing down on you at top speed! This sort of thing happens constantly. In crowded areas, drivers of every sort of vehicle often pass other vehicles and pedestrians with only an inch or two to spare.

Sidewalks in India, when there are any, are not always available for pedestrians. If they are not blocked by sleepers, beggars, families cooking lunch, itinerant vendors, illegal shops, bicycles, motor scooters, cows, buffaloes, sleeping dogs, piles of gravel, open ditches and other obstacles, then the local men have been using the adjoining walls as a toilet, rendering them unfit for use because of the horrendous stench.

Drivers coming up behind you usually honk to tell you to get out of their way. Unfortunately, they often wait until they are about three feet away from you to do so. But it's even worse when they sneak up on you without honking, because if you happen to step to the side to avoid an obstacle just as they are passing you, the result could be disastrous. You're much safer walking on the right side of the road facing the traffic so you can jump out of the way if necessary, even though Indians usually walk on the left side of the road going with the traffic. But even if you are walking on the right, bicycles and scooters may come up on you from behind if they are heading for a turn or a parking spot on the right side of the road. Glance over your shoulder whenever you hear a vehicle coming up behind you so you can move aside if necessary.

Walking around town absorbed in listening to your iPod is not such a good idea for the same reason you shouldn't walk around talking on your cell phone unless, perhaps, you are in an area with useable sidewalks or little traffic. You need to be able to hear what's coming. If your attention is on what you are listening to, you simply won't be alert to what's going on around you.

Whenever you are out walking at night, always carry a flashlight ("torch" in Indian English) so you are easily visible to drivers who might not see you otherwise, especially in areas where many drivers don't use lights. Of course, a flashlight is also useful in order to avoid tripping on uneven sidewalks, falling in uncovered ditches or stepping in undesirable substances.

Trekking

The Himalayas are foremost among the world's trekking destinations, and many routes are extremely challenging. Trekking alone is extremely risky. It's best to find others to go with you, including an experienced, reputable guide (who may also do all the cooking). There are many trekking companies who can organize all the details for you.

If you are planning a trek, get yourself in the best physical condition possible before you start out. If you have a history of heart or circulatory problems, don't neglect to consult your doctor before planning a trip to high altitudes.

Make sure that someone knows your itinerary and who you are trekking with. Before setting out, get the best maps possible and the most detailed information on your route and the surrounding area. It's hard to get decent maps in India. Much better maps are available overseas, so try to get them before you come. If possible, bring a GPS as well. While it might seem like a great idea to bring a satellite phone, don't even think of bringing one without declaring it, or you could get arrested on suspicion of spying.

Always carry cold-weather gear even in summer, and more supplies than you expect to need. Even in the middle of summer, temperatures can suddenly plunge to freezing at high altitudes, especially at night.

Symptoms of Acute Mountain Sickness (AMS) usually develop during the first 24 hours at a high altitude, but they can take as long as two or three weeks to appear. Milder symptoms include dizziness, headache, lethargy, loss of appetite and difficulty sleeping. Severe symptoms include mental confusion, irrational behavior, breathlessness, vomiting, dry cough, drowsiness, lack of coordination, lack of balance, and severe headache.

If you start feeling sick, don't try to conceal it from your companions or to pretend that it's not as bad as it is. Many people do so for all sorts of foolish reasons. Your life is much more important than some deadline or concern about what people might think. Anyway, no intelligent person is going to think that you are weak because you get altitude sickness. After all, many of the strongest and most intrepid adventurers on the planet have suffered from it. If you deal with AMS in a timely manner, it's not a big problem. If you don't, it can even be fatal.

While it is not possible to prevent altitude sickness altogether, there is no reason why anyone should die of it, since the onset is relatively slow and the progression of the disease is predictable. The real dangers are where one is either trapped in a situation where it is impossible to descend, or else forced to keep moving by people who are determined to push on at all costs. The best prevention for severe altitude sickness is simply to refrain from going higher until all moderate symptoms are gone. Above 10,000 feet or so, it is recommended to increase your altitude by no more than 1,000 feet a day, with a rest day after every 3,000 feet of elevation gained. Adding some extra days for your trek will allow you time to rest in case of need. If you show symptoms of even moderate altitude sickness, wait to go any higher until they subside. If your symptoms continue to get worse, immediately descend to a lower altitude.

Altitude sickness is not much of an issue if you are only crossing a high pass and then descending again to an altitude that is not significantly higher than the one where you spent the previous night, because the onset takes several hours.

In addition to concern for your health, do give some attention to the environment. There are many parts of the Himalayas that are still quite pristine, so if you go trekking, please do your part to keep them that way and carry out everything you might have brought along that is not biodegradable. If you use toilet paper, bury it. Generally be sensitive about the environment. Don't cut trees for firewood or any other purpose. And refrain from polluting streams and lakes with detergent, human waste, etc.

• • •

Food & Health Issues

Indian Cuisines

THERE IS NO SUCH THING AS a homogeneous Indian cuisine. Every region has typical cuisines that are distinct, but there are endless variations on the themes and locals always know where to get the best sweets or *masala dosas* or *namkin* (savory snacks), etc. In every town, you will find certain shops or restaurants famous for their particular goodies, and people often travel long distances to get them. Whenever you go anywhere, ask the people you meet to tell you about the local specialties.

Indians in every part of the country take great pride in the way they use spices. The generic curry powders that we know in the West are all but nonexistent in India. Even though prepared masala mixes are becoming more popular, there are many distinct varieties. And most Indians still make their own, with every dish being spiced individually. Family recipes are jealously guarded, and the same dish made by any two cooks can be quite different. Since the Indian climate ranges from tropical to alpine, the range of available ingredients is huge.

Religion plays a major role in Indian cuisine. Jains are typically vegetarian and do not eat any root vegetables, including onion and garlic. Some also don't eat tomatoes. Traditional Hindus are vegetarian, but even those who aren't don't eat beef. Except for Sufis, most Muslims are meat-eaters, but they won't eat pork. Buddhists are generally vegetarians, except for some Tibetan Buddhists. The vast majority of restaurants, even exclusively non-vegetarian ones, serve neither beef nor pork. If these items are not on the menu then asking for them may be offensive.

Food is an important part of Indian culture in everyday life as well as in festivals. Dinner is the main meal of the day, and for many people it is the only meal apart from tea, which may be accompanied by *chapatis, samosas*, biscuits, sweets, etc. Every important celebration includes a feast or, at least, sweets.

Tea is a staple beverage throughout India, and it is usually the first thing offered to a guest. Most Indians have several cups a day. To make *masala chai*, the famous spiced tea that is popular throughout India, tea leaves are boiled in milk with a mixture of spices, and plenty of sugar is usually added. Coffee is more popular than tea in parts of South India, though it is much less common elsewhere. South Indian coffee is typically made with milk and sugar, and may have chicory or spices added as well.

Local restaurants *(dhabbas, hotels* and *bhojanalayas)* often have wonderful food, but ask around or look for those that are really popular to find the best ones. All large cities and tourist destinations have restaurants serving various international foods, Continental (a vague designation that seems to include anything that might have originated in Europe or even the US), Italian, Chinese and Israeli being the most common.

Vegetarianism is Not a Special Diet

India is a vegetarian's paradise, since it is one of the few places in the world where vegetarianism is not considered a special diet. In fact, restaurants that serve both vegetarian and non-vegetarian food usually list vegetarian first on their sign. There are far more vegetarians in India than meat-eaters, which has resulted in the greatest variety of vegetarian foods in the world.

Although most Indians are vegetarians, many Indians assume that foreigners generally aren't. In Indian English, vegetarian and non-vegetarian are commonly referred to in both speech and writing as "veg" (pronounced "vedge") and "non-veg." If you are pure vegetarian, you can say you are "pure veg," or, in Hindi, that you are *shudh shakahari* or *sampurn shakahari*. Saying merely veg or *shakahari* implies that you are less strict. The word for non-vegetarian is *Mamsahari*.

Vegan and macrobiotic diets are somewhat challenging to maintain in India because the concept is practically nonexistent here. Milk products are extensively used in the Indian diet, as is honey, although some strict Jains abstain from eating them. Vegans do best asking for *Jaini* food and going from there. For Indians, the distinction is between pure vegetarian (which, strictly speaking, includes no eggs or onions or garlic), vegetarian (which usually includes onions, garlic, eggs, and sometimes even fish), and non-vegetarian. *Vaishnava bhojan, sattvik bhojan* and Jain food are all without onions and garlic. Milk products are considered pure vegetarian, while eggs are not. Since conventional cheese (i.e., anything other than *panir*, which is a kind of fresh cheese) is usually made with animal rennet, strict vegetarians usually avoid it.

Incidentally, all packaged food products in India are supposed to be labeled either with a green dot (vegetarian) or red dot (non-vegetarian).

Communicating with Waiters

Signaling with your hand or making eye contact while jerking your head up slightly is the best way to get a waiter's attention. Refrain from shouting or snapping your fingers. When you want the bill, gesturing as if you are writing with one hand on a pad held in the other gets the point across, no matter what language the waiter speaks.

Don't engage the waiter in unnecessary conversation until your order has reached the kitchen; otherwise, the order might undergo undesirable transformations. Keep your order as simple as possible.

It helps to point to the item on the menu, if a menu is available. Ask the waiter to repeat your order back to you, especially if you have given any special instructions. Even if you have given a list of special requirements, getting him to write them on your order will increase the odds that you will get what you have asked for, though it's never certain. One reason this strategy won't always work is that waiters are often illiterate, especially in local restaurants and *dhabbas*, though many waiters who are fairly literate don't bother to write down their orders, anyway. The biggest problem, however, is that many cooks are fixed in their ideas of how food is prepared.

If you find the local food too hot, don't hesitate to ask for less spicy food or even for no spice at all. Hindi for *chilli* is *mirch*. If you really want no chillies at all, for instance, try adding, "not even a little for flavor, and no *mirchi masala* (chilli powder)" in order to keep the cook from adding a lot of chilli powder to compensate for the lack of chillies, as chilli powder is regarded as something different than actual chillies. Sometimes this approach works. Of course, the cook may decide to compensate by adding an excessive amount of something else, such as black pepper or ginger, for fear that the food will be tasteless otherwise.

Strangely, if you order a vegetable dish without chillies, many people will immediately infer that you want plain boiled vegetables. Sometimes, in spite of your best efforts to tell him that you like other spices, it's completely impossible to get a waiter or cook to understand that there is anything in between fiery hot food and plain boiled vegetables.

Food Etiquette

In India, it's customary to refuse the first and even the second offering of food and beverages, and this also applies when asked if you would like more of any item at dinner. It's generally considered impolite to enthusiastically accept the first offer. Incidentally, when Indians go abroad, they often go hungry because they politely decline the initial offer, expecting that it will be repeated.

It is essential to wash your hands well before eating, both for cultural and hygienic reasons. Incidentally, long fingernails are considered unhygienic.

The vast majority of Indians eat with their hands, and you should feel free to do likewise. Eat exclusively with your right hand, using your thumb and first three fingers only, even if you are naturally left-handed. Eating with the left hand is considered extremely unhygienic and ill-mannered, since in India the left hand is reserved for toilet purposes. Although people may not comment if you use your left hand, they will most certainly notice, and they will appreciate it if you make the effort to use your right hand. Food is served and passed only with the right hand as well. However, once you have started eating, it *might* be OK to pass and receive *chapatis* (flat bread) or other items with the left hand, since once your right hand has touched your mouth, it is considered *jutha*, unclean. *Jutha* means that anything that has come into contact with your saliva either directly or indirectly is impure and unhygienic. Although in many places it's customary to use the right hand to take *chapatis*, in other places, you would use the left hand because the right hand is deemed more impure by the fact that it has touched your mouth. As usual, take your cue from your hosts.

Don't touch communal food with your hands. Always use a serving utensil. You can take *chapatis* with your hand, but be careful not to touch any that you aren't taking.

There are many rules about food, but the exact rules and the degree to which they are observed vary enormously from place to place, caste to caste, and even family to family. As a general rule, it's unacceptable to offer anyone else food from your plate, even your spouse. And sharing an ice-cream cone would be even more offensive. Food left on plates after eating is also *jutha*, impure, and there are often complex rules about who can and can't eat leftovers. Traditionally (in religious families), the cook does not taste the food while it is being prepared, as it must first be offered to God.

The habit of swigging water from a bottle is disgusting to the average Indian, and it is also considered antisocial since it means the bottle is unclean and therefore can't be passed around. Indians prefer to pour it into the mouth without touching the lips to avoid polluting it with their saliva. This isn't hard. It just takes a little practice.

Indians like to touch their food as much as they like to taste and smell it, so they don't take much delight in using cutlery. A certain Iranian Shah visiting India was deeply impressed by the habit of eating with the hands, so much so that at the end of his visit he commented that, "eating with a spoon and fork is like making love through an interpreter." In Indian cuisine, any food that is not too messy can be eaten with your hands. However, if your hosts use cutlery, it's more polite to do likewise. Although even the most cosmopolitan Indians may prefer to eat with their hands when they are alone with their families, they often prefer to use utensils when dining with foreign visitors.

North Indians tend to use some kind of flat bread, such as *chapatis*, *rotis*, or *nan*, to scoop up their food, and non-Indians can adjust to this eating style fairly easily. In the South, rice is the main dish, and *dal* (pulses) and vegetables are usually mixed with the rice and formed into a little ball that is popped neatly into the mouth. This takes quite a bit of practice. Rice is served last in many places, which makes it a bit more challenging.

There is an art to eating with your hands. Just watch what others are doing and do the same. You can ask for utensils if you are not comfortable eating with your hands, and usually they can be provided. Spoons are provided for soups and anything runny.

Break your bread with the right hand without using the left by holding it down on the plate with the middle and ring fingers and using the thumb and index finger to tear it. Watch to see how the Indians do it. It's easy once you have done it a few times. If the *chapatis* are cold, it's fine to ask for some hot ones unless you are in a setting where the request might create some difficulty. Usually, more will be brought even if you don't ask, except in restaurants where there's a separate charge.

If you find the food is too spicy, cool it down with yogurt, fruit or tomatoes. Water just makes the burning sensation worse.

In many homes and restaurants, food is served on a stainless steel plate (*thali*), with no utensils except a spoon for a watery *dal* soup or dessert. In South India, banana leaves are often used as disposable *thalis*. You may be given one that is pre-washed, or you may be given some water to wash it with, though you may want to surreptitiously dry it off or use your own water. Folding the leaf towards you when you are finished eating signals that you have had enough to eat and are satisfied.

The traditional Indian dining table is low, with cushions for sitting on the floor rather than chairs, though in simple homes there may not even be a table. Instead, there may be a cloth or newspaper on the floor doing duty as a tablecloth. However, Western-style tables and chairs are the norm in hotels and restaurants as well as most middle and upper class homes, especially in urban areas, so most places where you stay will have them.

Take off your shoes before entering a kitchen, but don't go in without being invited. Don't touch anything in the kitchen without permission, and allow your host to serve you whatever you need rather than helping yourself.

Staying Healthy

Non-Indians don't have a natural immunity for diseases that are endemic to India, so extra precautions are necessary. A strong immune system is your best defense against disease. Nevertheless, it's scarcely possible to know how much resistance you may have to completely new diseases, so it's best to be careful. You can also take antioxidants to help strengthen your immune system.

Some people can eat and drink anything and never seem to get sick, but, almost inevitably, even a person with a very strong immune system who is indiscriminate in his or her eating habits will fall ill eventually, though the illness may take years to manifest. Certain diseases, such as *amoebiasis*, can remain dormant for many months or years before they become active, by which time you might not even realize that your illness is something you picked up in India. By the time you figure it out, the disease may be so deeply embedded in your system that it is all but impossible to get rid of it. It's just better to be careful.

Generally speaking, traveling to India is not advised if your health is poor, unless you are coming as a medical tourist and will be staying in a good facility. Otherwise, if you can afford to stay and eat in five-star hotels all the time, you will be fairly well insulated from most health problems. However, even if you are staying in a five-star hotel, don't just assume that you can eat everything on the menu with impunity. Mostly, you should be fine, but raw foods, shellfish and undercooked meat should still be avoided.

Before coming to India, see your doctor for a checkup as well as advice on vaccines and prevention of tropical diseases, etc. If your doctor has little experience with tropical diseases—which is true of most doctors—seek out someone with more experience. If you don't feel like asking your own doctor to recommend someone, contact the Center for Disease Control. Incidentally, there is recent evidence that vaccinations may have serious side effects that were previously unsuspected, so you may want to think twice about taking vaccinations that you don't absolutely need. For more information on vaccines, go to http://www.nvic.org.

A dental checkup is also a good idea before coming to India so that you don't risk having problems while you're here.

If you are always tired, your immune system will be weakened. Staying rested is your body's best means of resisting illness. Eating a balanced, healthy diet is also essential for keeping your immunity up. A constant diet of junk food weakens your resistance.

Don't be too rigid about following every single recommendation listed below or you may start to worry too much about what you are eating, and that's not good for your health, either. Depending on how strong or delicate your body is, you may be able to be a bit more relaxed about some points and still stay healthy; though that's something you have to determine for yourself. It's most important to use your common sense and pay attention to how your body reacts to different foods, etc.

Avoiding Disease from Food & Water

There is a common saying in India: "If you can cook it, boil it or peel it, you can eat it; otherwise forget it." This principle is relatively true, though it doesn't quite cover everything.

Always wash your hands before and after eating, and especially after using the toilet. The most common diseases you are likely to pick up in India, especially Travelers' Diarrhea (gastroenteritis, a.k.a. *TD* or *Delhi Belly*), are transmitted by poor hygiene, so washing your hands thoroughly—preferably with hot water and soap—will go a long way towards keeping you and those around you healthy. Since water for washing your hands is not always available when you are traveling, always carry some waterless hand cleanser, which you can bring from home or get in India.

Drink only pure water. Contaminated water is probably the single most common source of disease in India for Westerners. Water contaminated with viruses, bacteria or parasites can cause not only TD, but many other serious diseases as well. To ensure that you always have safe water, you need to plan ahead and pay attention. Purifying your own water is safer and more environmentally friendly than using bottled water.

Don't drink unpurified tap water; it's simply not worth the risk. Many Indians won't drink the tap water (or eat street food, either, for that matter), so you don't have to feel foolish about it. Ice is almost always made from unpurified tap water, and freezing doesn't kill the germs, so avoid ice unless you know it is made from pure water.

Any time that you are offered water from a communal cup or bottle, or if you are eating at a *dhabba* or other simple local restaurant, take care not to touch the cup or bottle to your lips. Indians never do because it would then be contaminated and unfit for others. In such places, cups aren't washed well, anyway—often just a rinse with cold water and nothing else. Learning to drink from a bottle in the Indian style will earn you brownie points for cultural awareness. You might want to practice in private to get the hang of it, though, so you can do it without spilling it all over yourself.

Even if you use bottled water for drinking, keep a small portable filter or some colloidal silver, iodine, or any other means to purify drinking water with you in case of emergency. It's safest to use purified water for brushing your teeth, as well.

Bottled water is not as safe as you might think since the reliability varies widely from brand to brand, and sometimes people refill the bottles with tap water and try to pass them off as the real thing (especially in budget hotels and restaurants, but sometimes in shops and other places, too). Apart from that, bottled water is commonly exposed to the sun and/or high temperatures, either of which cause certain toxins in the plastic to leach into the water, and these are very bad for your health. It's safer all around to take responsibility for your own drinking water by boiling it or purifying it by some other means. Not using bottled water at all not only much better for you and for the environment. It's also much cheaper.

A few years ago, there was a big scandal about the impurity of many Indian brands as well as some of the international brands (including the popular brands Bisleri, Kinley and Aquaplus, which turned out to be among the worst at that time). Even though they may be safe as far as microorganisms are concerned—though that's not always the case—tests found that many were contaminated with pesticides up to 104 times the levels considered acceptable by European standards.

If you do drink bottled water, never accept a bottle that has already been opened. Before opening a bottle, always test the seal and check for anything floating inside. Send it back if there is a problem.

Boiling your water is the safest way to ensure that it is free of bacteria, viruses, amoebas, etc. However, water should be boiled for at least 10 minutes, and you have to make sure it really boils. At higher altitudes, boiling takes longer (add 5 minutes at 2,000 meters, and more as the altitude increases). Once the water has boiled, let it cool to room temperature. You can add a small pinch of salt or pour the water back and forth between one container and another a few times to improve the taste.

The problem is that boiling water is not always practical. However, there are other means to ensure safe drinking water. Of the various types of water purifiers on the market, there are several that can render water virtually as safe as boiling it. If you are living in one place, you should get one for your kitchen. Properly purified water is safer and cheaper than bottled water. You can buy good home water purifiers in India, but make sure that you get one that provides maximum protection.

If you use a water purifier, be sure to check that it removes all the microorganisms that could make you sick. There are several brands that remove all bacteria, amoebas, parasites and giardia. The Center for Disease Control has an excellent guide to buying water filters for preventing *cryptosporidiosis* and *giardiasis*, which are two of the most common diseases that you can get from impure water. REI also has a good chart that compares various portable filters. (See *Internet Resources*, p. 290) Many filters that remove parasites may not be able to kill or remove smaller organisms such as bacteria and viruses. Portable purifiers that use ultraviolet light do an excellent job of killing microorganisms, although they don't remove pesticides or other contaminants from the water. Nevertheless, they are particularly useful because they are so easy to use and carry.

Chemical disinfection with iodine is an alternative method of water treatment, but chemically treated water should not be used over the long term, and it shouldn't be used at all by pregnant women or people with thyroid problems. Also, because its efficacy varies greatly with the temperature, pH, and organic content of the water to be purified, it's not as reliable as many other means.

Colloidal silver is a natural antibiotic that can also be used to disinfect water. Check with the manufacturer to make sure how much you need, how long to let the water stand, etc. Grapefruit seed extract is another natural antibiotic, but it tastes terrible. I sometimes use it for disinfecting fruit and salad greens, and it works well for that purpose, but it wouldn't be a top choice for anything else.

It's good to brush your teeth with purified water, especially when you first arrive, as well as in places where the water is known to be contaminated. If you use tap water, take care not to swallow any. Some cities have a water purification system, and the water may be chlorinated, but you can't completely rely on it. Chlorination doesn't always kill giardia, even a single cyst of which is enough to make you sick. It's good to change or sterilize your toothbrush fairly often. When bathing, also take care not to swallow the water. If you have small children with you, you need to be extremely careful.

Ganges water is said to be self-purifying due to some microorganisms in it that remove impurities if it sits for some time, and you do see people drinking it, but the reality is that the river is dangerously polluted. If you want to drink Ganges water, either purify it first or buy bottled Ganges water.

Pay Attention to Your Body

Pay attention to what your body tells you and learn to trust your feelings. You may not be used to doing this, but if you make a point of it, you'll find that it comes much more easily than you expected. If your intuition tells you that something will make you sick, don't eat it, no matter how hungry you are. You'll be better off throwing it into the garbage than into your stomach. Your body is not a garbage can! Never let your friends persuade you to eat or drink something against your better judgment.

Just because your gross senses can't perceive anything definitively "wrong" with that salad in front of you doesn't mean that your body can't feel something amiss on a subtler level. If you have a feeling that you shouldn't eat something, then don't, even if you have no idea why. On the other hand, don't let yourself get carried away with thinking everything will make you sick—or it probably will.

If you just can't face another bite of Indian food, treat yourself to a really good meal at a nice restaurant, with the kind of food you are used to eating back home. There is a great Ayurvedic principle called *okasatmya*, which means that eating the kind of food you have eaten since childhood (especially your favorite comfort foods) can help restore balance to the system. I experienced this dramatically when I was recovering from a severe case of food poisoning and my friends insisted on taking me out to an Italian restaurant for my birthday even though I was still quite unwell. To my astonishment, by the end of the meal all my symptoms were completely gone and I felt great! Obviously, it won't always cure you, but there are times when it really helps to have some good comfort food. All the big cities and most of the tourist places have a wide variety of international cuisines available, so you can almost always find something familiar to eat.

In addition to paying attention to what you are eating and drinking, you should also pay attention to any sudden changes in your body weight; your energy level, especially when the weather is hot; your allergies, especially if you seem to be acquiring new ones; as well as to your bowel movements, especially if there is any abnormality.

If you are a woman and having your menstrual cycle, you should also pay attention to your body's need for more rest. You are more likely to get sick if you keep running around when you need to rest.

What's Safe & What's Not

In general, refrain from eating raw fruit and vegetables unless you wash, dry and peel them yourself. Bananas and oranges are great because you can peel them without a knife—and they make ideal snacks—but take care not to touch the inner fruit with unwashed hands.

Salads should be avoided unless you make them yourself. To eat salad greens or unpeeled fruits such as grapes, first wash them thoroughly to remove any dirt and insects, and then soak them in a solution of pure water with apple cider vinegar, colloidal silver, grapefruit seed extract or iodine in order to kill any lurking micro-organisms. Use the amount recommended by the manufacturer, or 1/4 cup per liter for cider vinegar. I don't recommend using potassium permanganate, as it is poisonous. Soaking time varies from 15–30 minutes. After soaking, rinse again with purified water.

Be discriminating about where you take fresh fruit, fruit juice and fruit *lassi*. Ultimately, they are best avoided unless you make them yourself. Most of the *juice-walas* don't keep their equipment clean, nor do they wash the fruits with pure water. Moreover, they often add water to the juice. Packaged fruit juice is usually OK, but check that the packages are properly sealed.

Tea is almost always safe because the water is usually boiled a long time, and the same goes for coffee. If in doubt about boiling times, ask. If you take milk with your tea, make sure it has also been properly boiled. Usually *masala chai* (spiced tea) is made with the milk and water boiled together, although you can also get the milk separately. South Indian coffee is also made with milk. Avoid tea, coffee or unsealed drinks from dispensers as the machines may not have been properly cleaned. Carbonated drinks like Coke™, Pepsi™, Thums Up™, etc. are generally safe. However, avoid the diet versions and anything else made with aspartame. Research has indicated that it is a carcinogen even in normal conditions, but the toxicity increases dramatically when exposed to heat.

Dairy products can be risky. In hot weather, avoid all dairy products except curd (yogurt) unless you are sure they have been refrigerated properly—which will not be the case if there has been a power outage without a backup generator. Curd is safe if it is properly made and hasn't been sitting uncovered where flies and dust can get on it. Since it is made at room temperature, it doesn't have to be refrigerated, although it becomes sour if it isn't. If there are many power outages and the weather is hot, you really have to be careful about dairy products. When buying dairy products, check whether there is a generator (known as a "genset" in much of India) and whether it has been running. Ask around to find out which dairy is the best. A lot of dairy products are made from buffalo milk rather than cow's milk, especially in the North. It has a much higher fat content than cow's milk and also has a stronger taste and smell. If you want only cow's milk, you have to ask for it.

Lassi, a delightful drink that is made from yogurt, is usually safe as long as water, ice or fresh fruit hasn't been added to it. Many people never add water, although from an Ayurvedic perspective, *lassi* is better that way. If it's made with water, the water should be purified.

Milk must always be boiled unless you are opening a fresh package and you are certain it has been pasteurized (though with local brands, that may not be an absolute certainty). Ayurvedic doctors recommend boiling milk so that it foams up three times (taking it off the heat for a short time in-between) to render it more digestible as well as safe, but this might not always be adequate, especially at higher altitudes. Unpasteurized milk is extremely risky and can be a source of tuberculosis. Sometimes milk is watered down or adulterated, and this can be the case even with packaged milk.

Ice cream (my ultimate comfort food!) is best avoided, but if you really crave some, be discriminating about it. If you have even the slightest suspicion that the ice cream has melted and refrozen—a great risk with frequent power outages and no backup generator—don't eat it. Improperly frozen ice cream is a common source of food poisoning. If the ice cream comes in a wrapper or other package and you see even a slight opening or tear, or if it seems unclean or suspicious looking in any way, don't even think about eating it. Never take ice cream from a street vendor or a low-class place, or even from a high-class one that doesn't have its own generator, nor from any restaurant that isn't squeaky clean. There's just too much danger of contamination.

Indian ice cream is often not up to Western standards hygienically. But it also tends to have more synthetic additives. If you are living in India and you really love ice cream, your best option is to buy an ice cream maker and make your own using properly pasteurized cream.

Vegetables, rice, *dal, chapatis, iddlis* and *dosas* are usually safe, as long as they are thoroughly cooked and served fresh and hot. Avoid eating any foods that have flies on them, or cooked food that has been sitting around for a while, especially if it's cold. Getting it reheated isn't a guarantee that it will be OK.

India's cuisine has many wonderful deep-fried delicacies like *samosas, pakoras* and *puris*, which are difficult to resist. However, it's necessary to be discriminating about where you get them and be sure they are hot and fresh. Although you might think that deep-frying would kill all the microorganisms, this isn't necessarily the case. Deep fried foods can also make you sick either because the oil is bad or because the high heat has not penetrated all the way to the center of the food. *Panir pakoras*, for instance, can give you food poisoning if the *panir* has been left without refrigeration in hot weather (as I know from personal experience). Also, mishandling after preparation can contaminate food that would have otherwise been OK. Never take *pani puris* from a street vendor. The water used in the preparation is virtually always impure.

Non-vegetarian food of any kind must be especially well cooked. Eating undercooked meat, etc. is an invitation for a serious case of food poisoning. Shellfish should be avoided altogether. Since meat, seafood and chicken are commonly mishandled in preparation, even non-vegetarians may want to consider a vegetarian diet while they are in India. Passing through the lanes where butchers have their shops may be enough to convert many people to vegetarianism, at least temporarily. The sight is not for the faint of stomach. The vegetarian cuisine of India, on the other hand, is so marvelous and incredibly varied, that forgoing meat is no great hardship.

Packaged biscuits are generally safe from a microbial point of view, as are packaged potato chips and similar snacks.

The packet of spices etc. wrapped in betel leaf that is sold everywhere on the streets and that is often served after meals is not safe. *Pan* is a mild intoxicant that is supposed to be a digestive aid. Chewing *pan* is rather messy, as you have to spit it out. Lower-class apartment buildings and office buildings often have stairwell corners stained red with *pan*. Many people chew *pan* instead of smoking, but *pan* is also somewhat addictive. Moreover, it not only stains the teeth and the mouth with repeated use, it also rots the teeth. Since all of the ingredients are raw, it can also lead to a bout of Delhi Belly, so it's better to avoid it. If you do take *pan*, it's best to stick to the simpler varieties.

Restaurants often serve a mouth freshener made of a mixture of fennel seeds etc. at the end of the meal, often with the bill or your change sitting on top. Apart from whatever might be lurking on the currency, many people may have had their hands in it if there's no spoon, so you may want to skip it. If you like to have a mouth freshener after meals, you may want to carry a little tin filled with your own mix.

In general, avoid buying food from street vendors. Some people eat street food regularly and go for many months or years without having any trouble, while others—even Indians—get sick almost every time. Non-Indians are more prone to getting sick from street food, though not necessarily every time. However, getting sick even once is too often, especially if you end up in the hospital.

If you do patronize the street vendors, be discriminating about the cleanliness of the stand and how the food is prepared. Choose a vendor who has plenty of customers, and try to watch for a couple of minutes to see how he works before you decide if you want to eat there. In any case, never accept food that is already cooked, even if the vendor insists that it was taken off the grill just seconds before you walked up. The food should be cooked in front of you and handed to you immediately on something clean and dry.

Many foods are served wrapped in newspaper, which isn't too bad if the newspaper is clean. On the other hand, you can assume that any plates or cups used by street vendors are filthy. Normally they are rinsed in cold, dirty water and wiped with an even dirtier rag, which does nothing more than evenly distribute the germs.

Alcoholic beverages are safe from microorganisms, but stick to reputable brands. Home-brewed liquor, which is sometimes served at weddings (most commonly in Gujarat, which is a dry state, but also in other places), is risky because it is often adulterated with substances that are not fit for human consumption, and you are more likely to get sick from it than to have a good time. Hundreds or possibly thousands of people die from bad booze every year in India, and many more become blind from it.

Sometimes due to circumstances beyond your control you may find yourself having to eat questionable food. If this happens to you, take a couple of bismuth tablets (like Pepto-Bismol™) before you eat. This prevents many disease-causing microorganisms from being absorbed into your system by lining the stomach. While it's a good preventative measure, it's not advised to do this every day for more than three weeks.

Avoiding Mosquito-Borne Diseases

Mosquitoes, which are found throughout nearly the whole of India, are carriers of malaria, dengue fever, and other diseases. Although there is an anti-malaria drug you can take, it is not really effective. And it will almost certainly make you feel sick. Since you are meant to take it the whole time you are in India, this is a particularly undesirable side effect.

Ultimately, the only really effective way to prevent malaria and other mosquito-borne diseases is to avoid getting bitten. Although they proliferate in the warmer months, mosquitoes can turn up almost anywhere at any time of year. Global warming may be the reason for this.

Even if you don't expect to be in an area with mosquito-borne diseases, you should still carry a mosquito net and mosquito repellant, as outbreaks can occur unexpectedly. A mosquito net is the single most effective means to avoid getting bitten by the mosquitoes that spread malaria, as they bite between dusk and dawn. However, you also have to take care to avoid mosquito bites in the daytime, as Dengue is spread by day-feeding mosquitoes. Since you won't know what kind of mosquitoes are out and about in any given place, do your best to avoid all of them.

Mosquitoes don't like to fly high if they can get enough to eat closer to the ground, so rooms that are on the second or third floor of a building tend to get fewer mosquitoes than the lower floors. Since mosquitoes have extremely light, fragile bodies, it doesn't take much of a wind to blow them away. A fan or air-conditioner will often keep them down, though they will happily emerge from their hiding places as soon as it is turned off.

In the South, cotton mosquito nets are readily available, but nylon is more common in the North. The cotton ones are cooler and more comfortable, though you have to wash them to make them soft. You can get two basic types of mosquito nets in India: rectangular ones that are suspended by strings attached to six or eight loops fastened to various points around the room, or round ones that have a single suspension point enlarged by a ring at the top, which require only two connection points. The freestanding ones with tent-like frames are not commonly available in India.

White is the best color for a mosquito net, since mosquitoes can be easily seen against it. If your net gets a hole or tear, mend it immediately because mosquitoes will inevitably find the hole. They can also bite you right through the net if it is against your skin, so be sure that it is stretched well away from you. You can spray the net with repellent if the mosquitoes are really bad. Before going to bed, if the windows are closed or if there are screens, take the time to kill all of the mosquitoes you can find. Check behind curtains, under beds, in closets, etc. If there are holes in the screens or your net, patch them with a little duct tape. After you have switched off the lights and tucked yourself in, checking for gaps, use a flashlight to see that no mosquitoes have snuck in with you, or they will happily feast on you all night long.

Many people use mosquito coils, which burn like incense, or else mats or a liquid, both of which are burned in little electric devices you can buy anywhere. Sensitive people may feel uncomfortable as soon as they enter the room where these chemicals are burning, but most people don't even notice. "All Out" is said to be the least toxic brand, though it is still harmful. In any case, its smell is barely noticeable, which is not case with some of the others.

If you use these chemicals, burn them when you are out of the room and turn off the burners when you come back in order to minimize negative effects. There are also some all-natural, nontoxic varieties on the market. You can also burn your own blend of oils in the machines that take the liquids. You can also add your own oils to the mats.

DEET is frequently recommended, but remember that it is a highly toxic substance, so if you choose to use it, take care to follow the instructions. It's better to use DEET on your clothes than on your skin, and it shouldn't be used on children at all.

Makers of DEET have long promoted the idea that natural mosquito repellants aren't effective, but the CDC (U. S. Center for Disease Control) has found lemon eucalyptus to be as effective as DEET. Moreover, it has no side effects, whereas DEET comes with all sorts of warnings, as it is quite toxic. On commercial products, the label is likely to read p-menthane 3,8-diol or PMD, but it's the same thing.

You can get lemon eucalyptus oil in pharmacies most everywhere in India. Try mixing it with other oils such as neem, citronella, lavender, lemongrass, and eucalyptus in a base of a carrier oil such as coconut, apricot, or almond oil.

The effectiveness of any given oil or mixture seems to vary from individual to individual, indicating that how these substances interact with the body's chemistry is a key factor.

Some people recommend taking vitamin B1 because mosquitoes seem to be repelled by it.

Mosquitoes find their victims by smell, so you should bathe as often as possible and avoid wearing perfumes or other scented products, including scented deodorants. Plain lemon juice is a powerful odorless deodorant that doesn't attract mosquitoes.

It's better to wear light colors because mosquitoes are more attracted to dark ones, possibly for reasons of camouflage. If you are in an area with a serious mosquito problem, you should wear long-sleeved shirts, long pants and socks, if possible, and apply insect repellent to any exposed skin.

If you are living in an area with lots of mosquitoes, check in your home and the neighborhood for standing water. A perpetually wet corner of the bathroom, the saucer under a plant, an old rubber tire, or anything else that could hold stagnant water is an ideal breeding ground for mosquitoes, as are any swampy areas and pools of water than remain for more than a few days after the rains so dry out any vessel that can be emptied. Mosquito larvae are tiny and screw-shaped, and you can see them wriggling around under the water if you look closely, while mature mosquitoes can often be seen resting at the water's edge. If you are living next to a mosquito-breeding pond, there may be little you can do short of calling an exterminator or moving.

If you get bitten, apply neem oil or lemon juice, or rub the bite with the side of a cup of hot tea in order to relieve the itching. Avoid scratching insect bites or they could become infected.

While there are various allopathic remedies on the market, there are also many natural remedies against malaria, including fava bean, quinine and *artemisia annua*, that have been developed in various parts of the world. Chinese wormwood, *qinghaosu,* is reputed to be highly effective. There are also Ayurvedic remedies that are said to be effective in preventing malaria. Always consult a doctor before taking any remedies, whether allopathic or herbal.

Other Health Tips

If you get any cut or scratch that breaks the skin even slightly, clean it thoroughly and treat it with an antiseptic cream or iodine. Keep it clean and covered until it's healed. The potential for truly miserable infections is much higher in India than back home, especially since we don't have the local immunities. Scratches or bites from animals should be seen by a doctor immediately. If possible, catch the animal and get it tested for rabies; otherwise, you'll have to get rabies shots. Rabies is more common in India than many other places, so this should not be ignored.

Avoid walking barefoot outside. Dust can harbor parasites, some of which (such as hookworms) can penetrate right through the soles of your feet. Rubber thongs are essential if you are using shared baths or squat toilets. Get into the habit of washing your feet often, as well as your shoes, if you wear washable ones. In cooler weather, wear socks. Take care of your feet. It's helpful to massage them every day with a good antiseptic foot cream, preferably one that has tea tree oil or neem in it. It will keep your feet soft and in good condition and less vulnerable to infection and dust-borne parasites.

Don't lick your fingers when counting money. It is strange that many people in India have the habit of licking their fingers when counting paper money or shuffling through papers, because saliva is regarded as extremely impure. It's like spitting on the money or paper before giving it to someone, which is pretty disgusting. At any rate, due to this habit, paper currency tends to harbor a lot of disease-causing microorganisms, but coins are certainly not clean, either. Don't worry about it, though. Just make a habit of washing your hands before eating or putting your hands to your mouth or rubbing your eyes.

Take care to protect yourself from the sun, which can be intense. In hot weather, and especially in the mountains where the air is thin, you need to wear a hat or carry an umbrella to protect yourself from sunburn and heat stroke. Use a good sunscreen, even if the weather is cloudy. In the mountains, even ten or fifteen minutes exposure can be enough to cause a sunburn if you have sensitive skin.

AIDS/HIV is a huge problem in India, for which reason you should take maximum precautions not only when engaging in sex, but also any time you have to have an injection. If you have to have a shot, the needle should be new (unwrapped in your presence). If that's simply not possible, then it must be thoroughly sterilized. If you have to have a blood transfusion, verify that the blood has been properly screened. The needles etc. used for an intravenous drip feed should also be new.

If You Do Get Sick

If you are careful, you probably won't get anything worse than a little Travelers' diarrhea, or perhaps a cold, but if you have severe diarrhea lasting for more than a couple of days, you run a high fever, you have fever and chills, you become really weak or you have any unusual symptoms, you should see a doctor. While good allopathic care is available in various places, you will also find many physicians practicing traditional forms of medicine.

Delhi Belly is a relatively mild condition that is common among foreigners traveling to India. It can be caused by food your body is not used to, jet lag, change of altitude, change of climate, or contaminated food and water. Many people get it in the first week or two they are in India, though it can occur at any time. Usually, the symptoms—diarrhea (3–6 loose, watery stools in a day), cramps, nausea sometimes accompanied by vomiting—come on suddenly, last for a day or two and then pass by themselves.

Whenever you have diarrhea, avoid spices, fried food, raw fruits and vegetables, as well as alcohol and drinks containing caffeine. Drink lots of water or other clear liquids such as chamomile tea, hot, freshly cooked, clear broths, or packaged fruit juices diluted with safe water. Vomiting and diarrhea depletes your body of essential electrolytes—potassium, sodium, and glucose. You can replace them by sipping tender coconut water (said to be the best fluid replacement by many Indian doctors); commercially prepared electrolyte products or oral rehydration salts (available at most medical stores); or a home-made mixture of packaged fruit juice (for potassium) with 1/2 teaspoon of honey or sugar (for glucose) and a pinch of table salt (sodium chloride); or else you can mix 6–8 level teaspoons of sugar plus 1 level teaspoon of salt in 1 liter of pure water. *Nimbu pani* (which is basically lemonade), made sweet and salty, is also an excellent rehydration fluid. It's also delicious. If it's made well, it is even better than regular sweet lemonade. Be sure to sip slowly so you don't bring on more vomiting.

If you pinch the skin on the back of your hand, it should spring back quickly. If it doesn't, it means you are dehydrated and you need to drink more. It's a good idea to keep some electrolytes on hand because if you do get a little sick, you may not feel up to going out to get some.

Defizzed Coke has a settling effect on the stomach and can be quite helpful in cases of TD. However, soft drinks should only be taken flat and warm; otherwise, the carbonation can irritate the stomach even more. Pouring a carbonated drink back and forth between two glasses will get rid of the bubbles quickly.

Once your stomach has settled and the diarrhea and vomiting have subsided, you should wait at least a few hours or even a day before beginning to eat again. Start with bland, easily digestible foods such as hot applesauce, fairly watery hot cereal, thin soups, or soda crackers, before progressing to something simple but a bit more substantial like *iddlis* (which also make nice dumplings in soup broth.) Dairy products should be avoided, although you could try a thin *lassi*—salty *lassi* would be better than sweet, in this case. To make thin *lassi*, mix 1 part fresh yogurt with 6 parts pure water and stir vigorously (2 minutes in a blender is better); add salt to taste. For at least a day or two, you should avoid spicy, greasy, acidic, high-fiber, heavy, or sugary foods, as well as caffeine and alcoholic beverages; then resume your normal diet gradually. Continue to drink lots and lots of pure water, preferably warm or hot, as well as other liquids. The kind of food that your system is used to will often help you feel much better if you are still feeling a bit low once the symptoms have subsided.

While some doctors recommend anti-diarrheal products like Immodium™, Lomotil™, or bismuth tablets (all of which only address the symptoms), others contend that they may interfere with the body's ability to fight the infection.

According to many naturopathic physicians, grapefruit seed extract (10–15 drops in water or defizzed Coke) or colloidal silver is beneficial, and can help to alleviate the symptoms quickly. A few drops of grapefruit seed extract or colloidal silver in your water every day is thought to be helpful for preventing Delhi Belly. There are also Ayurvedic preparations that are excellent preventatives. Check with an appropriate health professional.

In the case of infants, elderly or weak people, TD can be life-threatening, so medical attention should be sought immediately. Zinc tablets combined with rehydration salts are frequently given to children suffering from diarrhea, but they may be appropriate for adults as well. You may want to ask your doctor about this.

If the symptoms are especially severe, they could be indicative of food poisoning, which is much more serious, and in which case you should see a doctor right away. Food poisoning comes on suddenly and is far more intense than ordinary TD (which can also be caused by contaminated food). The warning signs are usually no more than a few minutes prior to the onset of severe symptoms. Get to a doctor if possible. Food poisoning can be deadly, so you shouldn't wait around to see if it gets better on its own. Don't resort to anti-diarrheal medications, because your body is frantically trying to rid itself of the offending organisms and you don't want to hinder the process. As with TD, rehydration is essential. Drink a lot of pure water together with whatever rehydration method is available. If you go to a hospital, the doctors will probably want to give you an IV (intravenous drip), but they may consent to give you oral rehydration if you ask.

If you have diarrhea with blood or mucus, any fever, or there is no improvement after about 48 hours or so, you may have dysentery instead of ordinary TD, in which case, you should see a doctor immediately and get a stool test to determine exactly what you do have so it can be properly treated. However, don't take any medications, including anti-diarrheals, without the doctor's advice, as they could make your condition worse.

Hospitals in India, whether allopathic or Ayurvedic, are often quite different than in the West, with the exception of some of the new super-modern hospitals that you will find in the metropolitan areas (these are often ISO certified, which means they have international standards). Always go to the best hospital available, if you have any choice in the matter.

If you ever have to be hospitalized, especially in a hospital that is not up to international standards, you need to have someone staying there with you most of the time. She will be responsible to bring you food, medicine from the pharmacy, surgical supplies, etc. These things are usually not part of the package. She should also stay with you whenever the doctor visits, and she should not be shy to ask about everything and to insist on necessities like new needles rather than reused ones, and to check on sterilization of instruments, etc. Don't take anything for granted. A bi-lingual dictionary is essential if the nurses don't speak English and you don't speak their language. If one is not available, get someone to write down the most necessary words in the local language.

Western doctors are available in every city, as are pharmacies (usually called "medical stores"). Medical care is astonishingly cheap, except at some of the big hospitals, but even those are still far cheaper than their Western counterparts. A consultation with a private doctor, even a specialist, is usually only about Rs.100–500, though specialists in big hospitals may charge more, while government hospitals are free. In case of a serious emergency, try to get to the best and the most modern hospital available. If you have health insurance, always carry proof with you.

Most medicines are available in India and they are much cheaper than in the West, but their quality is variable. A recent article in *The Hindu* estimated that counterfeit drugs may account for about 60% of the drugs on the market. Many of these just don't have any beneficial effect, but others are dangerous.

Ayurveda is the leading indigenous system of medicine in India. It is an ancient system, and because it is effective when well practiced, it has become increasingly popular in the West. It is highly recommended for non-acute health problems—especially chronic ones—although its ability to deal with acute emergencies is not nearly as well developed as Western medicine.

Ayurveda is essentially prevention-oriented, and Ayurvedic medicine doesn't have the horrendous side effects that frequently result from allopathic medicines. I would hesitate to say that there are no side effects at all, but they are certainly far, far fewer and more benign. Moreover, with Ayurvedic herbs, the vast majority of side effects are merely a matter of physiological purification, which puts them in a different category altogether from the side effects associated with allopathic medicine. Of course, there can also be problems caused by herbs that have not been properly prepared or have been accidentally taken in the wrong combination or in the wrong quantity, but even these are unusual. In such cases, they are more likely to be ineffective than to cause any damage. Your best option is to go with the most reputable brands of Ayurvedic herbs, such as Nagarjuna™, Nidco™, Maharishi Ayurveda™ or Trigunayu™. Note that some brands have similar names (e.g., Nagarjun instead of Nagarjuna), so read the labels carefully. If none of these are available, ask your *vaidya* (Ayurvedic doctor) which locally available brands are the best.

In cases where Ayurvedic doctors charge only for prescribed herbs and charge nothing for the consultation, patients who can afford to do so customarily make a donation, which covers costs for those patients who can't afford the medicines. Ayurvedic herbs are extremely economical in comparison with allopathic medicines, though there are a few very special preparations that contain gold and other precious substances and are expensive.

There are about 3,000 Ayurvedic hospitals in India, most of which are functioning in conjunction with allopathic institutions.

Although most practitioners are institutionally qualified, Ayurveda has mainly been passed down through various families of *vaidyas* (Ayurvedic physicians), there are still many *vaidyas* who simply carry on the family tradition without a formal degree. Stemming from diverse family traditions, Ayurveda has many branches, and each of these has its specialties, some of which have been preserved better than others. While there are colleges dedicated to Ayurvedic medicine, most other medical schools in India also offer specialization in Ayurveda.

The Ayurvedic clinics that you find in tourist areas generally don't offer much more than a nice massage to relax your muscles, and they rarely have a qualified *vaidya*, so they wouldn't be a good choice for people with serious health problems. However, there are several renowned Ayurvedic hospitals and clinics in various parts of India that are well equipped to deal with serious problems.

Siddha and Unani are less well-known systems of traditional medicine, but like Ayurveda, they are also recognized by the World Health Organization. Homeopathic medicine and naturopathy are also quite popular in India, as are many other varieties of natural medicine. As you travel around India, you may also encounter various sorts of indigenous healers, bone-setters, etc. Although they usually hold no medical degree, some of them are really good at what they do. Such people you only find by word of mouth.

• • •

Communications & Infrastructure

Phone, Fax & Internet

PHONE SERVICE IN INDIA IS STILL DEVELOPING. Although it has certainly improved in recent years, it is not yet up to international standards. In some places it is difficult to get a good connection, and sometimes there will be no service for a few hours, or even days on end.

Phone numbers and area codes seem to change every couple of years. Finding a current phone book is usually difficult, and they are never complete. Directory assistance is improving but is not always helpful, although there is usually an automated number you can call to find out numbers that have changed. Landlines are often out of order, and cell-phone service, though cheap, is far from being world class. Nevertheless, the situation is slowly improving.

Public phone facilities are indicated by signs saying PCO (for local calls), STD (for long-distance within India) and ISD (for international calls). You may be able to use a prepaid phone card to make a long distance call from a PCO office that doesn't offer long distance. Sometimes the STD/ISD places also have fax machines where you can send and receive faxes.

All phone numbers in India are 10 digits long. The length of the city code determines the number of digits in the local number, which means they vary from place to place. Cell phones (more commonly called "mobiles") also have 10 digits, all of which begin with a '9'. When calling within India from a mobile, you use the full number, even if you are calling a local landline. To call a local number from a landline phone, you only dial the local number without the city code (but there may be an extra '2' at the beginning). For numbers within the same area, you have to add '95' at the beginning. To call elsewhere within India, dial '0' followed by the city code and number. For international calls from any phone, prefix '00' to the country code, e.g., to call the US or Canada, you dial '001' and then the number.

Toll-free numbers start with 1-800 or 1-600, but you can only call from the same service that hosts the number (or, in some cases, a few particular services), so you may not be able to call a BSNL toll-free number from a Reliance phone, or a Reliance number from Airtel, etc. Unfortunately, it's not always easy to figure out to which service a toll-free number belongs.

Prepaid phone cards are available from MTNL and other phone companies. Rates are usually the same as the standard government rates from an STD/ISD place. These cards are useful if you are staying in a hotel that has a high surcharge because then you only get billed for local calls in addition to the normal ISD or STD rates, which are pretty cheap. Otherwise, hotels may double or triple the rates. Prepaid cards are also useful if you are staying in a place that doesn't have STD or ISD, which is not uncommon. If you are using a phone that doesn't have tone capabilities, you can still switch to tone dialing by pressing the star (*) key after dialing the access number and before dialing your code.

International calling cards from ATT and other companies are useless in India because they are usually blocked. Moreover, they are far more expensive than the prepaid Indian calling cards.

Most STD/ISD places don't allow collect calls, but some allow callback. However, by far the cheapest way to call overseas is to use the Net2Phone service that many Internet cafes offer, or else a service like Skype.

Telegrams within India are extremely cheap, and you can send them from many post offices or telegraph offices.

Mobile phones have now become more common than landlines. Coverage is pretty good and rates are among the cheapest in the world, but customer service is deplorable. There are several services to choose from. Ask around to find which one seems to be the most reliable in a particular area or for roaming all over India.

To buy a SIM card with a prepaid account (which is what you need for your mobile in India), you have to provide a copy of your passport and visa, and two or three passport photos. In Kashmir, you also have to provide a local reference/address proof, which can be a letter from your hotel manager. The shopkeeper activates the both the new account and the minutes (which you purchase separately) while you wait.

There are various options for connecting to the Internet, whether or not you have your own computer.

Mobile devices that allow you to connect directly to the Internet can be used with various services in India. Pre-paid and postpaid plans are available throughout much of India, though 3G connectivity is not as widely available as the glacially slow 2G. In any case, not being dependent on Internet cafes or the vagaries of hotel phone systems is a major advantage.

Several companies now offer a wireless service that entails buying a special modem from them and enrolling in one of their numerous plans. You get either a USB modem or a PCMI card with a wireless connection, though connections tend to be excruciatingly slow and none are completely reliable.

If you have a modem and your own landline phone, you can sign up for a broadband connection from BSNL or other companies.

If you don't have your own computer or an Internet-enabled cell phone, you can still stay connected because virtually every city of has at least a couple of Internet cafes, and even small towns often have them. In addition to dedicated Internet cafes, you can often find Internet access at your friendly neighborhood STD place, business service bureaus, as well as at many hotels and guesthouses. Rates generally vary from Rs.10–100 per hour, depending on where you are. Many Internet cafes allow you use your laptop to connect with Ethernet. If you take your laptop to an Internet café to connect, be sure you have an up-to-date virus program, especially if you are running Windows.

Whenever you check e-mail on a public computer, use "Private Browsing," if it's available. In any case, always clear private data, close your browser window and log off at the end of your session. On most browsers, you do this by going to the Tools menu on your browser and selecting "Internet Options," then "Delete Cookies" or "Clear Private Data."

Avoid using your credit cards online at Internet cafes, as there have been many reports of credit card information being stolen by the use of keyloggers, which are devious invisible programs that record all your keystrokes, including passwords.

There are a few national franchises which offer broadband Internet connections and they are usually pretty good. Perhaps the biggest advantage they have over independent Internet cafes is that their systems are usually more secure, especially the ones such as Sify iWay that delete all your private info when you sign out.

If you find that the connection is excruciatingly slow, as it often is, especially in rural areas, try working in the evening or during office lunch times when usage is less.

When giving your e-mail address, instead of saying, "johnsmith at mac dot com," you will more easily be understood if you say "johnsmith at the rate of mac dot com." Indians typically say "at the rate of" for the name of the @ sign.

Time Difference

India has only one time zone, even though the country would normally cover two. Instead, they decided to simply average the difference, with the result that India Standard Time (IST) is half an hour different from almost everywhere else. It is 5.5 hours ahead of Greenwich Mean Time, 4.5 hours ahead of Frankfurt (3.5 during Summer Time), 10.5 hours ahead of New York (9.5 during Daylight Savings Time), 13.5 hours ahead of San Francisco (12.5 during Day-light Savings Time), and 5.5 hours behind Sydney time. Curiously, Nepal time is 15 minutes ahead of India.

Mail, Courier & Customs

The quality of postal service varies widely from place to place. In some places there is a huge amount of pilferage, while in other places there seems to be virtually none. Packages going out of India are usually safer than those coming in. Any time you mail something, have the clerk cancel *all* the stamps in front of you to make sure they can't be removed and reused, which is a common practice, and one that prevents a lot of mail from reaching its destination.

Most post offices have limited hours for services such as Speed-Post or sending parcels. 9AM to 2PM is typical. If you go later, they'll just tell you to come back the next day.

Letters should be well sealed in a sturdy envelope. You can get manila envelopes lined with cloth that are pretty strong. If you are going to register or insure a letter or parcel, you have to seal it with sealing wax, and the wax has to have some seal clearly impressed on it (an unusual foreign coin will do in a pinch). It is essential to insure anything valuable or important, but if the package is really impor-tant, it's safer to send it by courier. Never send anything without at least registering it.

If you have to send a check, be sure to either cross it (for deposit in India or Europe) or else write "For deposit only" and the name of the bank where it is to be deposited, along with the account number, if possible (for deposit in the USA). If you absolutely have to send cash or a cash equivalent that anyone could use (which technically you're not allowed to do), conceal it well. Letters are frequently opened and pilfered.

Express mail in India is called *Speed Post*. It's the most reliable way to send letters both within India and abroad. You can also send packages by Speed Post. The advantage of SpeedPost is that items rarely sit around long enough for idle hands to mess with them. Also, Speed Post packages under a certain size don't need customs forms, at least to some countries, including the USA.

Packages sent through the post must be sewn up in cloth. It's best to seal the items in plastic before taking them to the *packwala* (professional parcel packer), who can usually be found near a main post office. Good *packwalas* know how to pack things to minimize postage. Charges may range from Rs.5–150, depending on size, etc. If no *packwala* is available, go to a tailor.

Use plenty of padding or bubble wrap for anything breakable. You can ask the *packwala* to seal the package with sealing wax for you. In addition to the sealing wax, take some glue and drip it liberally along the line of stitching to prevent someone from carefully unpicking the stitches, removing items and then restitching it. Since the sealing wax can get knocked off in transit, the glue provides an extra measure of security.

Packages sent within India should always be insured, or at least registered, though registration gives no protection against pilferage. While it may be difficult to collect on the insurance, the mere fact that a package is insured will make it more likely to arrive safely. Packages and letters frequently sit around for days or, in certain cases, months, before they are sent out, and security in most Indian Post Offices is shockingly lax. Packages are commonly left sitting outside unguarded, where anyone could easily walk off with them—or where they could get soaked in the rain.

There are several options for sending parcels. Small items can be sent as Small Packets at a cheap rate, but they can't be insured or registered. Speed Post is fast and usually pretty reliable, and it can be insured. For overseas parcels, there is also SAL mail (surface/air/land), which can be insured or registered. Regular Airmail can also be insured and/or registered. Registered Book Post is cheap but slow (see below for special packing instructions).

It's best to send overseas packages from the Foreign Post Office (FPO). There are FPOs in several major cities. The FPO has a customs agent on site to check the packages before they are sent, which means they almost certainly won't get reopened along the way because of the customs seals. The package is examined before it is sealed to be sure that it doesn't contain any prohibited items. The FPOs have a separate counter for inspecting and packing jewelry that is to be sent overseas. Never send jewelry from a regular post office. There is simply too much risk that it will be stolen.

Customs regulations prohibit sending money, gold, dangerous goods, and banned items like *shahtush*, animal skins, ivory, drugs, etc. Items that look like they might be antiques require permission from the Archeological Survey of India to send out of India.

When sending packages from the FPO, you will need your passport, receipts for everything you are sending, and cash rupees for payment. Don't bring packages already sealed. The packages are examined in front of you and then repacked right there while you wait (for a fee), or you can do it yourself if you have all the necessary materials. The customs officer then seals the package. This process involves a form filled out in triplicate that has to be signed and stamped several times, so it can easily take a few hours. If you need to send herbal medicine or something similar, sending it from the FPO is the only reliable way to do so.

To send books by Registered Book Post, you need to leave the parcel open at one end for inspection. Wrap the books in clear plastic so the contents are clearly visible and then have them sewn with one end left mostly open. The parcel must also be tied with twine to ensure that nothing falls out. The plastic isn't required, but it protects the books from water and dirt.

Global Express mail (EMS) is the most reliable postal service if you need to have something important sent to you, since this service normally uses pilfer-proof packages, although insurance is not available.

Whenever you receive a parcel, don't take it out of the post office before weighing it. If the weight is less than the declared weight or anything looks suspicious about the packing, open it right there. Otherwise, if anything has been taken, they won't honor your claim. And, believe me, you can't always tell that a package has been opened, as many thieves are incredibly skillful.

Courier service to India is pretty reliable, but it is extremely expensive. Poste Restante (general delivery) is possible, but not highly recommended, as anything coming from abroad that's addressed to a foreign name tends to be carefully examined to see if it could contain money or anything else of value, and the longer it sits in the post office, the more likely that it will be opened. If you do use Poste Restante, you will need to bring your passport to claim your mail. It's better to have mail sent in care of someone local, if possible. Incoming parcels should always be registered and/or insured, no matter where they will be received.

Check the customs regulations of the country you are sending items to if you are sending more than small gifts. India has several courier companies that are quite fast and reliable. Sending packages from India using FedEx, DHL, etc. is much cheaper than sending packages to India using the same services.

Bring the packages in unsealed as the courier agents are supposed to inspect the contents before sealing them. Many courier agents don't keep packing materials on hand, so call ahead and ask whether you need to bring your own. Insurance for packages is usually limited to Rs.5,000.

If you are sending things to a small town in India, verify that the courier service actually delivers there. They may take your package and your money, and then notify you a few days later that they don't. To add insult to injury, some companies won't even refund your money even though it was their mistake.

There are several good couriers and some rather unreliable ones as well, so you should ask around to find out which ones are the most reliable. If you use a discount courier, your package may get repacked along the way (sometimes resulting in loss or damage), and delivery can takes a few days longer. Liquids can't be sent by courier.

About the Infrastructure

India's infrastructure is generally what you might expect of a developing country. While there are certain places in India that are quite well developed, this is far from being a universal reality.

Plumbing

Indian plumbing is a challenge for most Westerners. Water is not something that simply flows effortlessly from the taps 24 hours a day. In fact, it often doesn't flow at all. Where there's a municipal water supply, the water usually comes for an hour or two in the morning, during which time it is pumped up to a tank on the roof, so water is always limited. You have to be conservative with water and to fix leaks before they get too bad or you will run out.

It pays to find out how severe the water shortage is wherever you are going. Sometimes it's bad enough to warrant changing your plans. At times, there will be many days in a row with no water coming in the pipes, which is a major problem as the storage tanks are usually relatively small. There may be a water truck delivering water, in which case the supply is extremely limited. Even when there is water, however, there are many other difficulties.

Although bathrooms in upper-class hotels and homes are similar to Western ones, in most hotels, public facilities, and middle-class homes in India you will find squat toilets; little or no hot water; bucket baths rather than showers or bathtubs; and no shower curtain to keep the water from drenching the bathroom when you bathe. Plumbing in India is still relatively undeveloped, so don't have high expectations unless you are staying only in upscale places. Most rural homes in India don't have running water, and many places don't even have any safe drinking water nearby.

Indian squat toilets are a bit of a stretch for many Westerners, but many people prefer them because they feel that they are more hygienic and healthier than the sit-down kind. At one time, everyone used the squat method, and the majority of the world's population still does.

An Indian-style squat toilet consists of a hole in the floor with two slightly raised foot pads to either side. Since the floor can be wet and slippery, you need to be careful not to fall. Squat toilets are virtually never supplied with toilet paper. Instead you will find a water spigot with a small plastic jug or cup that you use to wash with and also to flush. You may also encounter a curious sort of hybrid toilet that has a seat that can be used either as a squat toilet or a Western-style toilet.

Indians are comfortable squatting with their feet flat on the ground, but this position is impossible for many Westerners, so balance can be a problem. Indian-style toilets can be especially challenging for older people and those with knee problems.

If you are unfamiliar with how to use an Indian-style toilet, here's how you do it: first, fill the little container with water; next, stand on the two foot pads that are on either side of the bowl, with the narrow end in front and squat over the bowl, holding onto the faucet if necessary. When you are finished, if you aren't using toilet paper, take the container of water and pour it with your right hand while washing yourself with your left hand. Keep washing until you feel clean, and wait a minute to dry off. The toilet may have a conventional flush lever or a pull chain. If there is neither, fill the jug again and pour the water into the hole. Men using the squat toilet as a urinal should rinse off the foot pads all around.

If you can't manage without toilet paper, you may need to carry your own. You can buy it in almost any large town, but it's usually unavailable in villages. Try to use the very minimum, as plumbing is often delicate. Sometimes in places with extremely poor plumbing, you will find signs asking that you don't use toilet paper. There may even be a dustbin (wastebasket) in which to deposit used toilet paper instead of putting it in the toilet.

Indians normally keep a pair of rubber *chappals* for use in the bathroom, and it is recommended that you do likewise, especially with Indian-style toilets or where the bathrooms are shared. Never use a squat toilet with bare feet, especially a public one.

Public toilets rarely have anywhere clean and dry to put stuff, so carry a spring-loaded carabineer (the kind you use for keys) to hang your bag on the door handle or wherever.

Most people in India take bucket baths rather than showers. You have a bucket of water and a little plastic cup to pour the water over you, and maybe a little stool to sit on. It's quite nice once you get used to it.

Even when the taps are functional, sometimes a shower fixture can only provide the merest trickle of water or it might not seem to work at all. You may have to wait for half a minute or more to see if any water is going to come out. If you hear noises in the pipes, there is a good chance that water will come eventually. Sometimes no water comes out of the showerhead just because the holes are completely clogged with mineral deposits; if so, you can try to open them up with a pin. Sometimes, the shower won't even be hooked up. In places with low water pressure, it is often far easier and more comfortable to simply take a bucket bath even if there is a shower.

Hot water is not something to be taken for granted. It's a luxury for most people in India. Even many affluent homes don't have hot water in the kitchen or bathroom sinks, though there may be a geyser for bathing. It's extremely rare to find hot water in public facilities. Even the toilets located in the public areas of five-star hotels often do not have hot water. Most Indians feel that for washing hands, cold water is sufficient. Soap is not always available. Cold water is used nearly everywhere for washing cooking utensils, dishes and clothes, etc.

Better hotels normally have 24-hour hot water, though you may have to turn on the geyser (water heater) yourself. When there is a geyser, you may need to ask where the switch is if it isn't obvious. In some hotels, you may have to ask for someone to go up to the roof and open the valve when you want to use hot water early in the morning even though the hotel advertises 24-hour hot water. Many places have hot water only during certain hours; others have it only by the bucket on special order; and sometimes it is not available at all, so you may want to ask before you check in.

Laundry & Dry-Cleaning

Laundry services are cheap almost everywhere in India except in the big hotels. A *dhobi-wala* or *dhobi* is a person who washes clothes, usually by hand. You send your laundry out early in the morning and get it back the same evening or the next day, though during the monsoon, it can take rather longer. In the heat of south India, you might even get your laundry back in two or three hours, all washed, dried and pressed. However, even if you give everything else to a *dhobi* or a servant to be washed, it is customary to wash one's own undergarments and to hang them to dry out of public view.

Washing by hand does not assure gentle treatment for your clothes, however. If there is a river or tank (pool for washing and bathing) nearby, the *dhobi* may take your clothes there and beat them on the rocks, laying them out on bushes or steps or on the bare ground to dry. Otherwise, the *dhobi* may wash them in a bucket with a brick in it or scrub them vigorously with a brush. This treatment is pretty hard on your clothes, so they sometimes come back in worse shape than they were originally. Buttons break or fall off, and sometimes new spots appear, while knitted items such as socks get stretched out because they will probably be ironed if you forget to tell the *dhobi* not to. Moreover, after a few washings, your clothes become noticeably thinner. Don't give an untested *dhobi* anything delicate or anything you are particularly fond of.

If you prefer to wash your own clothes, you can still take them to the local *press-wala* to be ironed. Most *press-walas* use irons made of cast-iron that are filled with hot coals rather than electric ones. Often you will find them with their tables set up under a tree right on the street.

If your clothing needs dry cleaning, ask around for a reputable cleaner. Many—but certainly not all—are pretty good. Some are excellent. And some are so bad you wonder how they stay in business. However, in large cities some dry cleaners also have laundries that wash your clothes, often in washing machines.

Electricity & Electrical Appliances

Electricity in India is extremely problematic. Like water, it's not something that is always available 24 hours a day; and when it is, you can't count on it being stable. There are several considerations besides differences in voltage and plugs, so if you are using any electrical or electronic items, don't skip this section. It does get technical, but if you are using foreign equipment or sensitive electronics, then you need this information.

Electric outlets always have an on-off switch next to them. To turn the outlet on, push in the lower part of the switch (the "down" position). Try to remember to switch them off when not in use. Because Indian wiring is often not perfectly done, you should always turn off and unplug appliances, including air conditioners, whenever they are not being used.

Outlets are generally not grounded, though they may appear to be, as they often have five holes to accommodate different configurations. However, many 3- or 5-hole outlets don't allow you to insert a two-pronged plug so you may need an adapter plug. If you don't have one, then with the outlet switched off, you can insert a pencil into the ground hole and maneuver the plug in.

Both the US and Canada use 110/125V current, while electrical current in India is 220–240V, but fluctuations, which can be really extreme (from 0-300V or more), are not uncommon. Moreover, low current is the norm in many places, and this is a more insidious problem because it can also destroy your equipment, even if it's steady. If a 110/125V North America appliance is plugged directly into a 220/250V outlet, it will quickly burn out, so it's necessary to convert (or step-down) the 220/250V with either a converter or a transformer.

Many 110/120V devices have dual voltage capabilities. This information is usually written somewhere on the device. Dual voltage appliances can be used on either 110/120V or 220/250V currents and do not require a converter or transformer, but only the proper adapter to plug into the wall. (For considerations related to electronic gear, see the section below on computers.) Irons, hair dryers, etc. usually have a manual switch that you have to flip, so you have to make sure they are on 220V before you plug them in or they will immediately burn out.

The type of appliance you bring to India (electric or electronic) and its wattage will determine whether you need a voltage converter or a transformer. You may need both, as they are not interchangeable. Always check the wattage of your appliances before using any voltage converter or transformer.

Converters are for electric products containing simple heating devices and/or for universal motor products that are not used continuously for long periods of time, such as garment steamers, irons, curling irons, hair dryers, electric razors, CD players, etc. Step-down converters convert 220/250V electricity to 110/125V electricity by reducing the voltage flowing into the appliance by half. The wattage of the appliance determines which converter you need. If this information isn't printed on the appliance label, then you can figure it out by multiplying the Voltage by the Amperage: Volts x Amps = Watts (e.g.: 120V x 6A = 720 Watts).

Converters are available for appliances up to 2000 watts. Appliances rated under 25 watts (such as radios, CD players and electric razors) require a low wattage converter, while appliances rated over 25 Watts (such as irons, steamers, hot pots, and hair dryers) require a high wattage converter. Dual wattage converters can handle both. Converters are designed to be used only for short periods of time. They shouldn't be used with electronically controlled items using digital timing or auto shut-off, or with any electronic device over 25 watts.

Appliances such as computers, answering machines, TVs and fax machines that have electronic circuitry (computer chips or integrated circuits), as well as power tools, etc., require transformers rather than converters. This is because electronic devices and appliances require more power and are used continuously for longer periods of time. The wattage of the appliance determines which transformer to use. It should be one that is rated at least 10% higher than the wattage of the appliance.

Computers & Electronics

Using your computer in India can be challenging, though it mainly requires a bit of extra vigilance and patience. First, you have to check whether or not your equipment is compatible with the line voltage (220 Volts) and frequency (50 Hertz). Laptops use an external power supply that plugs into an AC electrical outlet and converts the power into DC, whereas desktop computers have built-in power supplies.

Most laptops and peripherals have dual-voltage capabilities, which means they are manufactured to accept both 110V 60 Hz and 220V 50 Hz electricity. Look for a label on the power adapter or on the device itself to be sure. The label indicates dual-voltage if it says something like "Input: AC 100V - 240V, 50/60Hz." On the other hand, if it reads "Input: AC 120V, 60Hz" or something similar, then you need a step-down transformer. If you are unsure, check with the manufacturer. The wrong voltage will destroy your equipment.

If your computer is dual-voltage, which is certainly the norm for laptops, then all you need is an adaptor plug, which does not affect the current at all. Many dual-voltage devices have a built in detector that determines the local line voltage and automatically adapts, but some older devices have a manual switch. If there is a switch, remember to have it on the correct setting for the local voltage or you will fry the device the first time you plug it in! You may want to attach a reminder label to the plug to prevent this from happening.

The biggest problem with using a computer or other sensitive electronic items in India is unstable electric power, which can cause data loss as well as physical damage to the hardware. Spikes and surges cause the majority of all problems experienced by electronic equipment, and India will definitely challenge your equipment in this way. Power disturbances, including blackouts, brownouts and spikes, are common everywhere in India, and they are certainly among the most extreme in the world. A really bad power day in India might start out with 6–8 hours of no power, followed by a couple of hours of reasonably steady power to lull you into complacency, followed by an hour or two of incredibly unsteady power where it briefly goes off for a second or two and then spikes, settling down for a couple of minutes before going off and spiking again. Needless to say, if you don't have good protection, your equipment is likely to burn out in such conditions. Such extremes are most common in rural areas, but all the cities also have power problems.

All sophisticated electronic equipment, can be damaged by unsteady power, so you should never plug such items in without at least a surge protector. To be on the safe side, take the same precautions as you would with your computer.

To safeguard your equipment, it is absolutely essential to have a reliable surge protector. Get a branded surge protector with a warranty. The locally made power strips that look like surge protectors are worthless. Unfortunately, a surge protector by itself is not enough, since high, low, or fluctuating voltage can burn out the power supply or even the hard drive, but there is currently no practical, lightweight solution.

You might be lucky and get away with using only a surge protector (also known as a *spike protector*) for long periods of time without trouble. However, since India has so many power fluctuations, it is highly recommended to invest in a system to filter the power line. Clean power is essential to ensure optimum performance from your computer equipment. You can use a UPS (uninterruptible power supply), CVT (constant voltage transformer), or voltage regulator. Laptops have a far greater tolerance for unsteady current than desktop models do, but the power situation nearly everywhere in India is bad enough that going without good protection is risky. If you have a desktop computer with you, protection is absolutely necessary. If you have a modem that connects to the Internet via a phone line, you need to protect the modem as well.

A UPS has a battery backup (typically 10–30 minutes) that gives you time to save your work and shut down safely. It maintains a continuous supply of electric power to the equipment connected to it by supplying power from a separate source when utility power is not available. There are three types of UPS: off-line, line-interactive and on-line. However, the first two types don't supply perfectly continuous power. There's a brief interruption when the power source is switched.

The on-line UPS is recommended for especially difficult conditions or for equipment that is sensitive to power fluctuations. It provides clean power to your equipment from its reserves while at the same time continuously replenishing those reserves from the AC power. The on-line type of UPS (also known as a power conditioner or a line conditioner or double-conversion UPS), in addition to protecting against blackouts, provides protection against all common power problems. It essentially provides an electric firewall between the incoming power and your equipment, whereas a standby or line-interactive UPS only filters the input power. Since you can control the frequency and output voltage regardless of input frequency and voltage, the on-line UPS is the best for most conditions.

If you expect to have to rely on emergency generators (gensets), you'll need to buy an on-line UPS that is specifically rated to work with a generator. Some types of UPS don't function properly on emergency power: since a genset has a limited power output, there are frequent fluctuations as devices are turned on and off.

If you need a UPS, look for these features: a wide voltage window (at least 230VAC, +/- 20%) to enable you to work under poor voltage conditions; an Automatic Voltage Regulation (AVR) feature to handle voltage fluctuations; a resettable circuit breaker (rather than a fuse); sufficient backup time to allow for saving files and shutting down safely; built-in diagnostics to monitor the condition of the UPS; both audible and visual alarms (although the audible alarms can be annoying if you can't turn down the volume, especially in areas with low voltage); power management software to enable proper automatic shutdown before battery power runs out in case you are out; zero-delay clamping (which ensures maximum safety for your equipment, and should protect even from lightning strikes); and a good warranty. Most of the weight of the UPS is for the backup battery. If you are using it with a laptop, you may only need a few minutes of backup.

A Constant Voltage Transformer (CVT) evens out power fluctuations, maintaining both the quality and strength of the current, and they usually have a built-in surge protector as well. A CVT can keep you going during a brownout, but it doesn't have a battery backup, so your laptop battery needs to be sufficiently charged in case of power outages. CVTs can also provide enough current to run other items such as lamps or anti-mosquito devices even in the midst of a brownout—a big advantage, since brownouts may last many hours. A properly made CVT is fully automatic and isolates your laptop from the power supply.

A non-automatic voltage regulator or voltage stabilizer is an electrical regulator that requires constant monitoring in order to maintain a more-or-less constant voltage level, and it may not really isolate your computer from the power supply. A simple voltage regulator is smaller, lighter and cheaper than either a UPS or CVT; however, it may not be sufficient for your situation. Voltage regulators have a voltage meter, a switch to increase or decrease the voltage, and another switch to determine how much. They should also have an automatic cutoff if the voltage exceeds a certain limit, as well as a warning light. You have to watch them closely and make adjustments as the power fluctuates. They are better than nothing, but they are certainly not foolproof. If you do choose to use a voltage regulator, be sure to get one that is especially designed for computers, as there are different kinds. Many of the ones on the market are locally made, which means they have no guarantee, and the cheapest ones are made with aluminum wire, which is not recommended. Most of the local voltage regulators are hardly more than fancy surge protectors that protect only against power surges, so you need to examine the features carefully.

People have differing opinions about which option is best. Although an in-line UPS is best if you absolutely need the battery backup, many people say a CVT is better for all other purposes. Some people say that the voltage regulators only protect against spikes; others disagree. Probably the truth depends on how they are made. Whatever you choose, be sure to get a unit that has an ISO label rather than one that is locally made. Ask the local experts for help in determining which one will best suit your needs; but don't ask only in the shop where they are for sale. You may need to ask several people because often even merchants and people who run Internet cafes are entirely clueless about the differences between a UPS, CVT and a voltage stabilizer. If possible, check with the tech support people for your computer manufacturer here in India. There's no point in asking anyone in other countries; they won't have any idea about the extreme conditions in India.

The kind of voltage stabilizers that are used with certain major appliances such as refrigerators, air conditioners and TVs are definitely not appropriate for use with computer equipment because they only address the issue of low voltage rather than fluctuating current, and they can actually make the current more uneven. Although low voltage is a problem for computers because it places undue strain on internal components (which ultimately causes data glitches, system crashes and hardware failure), power fluctuations can destroy your equipment even faster, and these units don't protect against them.

If you are staying in one place—especially if you are using a desktop computer—don't even consider not getting protection of some sort for it. The problem for travelers is that UPS and CVT units are heavy and large, so it's a nuisance to carry one around. Voltage regulators are smaller and lighter, but still cumbersome. However, once you've had a hard drive wrecked by inconsistent power, the inconvenience seems much less significant. I can vouch for that!

Of course, if you are traveling a lot, you won't want to lug around extra equipment. One way to minimize potential damage is to charge the battery with the computer turned off. Although this approach won't protect your power adapter from ragged currents, it should at least protect your laptop's memory and hard drive. Instead of working with the computer plugged in, you would work off the battery. If you have the means to recharge the battery outside of the computer using a quick-charger, you can avoid ever plugging in the computer itself. Don't forget that you still need good surge protection for the quick-charger and your battery.

If you don't have a UPS or CVT, at least keep an incandescent light or fan on while you're charging the battery so you will notice if the power dims significantly or goes off, even if you're in the next room. If it does, quickly unplug your computer to avoid the surge when the electricity comes back on. If you run your laptop only on the battery, however, you'll need to replace the battery sooner than otherwise, and you may also have to replace a power adapter if it gets fried. You may want to check cost and availability of the power adapter and battery in India so you know what to expect.

Never leave your computer unattended while it is plugged in unless you have a system that is invincible. If you have a good UPS that shuts your computer down automatically, you don't have to worry much about all this unless there's a thunderstorm.

However you work, try to plug your computer into a circuit that has nothing else on it. In particular, avoid plugging the computer into the same circuit as a refrigerator, air conditioner, photocopier, water pump, geyser or any other equipment that cycles on and off. Also refrain from plugging irons, hotplates, hairdryers, and other heating devices into the same circuit.

Inevitably, many people just plug their laptop right into the outlet without any precautions at all because they rely on the flexibility of the power supply, but doing so is really foolish. They may get away with it for weeks or months or even years on end, if they are lucky, but eventually disaster is bound to strike. Someone whose equipment hasn't failed yet may well tell you that you have nothing to worry about. Beware of advice given with a cavalier attitude!

While sudden unexpected power problems can occur at any time, there are also intentional power cuts (load-shedding) that may last for several hours a day since the power supply is inadequate to service the whole city or town. The power may also be regularly unstable at certain times of day. If this is the case, you can simply plan to do other things or run the laptop off the battery at those times. Some places have their own generators that can maintain a steady current, including many five-star hotels, multinational corporate buildings, and luxury apartment complexes, but even in these places, there is often a spike or a gap when the power switches from city power to the generator.

Never hand-carry your laptop through a walk-through metal detector like the kind used at airports as these detectors can potentially damage the magnetic data on the computer and disks. The luggage scanner, on the other hand, won't damage the data.

Always keep a full backup or two of your hard drive and all your essential software someplace safe but accessible, including a bootable backup of your system. Also keep a list of the software registration codes in case you need to re-enter them. In addition, back up your current work frequently. Keep backups separate from your computer in case something happens to your computer.

Write down model and serial numbers, phone support lines and service contract info and keep this information where you can find it if you need it. India is hard on computers, so getting an extended warranty on your equipment is a smart move. Of course, you'll want to be sure that it is valid in India; many warranties are not worldwide.

• • •

Volunteering

"The best way to find yourself
is to lose yourself in the service of others."
—M.K. Gandhi

THERE ARE MANY OPPORTUNITIES for volunteer work in India, which you can do either as a full-time occupation, or even just an hour or two whenever you have time. If you do an Internet search on "volunteering in India," you'll find many organizations that need help. Some of these charge a considerable amount of money for the privilege of helping, but others are just happy to have your help. Ask around where you are staying and you may find an orphanage or hospital or other institution that needs help. Volunteering is not only rewarding, but if you are suffering from culture shock, it can also help you adjust. It's a great way to learn about the local culture and to make new friends.

You might also consider volunteering as a teacher, working on an organic farm, helping at an organization for abused women, or donating to a reputable organization that rescues children from life on the streets.

For more information on volunteering in India, see the *Guidebook for Volunteering in India* at <www.indiserve.org>, which lists many organizations that are looking for volunteers.

• • •

In Conclusion

THE REAL SECRET TO ENJOYING INDIA is learning to be in harmony with the way things function here. In order to accomplish this, you need to respect the culture, to relax and be flexible with your plans, and you need to be aware of what is going on around you as much as possible, including what happens behind the scenes. The more you can attune yourself to India, and the more you can learn to take everything as it comes, the more you will enjoy it. Indians are friendly, warm-hearted people, and getting to know them is a great delight.

If you are coming only to see the Taj Mahal, ride on a camel, and visit all the wonders you have been told about and nothing more, you will miss seeing India. As it has been so well said, "The traveler sees what he sees. The tourist sees what he has come to see."[20] The more you open your heart to the people you meet and your mind to their ways of thinking and living, the more India will open itself to you. Ultimately, it's mostly up to you whether you have a good time or not. Your attitude makes all the difference.

India is the land of all possibilities, the land where every day will bring you sights and sounds, smells and tastes that you have never before experienced or even imagined. May you enjoy it to the fullest!

• • •

Glossary

Adivasi	tribal person
ashram	place for spiritual practice
auto-rickshaw	three-wheeled mini taxi
auqat	status, position in society
ayah	nanny
Ayurveda	system of traditional medicine
bakshish, bakseesh	a tip, a bribe, or a gift to a beggar
bandh	labor or other strike when shops close, taxis stop running, etc.
bhat, bhatta	drivers' overnight allowance
bhojanalaya	local restaurant
bindi	forehead decoration worn by married women
Bollywood	Mumbai's film industry
Brahmin, Brahmana	priestly caste
Brahman	Supreme reality, in Vedic philosophy
chai	Indian tea
chapati, chapatti	flatbread
chappals	rubber sandals or thongs
charpoy	wood-framed rope cot
chillum	pipe for smoking cannabis
choli	blouse worn with a *sari*
chunni	scarf worn with an Indian-style ladies' suit
churidhar	narrow ladies' pants bunched at the ankle
Cloak Room	luggage storeroom at a railway station
coolie, *kuli*	porter [usage note: this term is usually OK for porters at railway stations, but never for hotel porters]
crore, *karor*	10 million
curd	yogurt

cycle-rickshaw	three-wheeled cycle that carries passengers
Dalit (or *Harijan*)	member of lowest castes
dacoit	highway robber
deva	personification of one of the forces of Nature
Delhi Belly	travelers' diarrhea (TD)
Diwali, Dipavali	Festival of lights
dhabba	open-air restaurant, esp. at a truck stop
dhanyavad	"Thank you"
dal	pulses (like lentils)
dharma	one's duty, what one is meant to do in life
dharmashala	pilgrims' lodge
dhobi, dhobi-wala	person who does laundry
dhoti	man's traditional unstitched garment
dosa	South Indian pancake, usually savory
dupatta	scarf worn with an Indian-style ladies' suit (*salwar-kamiz* or *churidhar-kamiz*)
Eve-teasing	sexual harassment or assault
genset	backup power generator
ghi, ghee	clarified butter used in cooking
godown	warehouse, storeroom
gunda, goonda	hoodlum
guru	spiritual guide, or a respected teacher
gurudwara	Sikh temple
hijra	eunuch
Hinglish	Hindi version of Indian English
hotel	can also mean a simple restaurant with no accommodation, esp. in South India
idli, iddli	steamed rice dumpling (South Indian)
ISD	public facility for international calls
izzat	honor, respect, self-esteem, prestige
Jaini food	pure vegetarian food
Ji	respectful or affectionate suffix, also used alone, like *Sir* or *Madam*

jugarh, jugadh	improvisation, creative problem-solving
juice-wala	fresh juice vendor
jutha	impure, contaminated by saliva
khadi	hand-spun, hand-woven cotton
Kshatriya	warrior caste
lakh	100,000
lassi	a popular drink made of yogurt
lathi	a police officer's staff used as a weapon
lehnga	long skirt
lunghi	man's informal traditional unstitched garment
mamsahari	non-vegetarian
mehendi	henna designs on the hands or feet
meherbani hai	"it is a kindness"
mirch	chilli pepper
naga baba	naked *sadhu*
namaste, namaskar	traditional greetings
namkin, namkeen	salty snacks
okasatmya	Ayurvedic principle of eating familiar foods
pan, paan	betel leaf wrapped around spices, etc. and chewed like tobacco
packwala	professional parcel packer
pakoras	vegetables or *paneer* coated with batter and deep-fried, like tempura
pallu	the end of a *sari* that is draped over the shoulder
pandit	a Vedic scholar learned in Sanskrit recitation and philosophy; can also be a priest
pani, paneer	fresh cheese
pashmina	cashmere
PCO	Phone call office, for local calls
petrol	gasoline
petrol pump	gas station

prasad	any food or other item that has been offered in a religious ceremony or at a temple
Punjabi dress	traditional ladies' suit (= *salwar-kamiz*)
punya	religious merit
puri	deep-fried flatbread
retiring room	short-term accommodation at an airport or railway station
rickshaw-wala	auto-rickshaw or cycle-rickshaw driver
roti	flatbread
salwar-kamiz	traditional ladies' suit
sadhu, sadhvi	male ascetic, female ascetic
sadhana	spiritual practice
salam aleikum	traditional Muslim greeting
Sanskrit	The ancient Vedic language
samadhi	transcendental pure consciousness
samosa	stuffed, deep-fried dumpling
Sanatana Dharma	'the eternal way'; correct, indigenous name for Hinduism
Sanyasi	Hindu religious mendicant
sardar	Sikh man
sari	ladies' unstitched garment
sattvik bhojan	pure vegetarian
sevashram	service-oriented ashram
shatush, shatoosh	finest hair from the neck of the Himalayan Ibex, an endangered species of wild goat
Shri, Sri	Mr., Sir
Shrimati (Smt.)	Mrs., Madam
shakahari	vegetarian
shudh	pure
Shudra	worker / servant caste
siddha	person who has yogic powers
Siddha	traditional system of medicine

siddhi	yogic power
STD	public facility for long-distance calls in India
swami	monk or religious teacher
taxi-*wala*	taxi driver
thali	stainless steel plate with compartments, also a full meal served on such a plate
thangka	Tibetan Buddhist scroll painting
thik hai	"OK"
tiffin	a light meal or snack, especially lunch
tilak	symbolic mark on the forehead
torch	flashlight
Unani	traditional system of medicine
vaidya	Ayurvedic physician
Vaishnava	devotee of Vishnu
Vaishnava bhojan	pure vegetarian food
Vaishya	member of the merchant caste
Veda	1) knowledge; 2) the ultimate reality, *Shabda-brahman*; 3) the source of creation; 4) the four Vedas: *Rig, Sama, Yajur* and *Atharva*
Vedic	pertaining to the Vedas
-*wala*	suffix meaning *one who* or *one that* or [*that . . .*] *one*
yatra	religious pilgrimage
yatri	pilgrim
yoga	The process of uniting individual consciousness with the Divine; also refers to the methods to achieve this goal (e.g., *raja yoga, dhyana yoga, hatha yoga, kundalinú yoga,* etc.)

Acknowledgements

I WISH TO ACKNOWLEDGE everyone who has in any way contributed to this book, whether knowingly or unknowingly. Thanks to my great friend and editor, Gerry Geer.

Thanks also to the following for permission to reprint copyrighted material:

Penguin Books, New Delhi, for extracts from: Pavan K Varma, *Being Indian*, 2004

HarperCollins, New Delhi, for extracts from: Roger Housden, *Travels in Sacred India*, 1996; Sanjeev Bhaskar, *India: One Man's Personal Journey Round the Subcontinent*, 2007

Dutton, New York, for extracts from: Gopi Krishna, *Awakening of Kundalini*, 1975

Scribner, New York, for extracts from: Mira Khamdar, *Planet India*, 2008

Tom Grundy, for extracts from: *Long-term Solo Travel—A Manifesto for Globetrotting Bliss*, <www.globalcitizen.co.uk>

In spite of efforts to acknowledge all sources, there may have been some that could not be located. Any omissions brought to my attention will be remedied in future editions.

Selected Bibliography

————, *Culture Briefing India,* Geotravel Research Center, Kissimmee, Florida, 2007.

Bhaskar, Sanjeev, *India*: *One Man's Personal Journey Round the Subcontinent,* HarperCollins Publishers, London, 2007.

Eck, Diana, *Darsan: Seeing the Divine Image in India.* Anima Books, Chambersburg, Pennsylvania, 1985.

Eliade, Mircea, *Yoga, Immortality and Freedom.* Bollingen Series, Princeton University Press, NJ 1973.

Grihault, Nick, *Culture Smart! The Essential Guide to Customs and Culture,* Kuperard, 2006.

Hall, Edward T., *The Dance of Life: The Other Dimension of Time,* Anchor Books, New York, 1984.

Housden, Roger, *Travels through Sacred India,* HarperCollins Publishers Pvt Ltd, New Delhi, 1996.

Kakar, Sudhir, *Indian Identity,* Penguin Books, New Delhi, 1996.

Kamdar, Mira, *Planet India,* Scribner, New York, 2008.

Krishna, Gopi, *The Awakening of Kundalini,* Dutton, New York, 1975.

Norberg-Hodge, Helena, *Ancient Futures,* International Society for Environment and Culture, *London, 1991.*

Sharma, Preeti, *Handbook for Medical Tourists to India,* Chillibreeze Publications, 2008.

Storti, Craig, *Speaking of India,* Intercultural Press, Boston, 2007.

Tully, Mark, *India's Unending Journey,* Rider, London, 2007.

Varma, Pavan K, *Being Indian,* Penguin Books India, New Delhi, 2004.

Wolpert, Stanley, *An Introduction to India.* Penguin Books, New Delhi, 1991.

Yogi, Maharishi Mahesh, *The Science of Being and Art of Living.* Penguin Books, USA, 1969.

Young, Isabel (Ed.), *Healthy Travel: Asia and India,* Lonely Planet Publications, Victoria, Australia, 2000.

Internet Resources

Accessibility: www.samarthyaindia.com; www.disabilityindia.org

Air travel and hotel search engine: http://ixigo.com

Business and cultural tips: www.culturalsavvy.com;
www.stylusinc.com

Central Bureau of Investigation: www.cbi.gov.in

Customs: www.cbec.gov.in/cae1-english.htm

Hospitality organizations: www.servas.org, www.couchsurfing.com

Postal rates and regulations: www.indiapost.gov.in

Transcendental Meditation: www.tm.org

Train information: www.indianrail.gov.in; www.seat61.com/
India.htm

Travel health: www.cdc.gov; www.bugbog.com

Travel tips: www.artoftravel.com

The U.S. State Department: www.travel.state.gov

Vaccinations: http://www.nvic.org.

Visa info: https://indiavisa.travisaoutsourcing.com;
www.mha.nic.in; www.mea.gov.in

Volunteering: www.indiserve.org; www.wwoofindia.org

Water purifier comparison charts: www.rei.com; www.cdc.gov—
factsht_crypto_prevent_water.htm

Women's travel: http://wanderlustandlipstick

Writings on religion, history and culture: www.williamdalrymple.com

Other useful websites: www.chillibreeze.com; www.indax.com;
www.transitionsabroad.com

A Note from the Author

SOME OF YOUR INDIAN FRIENDS may disagree with various points raised in this book. If so, please don't immediately jump to the conclusion that the information given here must necessarily be wrong. India is an extraordinarily diverse country, and cultural and regional differences can be extreme, so disagreements and differing viewpoints are unavoidable.

Also, as in any other country, Indians may not fully see certain cultural tendencies in their own community, and so your Indian friends may deny a description that seems quite accurate to you— just as you might do in your own country. In such cases, simply acknowledge their points of view and let your own experience and insight guide you to your own conclusions. You will also find that Indians are often surprised at some of the things that we as foreigners find challenging about their culture.

I've endeavored to give a balanced and realistic picture of what to expect in India, which has meant touching on subjects that are often ignored for one reason or another, but which, I feel, need to be understood in order to avoid problems. For the most part, I've tried to present the most prevalent Indian perspective, and not only that of the upper classes, who are definitely not in the majority.

There may well be some misinterpretations or other inaccuracies in spite of all my efforts to avoid errors, so if you do find any mistakes, or if you feel I have neglected an important issue that needs to be addressed, please contact me about it. This will help me in updating future editions. Positive feedback will also be greatly appreciated. Feel free to contact me by email at: <jdv@enjoyingindia.com>.

I hope this book will serve you well and will help you enjoy your time in India to the fullest.

Index

E

F

I

Indian Bradshaw 171
Indian English *50–51, 213, 217–218, 270*
India Standard Time (IST) *249*
infrastructure *162, 253*
Inner Line permits *19–20*
International Driver's License *201–202*
International Tourist Bureau *171, 180*
Internet access *246–247*
interpersonal relationships, importance of *4, 9, 44, 46, 57, 125*
Islam *101–102*
izzat 45–46, 67, 270

J

Jainism *79, 99*
Journalist Visa (J-Visa) *16, 217*
jugarh 48, 271

K

karma 103
Kashmir *69, 121, 139, 167, 247*
Kumbha Mela 147, 178–179

L

laundry & dry cleaning *20, 256–257, 270*
law enforcement *155–156*
Local Intelligence Unit (LIU) *37*
luxury tax *164*

M

macrobiotic diets *218*

T

About the Author

J.D. VIHARINI IS NOT THE NAME on my passport. It stands for *Jambu-dvipa-viharini,* an epithet of Ganga that means "one who wanders around enjoying India." I liked it and it fit perfectly. I chose it because I prefer, for personal reasons, to remain anonymous.

I was born in California, but have spent more than two-thirds of my life in other states and other countries. Having earned an MS in Vedic Studies in Europe, I came to India in 1980 and loved it immediately. In 1990, I began coming every year, spending more and more time here until I finally decided to stay. I have been living in India for several years.

Although I have an apartment in the Himalayas, I like to move around India with the seasons. At one time or another, I've spent time in nearly every part of India. Over the years, I've traveled around India first class, sardine class, and everything in between. From the Ritz to the pits, so to speak, I've stayed and dined in some of the most exclusive places in India and some of the least. I've stayed with families and attended their celebrations. I've rented apartments and learned how to contend with all that living here entails. I've experienced the intense, seething crowds of the Kumbha Mela and the serenity of the sparsely populated, high Himalayas. I've gone on pilgrimages and done business. I've been sick and learned how to stay well. I've made many friends and a new 'family', as well.

For all that, although most people think of me as being terribly adventurous because I'm a single woman who has mostly traveled and lived alone here, I'm not all that tough. However, with the help of many people I've met over the years, I've learned how to travel smart and to function in harmony with the culture. For me, living and traveling in India is a great delight. I love India and regard it as my home.

Notes

1. G.K. Chesterton, *All Things Considered, On Running After One's Hat*, 1908.

2. See the U.S. State Department website, <www.travel.state.gov>.

3. I learned Transcendental Meditation (as taught by Maharishi Mahesh Yogi) while I was in college. At the time I was so stressed out that I was all but suicidal, and my mind was so noisy I could hardly think straight. However, once I started meditating, my life began to change: the noise died down, and I became less and less frantic, less and less stressed out. My grades improved, as did my health and social relations. If I could meditate in such a state, anyone can. I've been meditating twice a day for decades, and it still keeps getting better.

4. Pavan K. Varma, *Being Indian*, Penguin Books, New Delhi, 2004, pp. 39–40.

5. Tom Grundy, *Long-term Solo Travel—A Manifesto for Globetrotting Bliss*, <www.globalcitizen.co.uk/other/travelmanifesto/manifesto>.

6. Mira Kamdar tells in *Planet India* (p. 41) of a couple who was arrested and fined "in lieu of serving a ten-day jail sentence in Rajasthan for kissing each other during their wedding ceremony. . . ."

7. Mark Twain, *Following the Equator*, 1897.

8. *Ekaṃ sat vipraha bahudha vadanti* (Rig Veda I.64.46).

9. Sanjeev Bhaskar, *India: One Man's Personal Journey Round the Subcontinent*, HarperCollins Publishers, London, 2007, p. 74.

10. *Travels through Sacred India*, p. 57.

11. Matthew 7:12.

12. *Travels through Sacred India*, p. XII. He further explains: "The natural world itself is for Hindus the display of the divine," p. 19.

13. This was a frequent saying of Maharishi Mahesh Yogi.

14. "None of the authoritative texts on liberation [the *Yoga Sutra* of Patañjali, the *Brahma Sutra Bhashya* of Shankara, etc.] recommend their use, nor do they describe drugs in the context of spiritual development—nor is there even the slightest hint that they could be useful in this regard. Where drugs

are mentioned at all, it is to indicate that they are a means of bondage, not liberation. How could sitting around in a hashish-induced stupor produce the extraordinary clarity of consciousness that is the hallmark of enlightenment? Drugs only give an illusion of spiritual experiences, and may ultimately damage the nervous system to the extent that it is no longer possible to have genuine ones." *Awakening of Kundalini,* Dutton, New York, 1975.

15. *Being Indian,* p. 23.

16. From the U.S. State Department website: "U.S. citizens, particularly women, are cautioned not to travel alone in India. Western women continue to report incidents of physical harassment by groups of men. Known as 'Eve-teasing', these incidents can be quite frightening. While India is generally safe for foreign visitors, according to the latest figures by Indian authorities, rape is the fastest growing crime in India. Among large cities, Delhi experienced the highest number of crimes against women. Although most victims have been local residents, recent sexual attacks against female visitors in tourist areas underline the fact that foreign women are also at risk and should exercise vigilance."

17. In the course of doing research for this book, I spoke with many women about their experiences with Indian men. Those who did not respect the Indian standards of dress invariably reported far more problems with harassment.

18. Jeremy Page, *South Asia Correspondent, Drug Dealers Blamed for Rising Death Toll in India's Hippy Paradise,* The Times, March 10, 2008.

19. From U.S. State Dept website: "If a driver hits a pedestrian or a cow, the vehicle and its occupants are at risk of being attacked by passersby. Such attacks pose significant risk of injury or death to the vehicle's occupants or at least of incineration of the vehicle. It can thus be unsafe to remain at the scene of an accident of this nature, and drivers may instead wish to seek out the nearest police station."

20. G.K. Chesterton, *All Things Considered, On Running After One's Hat,* 1908.

46580152R00170

Made in the USA
Lexington, KY
08 November 2015